Voicing Memories, Unearthing Identities

Studies in the Twenty-First-Century Literatures
of Eastern and East-Central Europe

Edited by

Aleksandra Konarzewska
University of Tübingen, Germany
Anna Nakai
Tokyo University of Foreign Studies, Japan

Series in Literary Studies

www.vernonpress.com

In the Americas:
Vernon Press
1000 N West Street, Suite 1200
Wilmington, Delaware, 19801
United States

In the rest of the world:
Vernon Press
C/Sancti Espiritu 17,
Malaga, 29006
Spain

Series in Literary Studies

Library of Congress Control Number: 2023906550

ISBN: 978-1-64889-624-8

Cover design by Vernon Press.
Cover image: Edward_Okuń_-_Autumn_leaves_-_MP_2409_MNW_-_National_Museum_in_Warsaw. Wikimedia Commons/public domain.

Table of contents

Acknowledgements

The volume's authors would like to acknowledge the importance of the contributions by their colleagues and scholarly mentors, without whose support, advice, discussions, and constructive feedback their chapters would not be the same: Davor Beganović (University of Tübingen, Germany), Stuart Dunn (King's College London, United Kingdom), Astrid Erll (Goethe University Frankfurt, Germany), Agata Firlej (Adam Mickiewicz University in Poznań, Poland), Elżbieta Górnikowska-Zwolak (University of Silesia, Poland), Anna Grabowska-Rogus (Emil Drobny Museum in Rybnik, Poland), Jiří Holý (University of Gießen, Germany), Reinhard Ibler (University of Gießen, Germany), Cody J. Inglis (Central European University, Austria/Hungary), Kimon Keramidas (New York University, United States), Alfrun Kliems (Humboldt University Berlin, Germany), Bogdan Kloch (Emil Drobny Museum in Rybnik, Poland), Éva Kovács (Wiesenthal Institute, Austria), Kateřina Králová (Charles University, Prague, Czechia), Ewa Kulik, and Schamma Schahadat (University of Tübingen, Germany), as well as the members of the Holocaust Memorial Monuments (HMM) Project and the participants and organizers of the 6th Future of Holocaust Testimonies Conference that took place in Akko in 2022.

We, the editors, also wish to express our gratitude to the Vernon Press editors for their invitation to start this project and for editorial support, including the engagement of the peer reviewers. Thanks to this generous opportunity, all papers received fair advice and suggestions before the final editing. The content of the book thereby became much more coherent, and each paper's statements were pronounced more clearly. Our special thanks go to Julia Furmanczyk, Ioannis Dimopulos, and Zuzanna Tymoftyjewicz, who vigilantly took care of consistency in terminology, orthography, and quotation style, and helped us manage extensive copy-editing. Additionally, during the preparation, the Suntory Foundation research grant helped one of the editors cover some costs.

Last but not least, we are truly indebted to each contributor to the volume. The project was launched in 2021, in the middle of the Covid-19 pandemic. Then, several months later, on February 24, 2022, Russia launched a full-scale invasion of Ukraine. All technical difficulties caused by the pandemic and the war aside, within a few months, the approaches within literary studies, Eastern and Central European studies, and memory studies changed so significantly that the volume took on a completely different meaning. However, we believe that precisely for that reason, the themes investigated in the following volume—memory and identity struggles—have proved their gravity in a new light.

Aleksandra Konarzewska
Anna Nakai

Germany, December 2022

Introduction: Literature, Memory, and Identity in the Twenty-First-Century Eastern and East-Central Europe

Aleksandra Konarzewska

University of Tübingen, Germany

Anna Nakai

Tokyo University of Foreign Studies, Japan

An immense wave of interest in memory studies has developed over the past twenty years.[1] Beginning primarily as a socio-historical experiment, analyses of memory have influenced other scholarly disciplines, particularly literary studies, with its mutual dependence on remembering as a collective action representing recollected historical events. Identity—mainly expressed in literary narratives—was closely connected to acts of remembrance and representation. New generations of authors working in this paradigm thus began to excavate public and private memories precisely for the sake of *remembering* instead of *overcoming* the past, pushing scholars to find a place for historical imagination. This book addresses the issue of identity as a pivot in studies of memory and literature. In this context, it addresses the question of cultural negotiation as it took shape between memory and literature, history and literature, and memory and history, with the help of contemporary authors and their works from Eastern and East-Central Europe.

In the region, the framework provided by memory studies became highly valuable for understanding the overloaded interpretations of and conflicting perspectives on events during the twentieth century. The trauma of two world wars, the development of collective consciousness according to national and ethnic categories, stories of the trampled lands and lives of people, and resistance to the reign of authoritarian and totalitarian terrors—these trajectories left complex layers of identities to unfold. Here we take the

---

[1] Cf. Anna Lisa Tota and Trever Hagen, eds., *Routledge International Handbook of Memory Studies* (London–New York: Routledge, 2016); Astrid Erll and Ansger Nünning, eds., *A Companion to Cultural Memory Studies* (Berlin: De Gruyter, 2010).

literature of countries such as Estonia, Poland, Serbia, and Russia as our point of departure and explain its significance in terms of geographical, theoretical, and thematic perspectives.

GEOGRAPHICAL SCOPE: EASTERN AND EAST-CENTRAL EUROPE

What we call Eastern and East-Central Europe is the geographical entity stretched from the east of the German-speaking area to Russia and the Caucasus, in other words, the regions that witnessed firsthand two totalitarian political regimes of the twentieth century: National Socialism and Stalinism. Until 1989/1991, most of these areas remained parts of the Eastern Bloc. The direct experience of genocide, ethnic cleansing, political persecution, censorship, and propaganda shaped the entire region, resulting in collective remembrances that significantly differ from those constituted in the postwar era in what is broadly understood to be the "West." In this way, the commemoration of the victims of Nazism—with a particular focus on the genocide of European Jews—is considered in the Western discourse the only memory duty with both unique and universal moral dimensions.[2]

This attempt at universality has often stood at odds with the collective memories of local nations and ethnic groups of Eastern and East-Central Europe, which became particularly visible after the fall of communism in those regions. As Ann Rigney asserts, associating any commemorative act with political meaning is not a simple outcome of unfortunate historical events but was installed, practiced, and therefore enforced throughout the latter half of the twentieth century:

> [T]he collapse of communism in the late 1980s and the major expansion of the European Union that followed in 2004 undermined this emerging consensus about the centrality of the Holocaust and the idea of a "bad conscience" to any master narrative of Europe. [...] Critically, the difficulty of integrating the former communist countries into the larger European master narrative was compounded by the fact that the legacy of Stalinist dictatorship introduced a new focus of

---

[2] Aleida Assmann, *Cultural Memory and Western Civilization: Functions, Media, Archive* (Cambridge: Cambridge University Press, 2011); Giorgio Agamben, *What Remains of Auschwitz: The Archive and the Witness.* (New York: Zone Books, 1999); Theodor W. Adorno, *Gesellschaftstheorie und Kulturkritik* (Frankfurt a. M.: Suhrkamp Verlag, 1975); Theodor W. Adorno, "Cultural Criticism and Society," in *Prisms*, trans. Samuel and Shierry Weber, ed. Thomas McCarty. (Boston: MIT Press, 1997).

memory that offered serious competition to the Holocaust as the dominant site of atrocity and victimhood.[3]

The abolition of censorship and the pluralization of the public sphere brought systematically oppressed and silenced voices and perspectives of minorities (Kashubians, Silesians, Rusyns, etc.) into sight. However, they simultaneously caused the reappearance of openly xenophobic discourses like blatant anti-Semitism and anti-Romism. One could also observe memory and identity conflicts at the very local level. Often, official interpretation or commemoration does not correspond to experiences shared by underrepresented groups. Minority perspectives thus question hegemonic memory discourses, and Silesian attempts to challenge the dominant Polish narrative would be an acute example of this.[4] Recently, this new angle was even more nuanced with the colonial understanding of the communist past in the region too.[5]

THEORETICAL CONSIDERATIONS: BEYOND POLITICAL MEMORY

Adding to regional interests in memory studies, the popularity of the field centered on the concept of collective memory as an analytical tool and therefore concentrated on social approaches.[6] This strong methodological inclination has been criticized for heavily highlighting the institutional and,

---

[3] Ann Rigney, "Ongoing: Changing Memory and the European Project," in *Media and Cultural Memory/Medien und kulturelle Erinnerung*, eds. Astrid Erll and Ansgar Nünning (Berlin–New York: De Gruyter, 2014), 345. Rigney also notes that "[t]here was a tendency among commentators in the former West [...] to view the 'new' members of Europe as belonging to an earlier stage of development in an implicitly stadial narrative in which 'overcoming' ethnic and political conflict was taken to be an inevitable stage in modernization and European integration." Ibid., 345. See also: Michael Rothberg, *Multidirectional Memory: Remembering the Holocaust in the Age of Decolonization* (Stanford: Stanford University Press, 2009); Ljiljana Radonić, "Post-communist invocation of Europe: memorial museums' narratives and the Europeanization of memory," *National Identities* 19, no. 2 (2017): 269–88.

[4] See Chapter 9 of this volume.

[5] To attempt to use postcolonial theory to analyze the communist past is "to elaborate a critical language pertinent enough to represent the complex histories of dependence in a region." See Dorota Kołodziejczyk and Cristina Şandru, "Introduction: On colonialism, communism and east-central Europe – some reflections," *Journal of Postcolonial Writing* 48, no. 2 (2010): 113–116, here 113. There is also research focusing on postcolonial reading on post-communist literature. Dobrota Pucherova and Robert Gafrik, eds., *Postcolonial Europe? Essays on Post-Communist Literatures and Cultures* (Leiden: Brill, 2015).

[6] Wulf Kansteiner, "Finding Meaning in Memory: A Methodological Critique of Collective Memory Studies," *History and Theory* 41, no. 2 (2002): 179–97.

thus, one-way transmission of historical memories. However, cultures of remembrance should be more broadly understood as processes of questioning the hegemonic construction and inflexibility of one's own identity. To use the terminology of Aleida Assmann, the politics of memory in the countries of Eastern and East-Central Europe struggle to this day between the politics of self-assertion (*Politik der Selbstbehauptung*) and the politics of regret (*Politik der Reue*).[7] The former emphasizes and venerates the continuity between the past and present, whereas the latter focuses on rupture and change.[8]

The tension created by both approaches also contributed to diversifying nuanced reactions vis-à-vis political memory. The politics of remembering encompasses not only the official policies of a given administration but also becomes a non-homogeneous result of initiatives launched by public actors who possess sufficient cultural and social capital and interest in participating in memory debates. This process involves governmental and non-governmental institutions (cultural centers, scientific units, and NGOs) and individuals (journalists, scholars, writers, and artists). Contemporary Eastern and East-Central European literature simultaneously echoes and creatively reuses memory tropes. It has thus acquired a prominent role as a (counter-)player in current collective and cultural memory debates.

Based on the idea that the encounter between social sciences and literary studies is a step toward pushing the boundaries of academic disciplines, French historian Ivan Jablonka provocatively states: "History is a contemporary literature."[9] If this statement holds some truth, it is possible to claim the converse, too: Contemporary literature becomes historiography. In fact, the literature of Eastern and East-Central Europe puts collective memory in fluid temporal transformation. The statement by Polish writer Jacek Dukaj confirms the point: "Judging by our literature, Poland has always existed more in the past and the future than in the present."[10] Dukaj's idea describes the reality of almost all countries in the region. Consciousness of the linear

---

[7] Aleida Assmann, *Ist die Zeit aus den Fugen? Aufstieg und Fall des Zeitregimes der Moderne* (München: Hanser, 2013), 308–11.

[8] Ibid.

[9] Ivan Jablonka, *History Is a Contemporary Literature: Manifesto for the Social Sciences*, trans. Nathan J. Bracher (Ithaca, NY: Cornell University Press, 2018). Jablonka wrote an epic biography about his grandparents—who were persecuted as communists in prewar Poland and suffered in Vichy France as Jewish immigrants—to reconsider the boundaries between history and literature as a historian; see Ivan Jablonka, *A History of the Grandparents I Never Had*, trans. Jane Kuntz (Redwood City, CA: Stanford University Press, 2016).

[10] Jacek Dukaj, "Wstęp," in *PL + 50: Historie przyszłości*, ed. Jacek Dukaj (Kraków: WL, 2004), 6.

development of time was disrupted by the location on the margins of Europe and witnessing both national and transnational tragedies. In this geographical realm, the question of 'what happened' takes on a significantly heavy, almost real presence, whereas the question of 'what could have happened' thereby acquires a special meaning as a matter of possibilities. At the same time, the present moment should be devoted to creatively maintaining the relationship between the past and the future.

In practice, literature helped preserve the memory, for future generations, of those who were persecuted and lost their lives too early. Even in countries with an unquestionably hegemonic status (such as Russia/the Soviet Union in the concerned region), the lack of political freedom and freedom of speech burdened literature with this additional task of remembrance. In the opening to her poem *Requiem*, the Russian poet Anna Akhmatova (1889–1966) commemorated the victims of the Great Terror in the 1930s in the Soviet Union:

> In the fearful years of the Yezhov terror, I spent seventeen months in prison queues in Leningrad. One day somebody 'identified' me. Beside me, in the queue, there was a woman with blue lips. She had, of course, never heard of me; but she suddenly came out of that trance so common to us all and whispered in my ear (everybody spoke in whispers there): 'Can you describe this?' And I said: 'Yes, I can.' And then something like the shadow of a smile crossed what had once been her face.[11]

Throughout the twentieth century, as shown in the case above, voicing one's account took on a particular communal role in representing both the individual and the collective. This trend has become increasingly evident in the twenty-first century, as the questions of identities have begun to gain more and more significance.

SEARCHING FOR A NOVEL LINK: MEMORY STUDIES AND LITERARY STUDIES

In twenty-first-century literary works from Eastern and East-Central Europe that thematize the question of memory, one can recognize new strategies, first and foremost, a vast need to (re)explore one's own identity, both individual and collective. It includes reconsiderations of one's transculturality/transnationality, investigations into a genealogy of people, things, and places (especially when their fates have remained unknown for years due to political reasons or

---

[11] Anna Akhmatova, "Requiem," in *Selected Poems*, trans. D. M. Thomas (London: Penguin books, s.d.), 87. Cf. Alexander Etkind, *Warped Mourning: Stories of the Undead in the Land of the Unburied* (Stanford: Stanford University Press, 2013).

personal traumata), as well as a rising interest in gender and queerness issues, not seldomly resulting in narratives that insightfully challenge and question already existing memory paradigms and taboos, both universal and local.[12]

Among such reconsiderations, one unique case is literature that openly delves into the identity struggles of the second and the third generation of Shoah survivors in very local, East-Central European contexts.[13] Together with the subjects of language, religion, and nationality (Ukrainian, Polish, Hungarian, etc.), they also include questions about the long-term consequences of ideological and political choices made by people's (grand)parents that in the authoritarian/totalitarian regimes could affect whole families (e.g., involvement in communist rule, or, conversely, participation in the anti-communist dissent). As Deborah E. Lipstadt and Eva Fogelman point out, "[i]n Eastern Europe many children of survivors grew up as children of Communists rather than children of Jewish Holocaust survivors. It would not be until *glasnost* in the U.S.S.R., and the Solidarity movement in Poland that confrontation with the past began, and survivor families were able to grieve over the dead and embrace their true identities and their links to a past that was destroyed."[14]

On the formal level, one can observe the appearance of ego-documents (memoirs, travelogs) and pieces of prose that consciously and creatively play with epistemological uncertainty and memory gaps—"Those speaking may be fictitious, but what they say is real. [...] It's the stories that can be authentic or not"[15]—as well as attempts to blur the distinction between the private and the political. Literature plays with collective memory paradigms by making up alternative versions of the past ("what could have happened if...") in

---

[12] See the longer poetic piece by Bożena Keff that concerns the taboos of maternity and mother–daughter relationships in the shadow of the Shoah: Bożena Keff, *On Mother and Fatherland* (Cambridge, MA: MadHat Press, 2017).

[13] Similar attempts to connect memory with identity can be found in: Jade McGlynn and Oliver T. Jones, eds., *Researching Memory and identity in Russia and Eastern Europe* (London: Palgrave Macmillan, 2022).

[14] Deborah Lipstadt and Eva Fogelman, "Children of Jewish Survivors," in *Encyclopaedia Judaica*, vol. 9, ed. Fred Skolnik (Detroit: Thomson Gale, 2007), 386. In her nonfiction book *Secondhand Time*, Svetlana Alexievich evokes the story of a Jew who, as a teenager, was in a Soviet partisan troop and had to hide his identity: "The partisan commanders had secret instructions from Moscow: Don't trust the Jews, don't let them into the regiments, annihilate them. They considered us traitors. We learned the truth about all of this thanks to perestroika." Svetlana Aleksievich, *Secondhand Time. The Last of the Soviets*, trans. Bela Shayevich (New York: Random House, 2016), 200.

[15] Mikhail Shishkin, *Maidenhair*, trans. Marian Schwartz (Rochester: Open Letter, 2012), 24. Cf. Katja Petrowskaja, *Maybe Esther*, trans. Shelley Frisch (London: 4th Estate, 2018) and David Albahari, *Götz and Meyer*, trans. Ellen Elias-Bursać (San Diego: Harcourt, 2004).

speculative fiction and genre fiction.[16] Simultaneously, authors are aware of the crucial paradigms of memory scholarship, particularly those that have been successfully adopted by literary criticism and literary studies—such as 'postmemory'—and make use of them consciously and creatively.[17]

Along with fresh topics and theoretical and formal approaches, the twenty-first century also brought new technologies that have allowed a reconsideration of mnemonic and archival tools and practices and rethinking such notions as the 'library,' the 'exhibition,' or the 'archive.'[18] In one instance, the Auschwitz Memorial Museum regularly posts a photograph of one former prisoner who was born on that day and provides a short note about their fate on their social media channels: "12 August 1941 | French Jewish girl Annie Nakache was born in Constantine, Algeria. She lived in Toulouse—a daughter of a swimmer Alfred Nakache. In January 1944, she was deported to #Auschwitz with her parents. She was murdered in a gas chamber with her mother, Paule."[19] At the same time, over the past three decades, digital cameras and recording and storage devices have become accessible (which also means affordable) for almost anyone, enabling new ways of active participation in commemoration actions. Mainly social media platforms and content management systems that offer intuitive user interfaces allow laypersons to share their family stories, memoirs, and discoveries and to also discuss them publicly. Considering internet platforms have already established their literary poetics ('Tweets', i.e., posts on Twitter, require similar rigid brevity as aphorisms or haiku),[20] one can see how the digital era connects literature with memory practices.

---

[16] Cf. Igor Ostachowicz's ironic horror novel *Night of the Living Jews*: Igor Ostachowicz, *Noc żywych Żydów* (Warszawa: Wydawnictwo W.A.B., 2018).

[17] On the concept "postmemory," see Marianne Hirsch, *Generation of Postmemory: Writing and Visual Culture After the Holocaust* (New York: Columbia University Press, 2012).

[18] Aleida Assman, "Canon and Archive," in *Cultural Memory Studies: An International and Interdisciplinary Handbook*, eds. Astrid Erll and Ansgar Nünning (Berlin, New York: Walter de Gruyter, 2008).

[19] Auschwitz Memorial/Muzeum Auschwitz, "12 August 1941. French Jewish girl Annie Nakache," Facebook, August 12, 2022.

[20] Cf. poetological analyses of Twitter and Facebook contributions: Ingunn Lunde, "Hashtag Poetics: Political humour on Russian Twitter," *Zeitschrift für Slawistik* 61, no. 1 (2016); Rebecca Romdhani, "Minor genres and marginal realities: Kei Miller's blog posts and Facebook notes," *Journal of Postcolonial Writing* 54, no. 1 (2018).

AIM AND STRUCTURE OF THE VOLUME

Literature functions as a compelling medium and creative force of remembrance and identity-making.[21] Hence the following volume's task is to introduce and analyze contemporary authors' attempts to engage with various mnemonic practices. The book offers case studies from Estonia, Georgia, Hungary, Poland, Russia, and Serbia, with some cross-national or trans-regional (Upper Silesia), ethnically diverse (including Jewish) perspectives. The articles deal with literary works from twenty-first-century viewpoints and exhibit how diverse authors could find strategies to work around monolithic identity-making processes through the flexible use of temporal frameworks, stretching the past into the present and sometimes into the future, or the other way around.

Voicing Memories, Unearthing Identities is divided into sections based on three different aspects of the literary approach to make sense of the self. As the book's title suggests, its aim was, first and foremost, to collect the *voices* of people exercising private and public remembrance. Through this practice and its setbacks, the identity/identities of the authors/protagonists *unearth*. Thus, one can see stages between voicing and reconfirmation step by step. To this end, the book is organized into three parts. The first of them, *Creating Identity*, includes articles that analyze the creative dependence between writing literature and fabricating identities. "Creating identities" is, admittedly, a standard feature of literary culture, yet the volume's contributors reinvestigate this question with the help of conceptual maneuvers such as the 'futures past,' the 'lie,' 'forgetting,' or 'archival writing.' Justyna Tabaszewska, for instance, examines a few works by Polish authors to illustrate how alternatives for our future could be conceived vis-à-vis historical events. She argues that works like Jacek Dukaj's anthology *PL+50. Histories of the Future* (*PL+50. Historie przyszłości*, 2004) and Ziemowit Szczerek's novel *Victorious Republic* (*Rzeczpospolita zwycięska*, 2013) demonstrate how the visions of the past frame stories of the future as "an active component of collective memory."[22] Jennifer Döring's article presents comparative analyses of three contemporary Russian authors (Lyudmila Ulitskaya, Mikhail Shishkin, and Andrei Gerasimov), referring to the concept of the lie as a powerful tool for both forgetting and preserving 'the truth' in specific circumstances. All authors portray the lie as a social venture passing on stories from one generation to another. A similar notion concerning generational memory is investigated by Alena Heinritz. In

---

[21] Astrid Erll, *Memory in Culture* (London: Palgrave Macmillan, 2011).

[22] Jacek Dukaj, ed., *PL + 50. Historie przyszłości* (Kraków: WL, 2004); Ziemowit Szczerek, *Rzeczpospolita zwycięska: Alternatywna historia Polski* (Kraków: Znak, 2013).

her article, she explores the importance of archives and documents in the context of the post-communist memory culture while analyzing prose by Kéthévane Davrichewy, Kateřina Tučková, and Lyudmila Ulitskaya.

In the second part of the volume, *Conflicting Identity*, the reader will find three chapters that deal with conflicts in identity molding. Today, we are aware of identities' fluid nature: their multiple facets are not free from apparent contradictions, and, moreover, not all elements of identity are level. One of the most striking uneven relationships in this regard is the Jewish–Polish juxtaposition throughout the twentieth century: the Jewish population in Poland, although speaking Polish and sharing specific social visions of the era, was seen (and saw itself) as the Other. Karolina Kołpak focuses on this very Jewish–Polish confrontation: The author claims that the term 'conflict,' often describing the historical relationship of the two ethnic groups normatively, hinders proper comprehension of the minority-majority imbalance. Her extensive analysis of Szczepan Twardoch's novels *The King of Warsaw* (*Król*, 2016) and *The Kingdom* (*Królestwo*, 2018) demonstrates that the Silesian author managed to show the asymmetry of the Poles and the Jews in interwar Warsaw.[23] Transitioning from the interwar era to the communist era, one will find Melinda Harlov-Csortán's article about another dark phase of Eastern and East-Central European collective memory. According to Harlov-Csortán, contemporary Hungarian writers and filmmakers (Péter György, György Száraz Miklós, and Márta Mészáros) touched upon the question of historical rupture in post-socialist memory. In their works, the lack of accounts of the past and deliberate silencing illustrates the difficulties of generational transmission of memory visions. The prose of contemporary Polish-Jewish authors (Agata Tuszyńska, Piotr Paziński, and Mikołaj Grynberg), analyzed by Elisa-Maria Hiemer, adds an intriguing layer to such struggles. Hiemer argues that for Jewish citizens, the lack of strong Jewish memory in Poland and the overall Polish national perspective (the combination of heroism and victimhood) became an additional obstacle in the process of identity formation. Identities are being shaped and shaken, but there are efforts to restore them throughout the changing times.

The three chapters from the last part of the book, *Preserving Identity*, cover a more comprehensive range of mnemonic practices that aim to ensure the consistency of the narratives. Philine Bickhardt's analysis of David Albahari's novel *Götz and Meyer* (*Gec i Majer*, 1998) explains the synthesis of differing testimonies of the Shoah between divided subjectivities.[24] The novel offers an extensive account of the perpetrator's view, but it is precisely thanks to such a

---

[23] Szczepan Twardoch, *Król* (Kraków: Wydawnictwo Literackie, 2016).
[24] David Albahari, *Götz and Meyer.*

step that 'the unspeakable,' i.e., the account of the victim, can be reconstructed. Here, Bickhardt argues, "[i]magination 'fills' the gap left by the witness and the document," the gap between the subjective and the objective. While purely textual attempts to preserve identities retain their scope, modern technology allows us to tackle this issue differently. Kseniia Tereshchenko and Antonina Puchkovskaia present the possibility of reinterpreting Gulag literature in the digital world. Their digital humanities project entitled "Notes from the Camp" focuses on the Gulag literature of Estonians, which was often overshadowed by the work of the same genre but written in Russian. Since Gulag literature, as a hybrid form of fiction and non-fiction, has complex cultural implications, the authors emphasize the importance of accessible resources to continue working on the memories of the Gulag, pointing out that the living collective can vary even within one country and one community. The chapter by Monika Glosowitz showcases such examples of the women's herstories of Upper Silesia, a historic mining region of contemporary Poland. Highlighting contemporary women writers such as Anna Dziewit-Meller and Joanna Fligiel, Glosowitz points out that there is a way in which Silesian women's expression would not be an insignificant part of official national myths (neither Polish nor Silesian nor German) but could become counter-narratives to the forced gender hierarchy in the economic dynamics in the region.

In sum, the chapters in the following book address a fusion of three academic fields: memory studies, Eastern and East-Central European studies, and literary studies, and invite further interdisciplinary dialogues on remembrance, oblivion, and recollection.

APPENDIX: UKRAINIAN ESSAYS

The editors started planning this volume in 2021, and the authors finished writing their chapters long before the full-scale Russian invasion of Ukraine began. While the book accommodates several diverse voices from different parts of the Eastern and East-Central European region, the feeling that the volume lacked a vital component could not be shaken off. Adding to the original volume's manuscript, we decided to include short essays on memory and literature that were kindly offered to us by four Ukrainian literary scholars. By having these variegated texts appear in one book, we wish to express our solidarity with the people whose voices have yet to be heard and whose search for identity via memory is to be continued.

REFERENCES

Adorno, Theodor W. "Cultural Criticism and Society." In *Prisms*. Translated by Samuel and Shierry Weber. Edited by Thomas McCarty. Boston: MIT Press, 1997.

———. *Gesellschaftstheorie und Kulturkritik*. Frankfurt am Main: Suhrkamp Verlag, 1975.

Agamben, Giorgio. *What Remains of Auschwitz: The Archive and the Witness*. New York: Zone Books, 1999.

Akhmatova, Anna. *Selected Poems*. Translated by D. M. Thomas. London: Penguin Books, 1992.

Albahari, David. *Götz and Meyer*. Translated by Ellen Elias-Bursać. San Diego: Harcourt, 2004.

Aleksievich, Svetlana. *Secondhand Time. The Last of the Soviets*. Translated by Bela Shayevich. New York: Random House, 2016.

Assmann, Aleida. "Canon and Archive." In *Cultural Memory Studies: An International and Interdisciplinary Handbook*, edited by Astrid Erll and Ansgar Nünning, 97–108. Berlin–New York: Walter de Gruyter, 2008.

———. *Cultural Memory and Western Civilization: Functions, Media, Archive*. Cambridge: Cambridge University Press, 2011.

———. *Ist die Zeit aus den Fugen? Aufstieg und Fall des Zeitregimes der Moderne*. München: Hanser, 2013.

Auschwitz Memorial/Muzeum Auschwitz. "12 August 1941. French Jewish girl Annie Nakache." Facebook, August 12, 2022. https://www.facebook.com/auschwitzmemorial/photos/a.10150892453251097/10158362489591097/.

Dukaj, Jacek, ed. *PL+ 50: Historie przyszłości*. Kraków: WL, 2004.

Erll, Astrid. *Memory in Culture*. Translated by Sara B. Young. New York: Palgrave Macmillan, 2011.

Erll, Astrid, and Ansgar Nünning. "Literaturwissenschaftliche Konzepte von Gedächtnis: Ein einführender Überblick." In *Gedächtniskonzepte in der Literaturwissenschaft: Theoretische Grundlegung und Anwendungsperspektiven*, edited by Astrid Erll and Ansgar Nünning, 1–10. Berlin–New York: Walter de Gruyter, 2005.

———, eds. *A Companion to Cultural Memory Studies*. Berlin–New York: Walter de Gruyter, 2010.

Etkind, Alexander. *Warped Mourning: Stories of the Undead in the Land of the Unburied*. Stanford: Stanford University Press, 2013.

Jablonka, Ivan. *A History of the Grandparents I Never Had*. Translated by Jane Kuntz. Stanford: Stanford University Press, 2016.

———. *History Is a Contemporary Literature: Manifesto for the Social Sciences*. Translated by Nathan J. Bracher. Ithaca, NY: Cornell University Press, 2018.

Keff, Bożena. *On Mother and Fatherland*. Cambridge, MA: MadHat Press, 2017.

Kołodziejczyk, Dorota, and Cristina Şandru. "Introduction: On colonialism, communism and east-central Europe – some reflections." *Journal of Postcolonial Writing* 48, no. 2 (2010): 113–116.

Lipstadt, Deborah, and Eva Fogelman. "Children of Jewish Survivors." In *Encyclopaedia Judaica*, vol. 9, edited by Fred Skolnik, 382–388. Detroit: Thomson Gale, 2007.

Lunde, Ingunn. "Hashtag Poetics: Political humour on Russian Twitter." *Zeitschrift für Slawistik* 61, no. 1 (2016): 102-118.

McGlynn, Jade, and Oliver T. Jones, eds. *Researching Memory and Identity in Russia and Eastern Europe*. London: Palgrave Macmillan, 2022.

Ostachowicz, Igor. *Noc Żywych Żydów*. Warszawa: Wydawnictwo W.A.B., 2018.

Petrowskaja, Katja. *Maybe Esther*. Translated by Shelley Frisch. London: 4th Estate, 2018.

Pucherova Dobrota and Gafrik Robert, eds. *Postcolonial Europe? Essays on Post-Communist Literatures and Cultures*. Leiden: Brill, 2015.

Radonić, Ljiljana. "Post-communist invocation of Europe: memorial museums' narratives and the Europeanization of memory." *National Identities* 19, no. 2 (2017): 269–88.

Rigney, Ann. "Ongoing: Changing Memory and the European Project." In *Media and Cultural Memory/Medien und kulturelle Erinnerung*, edited by Astrid Erll and Ansgar Nünning, 339–360. Berlin–New York: Walter de Gruyter, 2014.

Romdhani, Rebecca. "Minor genres and marginal realities: Kei Miller's blog posts and Facebook notes." *Journal of Postcolonial Writing* 54, no. 1 (2018): 95–107.

Rothberg, Michael. *Multidirectional Memory: Remembering the Holocaust in the Age of Decolonization*. Stanford: Stanford University Press, 2009.

Shishkin, Mikhail. *Maidenhair*. Translated by Marian Schwartz. Rochester: Open Letter, 2012.

Szczerek, Ziemowit. *Rzeczpospolita zwycięska: Alternatywna historia Polski*. Kraków: Znak, 2013.

Tota, Anna Lisa and Trever Hagen, eds., *Routledge International Handbook of Memory Studies*. (London–New York: Routledge, 2016).

Twardoch, Szczepan. *Król*. Kraków: Wydawnictwo Literackie, 2016.

PART I.
CREATING IDENTITY

Chapter 1

Future in Memory Studies and Functions of Alternative Histories

Justyna Tabaszewska

Institute of Literary Research of the Polish Academy of Sciences, Poland

Abstract: This chapter's main interest is the question of how the future, mediated through the different versions of alternate histories, can be a part of collective and cultural memory. The paper shows—by utilizing Ann Rigney's idea of remembering hope and Brian Massumi's notion of futures past—that certain visions of the future are a vital point of reference for at least some collective memory frames. The research material analyzed in the paper comprises mostly Polish novels, especially alternative histories created by Jacek Dukaj, Jerzy Sosnowski, Łukasz Orbitowski, Edward Redliński and Ziemowit Szczerek, and Jan Komasa's film *City 44*. These texts are interpreted in a twofold manner: as autonomous cultural texts and as media of memory. This approach allows to show how literature can contest different memory schemas and how— by creatively using both literary and memory clichés—literary texts are used to deconstruct affects standing behind contemporary politics of history.

Keywords: memory, future, alternate history, Polish novels, media of memory, futures past

***

INTRODUCTION[1]

This chapter's main interest is the question of how the future—both anticipated now and at a certain point in time—can be a part of collective and cultural memory. The first part of the paper lays the groundwork for the thesis that

---

[1] This article is a part of the project *Memories of "Future Past" as an Aspect of Creating* Contemporary Poetics of Memory, financed by the Polish National Agency for Academic Exchange, through the Bekker programme.

literature is that medium of memory that—if analyzed properly—can provide the clearest illustration of this complex research question. The next part of the text introduces three different conceptualizations of the future and underlines the most interesting ones—Ann Rigney's[2] idea of remembering hope and Brian Massumi's notion of futures past.[3] The following sections of the article analyze the complex and intriguing example of Polish collective memory and Polish literature to show how the future, especially the past future, is used to create, support or contest certain memory frames.

The intuition that the future past is a significant point of reference for collective memory is particularly important in the case of Polish culture and literature, which—as both critics and writers have noted—often flees from the troublesome present either into the past or the future.[4] This article will attempt to show that, in many cases, the direction of this escape is past future—the unrealized vision of a once possible future that nonetheless actively influences frames of memory.

The research material which will be analyzed in this paper comprises mostly Polish novels, especially alternative histories created by Jacek Dukaj (b. 1974), Jerzy Sosnowski (b. 1962), Łukasz Orbitowski (b. 1977), Edward Redliński (b. 1940) and Ziemowit Szczerek (b. 1978), although I will also refer to Jan Komasa's (b. 1981) film *City 44* (*Miasto 44*, 2014). Those texts are interpreted twofold: as autonomous literary and cultural texts and as media of memory. This approach shows how literature can contest the kind of politics of memory that dominated Polish public discourse in recent years and how—by creatively using both literary and memory clichés—literary texts are used to deconstruct affective facts and affects standing behind contemporary politics of history. The article, therefore, shows that although alternative histories are not often analyzed in the context of memory, they provide the perfect research material for memory studies, particularly in the context of how a merely anticipated future can influence the memory of certain events.

---

[2] Ann Rigney, "Remembering Hope: Transnational Activism Beyond the Traumatic," *Memory Studies* 11, no. 3 (2018): 368–80.

[3] Brian Massumi, *Ontopower: War, Powers, and the State of Perception* (Durham, London: Duke University Press, 2015).

[4] Cf. for example Jacek Dukaj, "Wstęp," in *PL +50: Historie przyszłości*, ed. Jacek Dukaj (Kraków: WL, 2004); Przemysław Czapliński, "Marginesy i centrum," in *Codzienne, przedmiotowe, cielesne*, ed. Hanna Gosk (Warszawa: Świat Literacki, 2002).

A FEW BASIC QUESTIONS AND A STEP TOWARDS DEFINING THE FUTURE IN MEMORY STUDIES

This chapter considers the peculiar exchange that takes place between literature and memory in the context of the future. To shed some light on the matter at hand and to delineate the research field, I first need to posit several questions and hypotheses. The primary one relates to the future: although memory research is not limited to what was but also looks at the relationship between past events and the current framework of memory, this way of perceiving things still rests upon a dynamic but merely a bidirectional relationship between the past and the present.[5] The future appears in memory studies as a point of arrival, which should guide current actions[6] rather than as an element that transforms the aforementioned dyadic relation into a triad. Indisputably, the relegation of the future to the outskirts of memory research comes from the inherent difficulty associated with writing about things that have not yet happened. Meanwhile, as this article attempts to show, the future—the one currently anticipated, the one imagined in the past, or the one that lives on as part of the memory of the things that once might have been—is a constituent of collective memory. And it cannot be treated as if it were not so, irrespective of the theoretical hardships that it brings. Therefore, the only path a researcher interested in, the triadic, dynamic memory, can take requires a direct reconsideration of the problem at hand.

Literature is a non-obvious but, nonetheless, invaluable aid in this confrontation. Those genres of literature that are interested in how imagination and memory work, are the particular area where the subject of the future was regularly considered, and they, therefore, provide invaluable source material.[7] As research from various fields of science indicates[8]—including neuroscience,[9]

---

[5] See Aleida Assmann, *Cultural Memory and Western Civilization: Functions, Media, Archives* (Cambridge: Cambridge University Press, 2011); Michael Rothberg, *Multidirectional Memory: Remembering the Holocaust in the Age of Decolonization* (Stanford: Stanford University Press, 2009).

[6] Karl Szpunar and Piotr Szpunar, "Collective Future Thought: Concept, Function and Implications for Collective Memory Studies," *Memory Studies* 9, no. 4 (2016): 376–89; Robert Crownshaw et al., eds., *The Future of Memory* (Oxford: Berghahn Books, 2010).

[7] It should be also noted that the future of literary research is a widely researched phenomenon, especially in the area of comparative literature. See Ursula K. Heise, ed., *Futures of Comparative Literature: ACLA State of the Discipline Report* (London: Routledge, 2017).

[8] Pascal Boyer and James V. Wertsch, eds., *Memory in Mind and Culture* (Cambridge: Cambridge University Press, 2009), 18.

[9] Martin Conway et al., "The Remembering–Imagining System," *Memory Studies* 9, no. 3 (2016).

psychology and sociology,[10] memory studies with its currently fast-growing subdiscipline: collective future though,[11] and literary research— the process of imagining and constructing coherent versions of the future strongly depends both upon the way our memory works (on the individual and collective level) and on literature's ability to entice the reader to actively remember and imagine different versions of reality. To put it simply: literature—and genres such as alternate history, utopias and dystopias in particular—can be treated as a medium of various forms of memory, including the memory of a possible and past future. Interacting with the visions of pasts and futures carried by literature can, therefore, as Meymune Topcu and William Hirst suggest, be the first step towards becoming actively engaged in the present reality.[12] Additionally, literature is better suited than history to dealing with the challenge of describing what could be or what could happen with our future: this advantage of literature comes from its singular status as a medium of memory, which is concurrently able to represent established frames of memory and influence those that are just emerging. This brings to mind the work of Astrid Erll, who points out that literary texts re-present cultural memories and that these texts also provide the patterns that inform our perception of the past.[13]

From the point of view of this paper, Erll's thesis ought to be extended and transformed: literature shapes our perception of the past and the future. In the latter case, it is more efficient than any other medium, as it is not limited by comparable constraints, and its ability to create fictional worlds is not a hindrance in this case but an asset. To better describe how the literary medium can be beneficial in the analysis of the compound problem of the future's place in memory research, it is best to begin with a general description of how the future is understood for the purpose of the current argument. First of all, when writing about the future, I do not refer to some futuristic vision of history's course, and I refrain from any speculation on which path it is most likely to take. Secondly, the future might be understood, at the least, in a threefold way: as that future which is currently anticipated, as the one which was awaited in the past, and the one which is presently considered to have been most likely in preceding times (though it was not necessarily so). The typology introduced here is in no way complete—it is

---

[10] Meymune Topcu and William Hirst, "Remembering a Nation's Past to Imagine Its Future: The Role of Event Specificity, Phenomenology, Valence, and Perceived Agency," *Journal of Experimental Psychology: Learning, Memory, and Cognition* 46, no. 3 (2020).
[11] Szpunar and Szpunar, "Collective Future Thought."
[12] Topcu and Hirst, "Remembering a Nation's Past."
[13] Astrid Erll, *Memory in Culture,* trans. Sara B. Young (New York: Palgrave Macmillan, 2011), 226.

considered to be a starting point that grounds the attempt to describe the influence of the future on current frames of memory.

FLUID FUTURES AND THE UNCERTAIN BOUNDARIES BETWEEN WHAT COULD HAVE BEEN AND WHAT WE WANT TO BELIEVE COULD HAVE HAPPENED

Anticipated Future and Futures Past

This part of the chapter will analyze the previously introduced distinction in greater detail and attempt to ascertain whether the backdrop of alternate history is constructed upon what might have been or rather on that which we want to believe was possible at some point. This task requires a working definition of the notion *currently anticipated future.*

This category is grasped intuitively as our present imaginings and expectations of the future. Most of us have some more or less precise mental image of what is to come—if not in the long term, then at least in the shorter run. Nonetheless, alongside this individual future, which might be equated with planning, we also speculate about it on a macro level. Sometimes these predictions are expressed directly (any political program is a blueprint for a particular future) or take the form of specialized analysis (relating to projected inflation, the job market, etc.). But they can also manifest as less particularized collective hopes or fears. The latter have become an important part of our everyday lives in the years of the COVID-19 pandemic, as the questions of the final curbing of the disease or its subsequent waves concern nothing else than our common future.

Sometimes—and not as rare as it might seem—literature becomes the carrier of such futuristic visions, expressing both collective and individual fears. This is often the case when cultures, nations, or groups across historical thresholds, inspire speculation on what will come next and how the future could substantially differ from the present.

This problem will be explained more closely later in this chapter, but now I would like to focus on the second type of the three ways mentioned above in which the future can be understood. The intuition that part of the memory of the past is also constituted by the once anticipated future is well illustrated by Brian Massumi's theory of futures past[14] and—on the other hand—by Ann Rigney's remarks on how we remember and build hope.[15] Massumi suggests that any anticipated event (for example, a possible terrorist attack) is henceforth remembered as possible, that is, as a future that could have

---

[14] Massumi, *Ontopower.*
[15] Rigney, "Remembering Hope."

materialized. When such an event is accompanied by strong affects, these turn into affective facts—the fear elicited by a terrorist threat is indisputably real, even though the threat might not have been. Massumi pays the greatest attention to fear as the most basic of affects, one which activates the memory of a possible future, but optimism[16] can be no less powerful in this regard. Massumi draws attention to a peculiar trait of such memory: it has identity- and community-building properties, as there is no other framework for collective identification as rigid as the one constructed around a traumatic event, even if the said event was only potential in its character.[17]

While Massumi argues that past futures and affective facts associated with them can be politically dangerous (because they are prone to manipulation), Ann Rigney claims that they can also be useful for building positive memory and social consciousness by showing that even in a traumatic past we can see hope for a future change. And that hope, as Rigney points out, should be used as a political and cultural tool, activating transnational activism.[18]

Despite obvious differences, Massumi and Rigney claim that past futures are an under-researched source of collective memory and identity. To better explain the gravity of this phenomenon, it is necessary to focus on specific cases. As was already mentioned, this paper explores mostly Polish frames of memory, as it is paradigmatical for the Central European countries, which were gravely impacted by the Second World War and underwent a sudden political shift during the 1990s after the dissolution of the Soviet Union. The choice of Poland is influenced not only by the rich Polish literature pertaining to the future and alternative histories but also by the permanent Polish obsession with the subject, which goes back in time much further than the start of the twenty-first century.[19] This example will allow me to highlight the tensions present at the intersections of the memory of certain events, the memory of affective facts, and the future's past that are associated with them.

---

[16] Cf. the notion of the cruel optimism: Lauren Berlant, *Cruel Optimism* (Durham, London: Duke University Press, 2011).

[17] See Brian Massumi, "Everywhere You Want to Be: Introduction to Fear," in *The Politics of Everyday Fear*, ed. Brian Massumi (Minneapolis, London: University of Minnesota Press, 1993), 3–37.

[18] Rigney, "Remembering Hope."

[19] See, among others Maciej Wierzbiński, *Zdobycie Gdańska* (Warszawa: Wydawnictwo Universum, 1931).

One of the best cases of negotiating memory about what might have been is the Polish memory of the Warsaw Uprising.[20] This event[21] is one of the most important nodes of Polish collective memory. Though experts differ in their assessment of the event itself, it can be interpreted either as a military defeat of the Home Army, an act of heroism sparked by the hope of liberating the city, or—according to the less popular opinions—an event that escapes easy ethical categorizations (alongside the obvious bestiality displayed by the Nazi forces there were some ethically dubious decisions taken by Polish leaders, such as allowing children to partake in war efforts).[22] The Warsaw Uprising is—according to Maria Kobielska, among others[23]—one of the crucial nodes of Polish memory, still vital after more than eighty years since it occurred. In my opinion, the singularity of this event stems from its fluid status—the assessment of what has happened rests to a great extent upon the *current* perception of Warsaw's possible future past: whether it was the total destruction of the city by the Nazis or rather a speedy liberation by the Red Army, stationed not far from the city at the time.

The memory of the Uprising is therefore framed not only by what has happened, not only by the judgment of actions of the Home Army's military command, but also by what *might have been*—and the fact that Warsaw's fate was uncertain in any case, feeds the discussion that has been ongoing for many years.

Further complicating the matter, the vision of the future anticipated by the insurgents was extremely optimistic: the German army was to be easily pushed back and forced to leave Warsaw by the Home Army. This affective fact is the cornerstone of many texts of culture that take up the topic of the Uprising, among them *City 44* (*Miasto 44*)—the motion picture directed by Jan Komasa—which aptly depicts the beliefs of the rebels in the first days of the Uprising. The hope was that the whole endeavor would take several days and that the approaching Soviet forces would join the fight if things did not go as

---

[20] The Uprising started on August 1, 1944, and it was the most important military effort led by the Polish Home Army. The aim of the Uprising was to liberate Warsaw from the Nazi forces before the arrival of the Red Army. It was a military defeat on a grand scale: more than 80% of the city was destroyed and around two hundred thousand Polish citizens were killed.

[21] I define the term 'Event' after Lauren Berlant, "Intuitionists: History and the Affective Event," *American Literary History* 20, no. 4 (2008): 845–60.

[22] The sociological and historical analysis of this phenomenon was already carried out by Lech Nijakowski, *Polska polityka pamięci* (Warszawa: WAiP, 2008) and Tomasz Łubieński, *Ani tryumf, ani zgon: Szkice o Powstaniu Warszawskim* (Warszawa: Wydawnictwo Nowy Świat, 2009).

[23] Maria Kobielska, *Polska kultura pamięci w XXI wieku: dominanty* (Warszawa: Wydawnictwo IBL, 2016).

planned. What had occurred was far from what was anticipated. The optimism of the first days gave way to the horror of failure on an unimaginable scale. Despite all this, as evidenced by Komasa's film, among other works, the possibility of victory still functions in Polish memory as one of the versions of the affective future past.

Traces of this belief can be found not only in contemporary political history, which underscores the inaction of the Red Army (transferring the responsibility for the massacre of civilians from the Nazi occupant, and in some sense from the commanders of the Home Army, onto the USSR), but also in literature. Maria Kobielska points to the novel of Łukasz Orbitowski, titled *Spectres* (*Widma*, 2012),[24] which explores such a vision of history where the Uprising never occurred. I will not summarize the novel here, but I want to highlight its peculiar aspect.[25] Although the book's starting point is the description of the reality in which the Uprising did not take place, the novel quickly turns into a story about Warsaw, where eleven years after the non-existent Uprising, history returns to its old tracks, obliterating everything that was destroyed in August 1944. On a meta-level, Orbitowski's novel shows the attachment of Polish collective memory to thinking about history as discrete. This means that individual events can be—in the novel literally, in the collective memory figuratively—closed in a box and removed from its course. What is interesting is the fact that specters of once possible pasts haunt the Polish imagination quite frequently; in some cases, they are even described simply as ghosts, returning to complicate the already quite complex present—like in the case of the Cursed Solders,[26] whose ambiguous history forms the background of Orbitowski's two other works: the short novel *It's coming* (*Nadchodzi*, 2017) [27] and the drama *Fire* (*Ogień*, 2012).[28]

The second event that provokes analogous memory responses in Poland was the introduction of Martial Law in 1981. Similarly, in this case, the collective perception of the event depends largely not on what happened (the Martial Law period is well researched by historians),[29] but on what could have

---

[24] Łukasz Orbitowski, *Widma* (Kraków: WL, 2012).

[25] I analyze this example in detail in the paper "Affective Future and Non-existent History: The Issue of Future Past in Memory Research," *Memory Studies* (preprint).

[26] This term is used mainly to describe the Polish anti-communist movement formed around 1945 by members of the Polish Underground State.

[27] Łukasz Orbitowski, "Nachodzi," in *Nadchodzi* (Kraków: WL, 2017).

[28] Łukasz Orbitowski, *Ogień* (Warszawa: NCK, 2012).

[29] The Martial Law was declared on December 13, 1981. The government drastically restricted everyday life to counter political opposition. The period of Martial Law is one of the most important nodes of Polish collective memory. Cf. Nijakowski, *Polska polityka pamięci*; Kobielska, *Polska kultura pamięci*.

happened, or more precisely—what we now view as possible scenarios of the future's past. If it is considered that introducing Martial Law saved Poland from Soviet intervention, it is usually assessed positively as the lesser evil. However, if it is considered that it only delayed the success of the Solidarity movement, it is considered an extremely negative event. Polish culture provides some interesting examples of alternative stories that elaborate on this event, the most interesting of which is Edward Redliński's *Hemorrhage* (*Krfotok*, 1998), which clearly supports the positive assessment, showing the negative effects of not introducing Martial Law (e.g. a military coup and civil war).[30]

Both above mentioned novels, despite their differences (the books relate to different historical events and Redliński does not use fantastic elements—his novel is kept in a realistic convention), can be considered examples of confronting the optimistic belief that Polish history could be completely different (and much better), if only one specific event were eliminated from it.

WHAT WE THINK COULD HAVE HAPPENED OR WHAT COULD HAVE HAPPENED? ABOUT THE FICTIONAL ADVANTAGE OF ALTERNATIVE HISTORIES

The examples, as mentioned above, allow us to expand the issue of the previously signaled distinction between what at a given moment was imagined or anticipated as a possible future and what is anachronistically reconstructed as such a past future. Orbitowski's book mixes these two categories: the future without the Warsaw Uprising was certainly anticipated, but it was not a future in which the uprising was prevented by supernatural intervention, while Redliński's novel explores scenarios of a future past that was possible, but probably much worse than the future anticipated in 1981. I draw attention to the fluidity of the seemingly obvious border between what was once anticipated and what is now considered to be possible in the past because the majority of alternative stories—as opposed to counterfactual history[31]—distinguish between what is or was possible and what may have been expected but never was possible. This is the case in two novels by Marcin Wolski (b. 1947): *Alterland* (*Alterland*, 2005),[32] in which the author explores three different scenarios of Hitler's assassination (an event that was possible, but whose outcomes were hard to predict), and in *Wallenrod* (*Wallenrod*,

---

[30] Edward Redliński, *Krfotok, czyli stanu wojennego nie było* (Warszawa: Muza SA, 1998).
[31] I define the term after Alexander Demandt, *History That Never Happened: A Treatise on the Question, What Would Have Happened If?*, trans. Colin Thomson (Jefferson: McFarland Publishing, 1993).
[32] Marcin Wolski, *Alterland* (Warszawa: WAB, 2005).

2012),[33] where the course of the Second World War is altered through the supernatural extension of Józef Piłsudski's life and by the activities of the Polish spy, Helena Wichmann.

It is worth underlining the shift I made in defining alternative histories in opposition to counterfactual history: it is to show why the alternative stories that do not have to avoid fantastic elements (which are unacceptable in the genre of counterfactual history, based on the assumption that alternative scenarios of history, explored in such genre, might not be very probable, as they may include many changes in the reality, but they all must be possible and logical)[34] but at the same time are not obliged to use them, are the medium more closely connected with the work of memory. The ability to create both realistic scenarios in which a given past could exist and to create cultural texts playing with the expectations and fantasies about the future past makes literature a medium that most strongly resonates with the already existing framework of memory, based not only on facts, but on the wishful politics of history.

Alternative stories created in the field of literature are often hybrid in terms of genres, drawing from philosophical concepts (especially the category of possible worlds),[35] and historical research—in which counterfactual history is understood as a specific thought experiment that allows for a better understanding of the mechanisms governing history—and from a vast literary tradition, spanning science fiction novels, spy novels, essays, biographies, and fictionalized gonzo reports.

The expansion of alternative histories is closely related to the political changes at the end of the twentieth century. Although other possible courses of reality were the object of philosophical investigations for a long time, the problem was recently introduced on a larger scale in literature and other texts of culture. As Catherine Gallagher points out, although some well-known alternative histories already existed in the 1950s, the 1990s are a time of growing

---

[33] Marcin Wolski, *Wallenrod* (Poznań: Zysk i S-ka, 2012).

[34] Counterfactual histories are most often used as an argument in the discussions about the strategic decisions in certain moments in history. For example, Piotr Zychowicz, a right-wing publicist, is trying to prove that Poland should have formed an alliance with Hitler, and not with Great Britain or France. See Piotr Zychowicz, *Pakt Ribbentrop-Beck czyli jak Polacy mogli u boku Trzeciej Rzeszy pokonać Związek Sowiecki* (Poznań: Rebis, 2012).

[35] See esp. David Lewis, *Counterfactuals* (Cambridge, Mass: Harvard University Press, 1973).

interest in the genre.[36] This expansion can be—as Matthew Schneider-Mayerson argues[37]—associated with the then-celebrated notions of the end of history,[38] which were consistent with the assumption that after the fall of the Berlin Wall, history will return to the "right track" and will develop according to the only possible scenario, wherein capitalism marks the final era in the advancement of societies. The period, which some historians name post-history[39] and that is sometimes interpreted as a time of immersion in the present and of abandoning great collective projects concerning the future,[40] is rich in texts that rewrite future past—as if, at the time, there was too little imagination that could produce a coherent vision of the future, and too much of it when it comes to rewriting history and contesting that what has already happened.

During that period, a simultaneous expansion and hybridization of two types of thinking about the future took place: on the one hand, the breakthrough of 1989 provoked the creation of a vision of a "new" future, especially in the countries undergoing political transformation at the time, on the other—it turned the past and the once possible visions of the future into a subject of discussion. These two kinds of futures thus became an active factor in the process of shaping collective identity and memory.

It is worth mentioning that the year 1989 and the changes taking place in Europe were a factor that triggered theoretical interest in the issue of the future, as well as the literary and cultural attempts to describe it. This phenomenon is discernible in the case of Polish alternate histories, which underwent a dynamic revolution in the 1990s, gradually becoming more and more elaborate and less embedded in casual historical thinking.[41] As both Catherine Gallagher[42] and Matthew Schneider-Mayerson[43] point out, this is why the genre of alternative history gained popularity at the time: its structure, based on counterfactual history but not constrained by the limits of what is or was possible, allows writers to confront both the fears and the hopes

---

[36] Catherine Gallagher, *Telling It Like It Wasn't: The Counterfactual Imagination in History and Fiction* (Chicago: The University of Chicago Press, 2018).
[37] Matthew Schneider-Mayerson, "What Almost Was: The Politics of the Contemporary Alternate History Novel," *American Studies* 50, no. 3/4 (2009): 63-83.
[38] Francis Fukuyama, *The End of History and the Last Man* (New York: Free Press, 1992).
[39] Hans Urlich Gumbrecht, *After 1945: Latency as Origins of the Present* (Stanford: Stanford University Press, 2013).
[40] Zygmunt Bauman, "Pięć przewidywań i mnóstwo zastrzeżeń," in *PL +50. Historie przyszłości*, ed. J. Dukaj (Kraków: WL, 2004).
[41] Przemysław Czapliński, "Alternowanie dziejów," *Teksty Drugie*, no. 3 (2022).
[42] Gallagher, *Telling It Like It Wasn't*.
[43] Schneider-Mayerson, "What Almost Was."

concerning the future and the disappointment connected with imperfect past. For the above reasons, alternate histories are better than other narratives about "what could / can be" at *representing* the currently dominant *politics of affect*, and they provide a perfect image of contemporary cultural memory for research. It is worth underlining that, especially Polish alternative histories are constructed as a tool to work through unresolved affects associated with the past, and they are most often based on exploring optimistic scenarios of some future past. As such, they are not following the path of classic American alternative histories, which are more pedagogical in their design, and they tend to create alternative histories as a warning against making old mistakes.

In conclusion, alternative stories, especially those which not only transform the past but also propose certain visions of the future, provide invaluable research material for memory studies, as they show in coherent form how thinking about the past changes under the influence of current experience and under the pressure created by anticipated future. The study of this phenomenon is particularly important in the case of Polish memory, characterized by its ability to combine distant experiences into a specific affect-memory knot, where what was and what may be intertwined seamlessly.

UNDER PRESSURE

To present this complex temporal and affective relation between what was and what can be, this part of the paper will explore the original anthology *PL+50. Histories of the future* (PL +50. Historie przyszłości, 2004), edited by Jacek Dukaj, who by then was already an established Polish writer.[44] The book was published in the year 2004, at a date that seems to be a turning point in Poland's history due to its accession to the European Union, and therefore— regardless of the assessment of this event—a breakthrough in international and economic relations of the country. The effects of joining the European Union are still felt by all Poles in their everyday experience, which is why it is a typical starting point for at least two questions: "what will come next?" and "what would have happened if Poland did not join the EU?" It is also— according to the theories connected with affect and memory studies—the Event that changes the structure of ordinary affects.[45] The effects of this event are as yet unforeseen and remain open, as evidenced by the recurring question in Polish politics about the possibility of Poland leaving the EU (which is sometimes even seen as a necessary "correction" of the past).

---

[44] Dukaj, *PL + 50.*
[45] Kathleen Stewart, *Ordinary Affects* (Durham, London: Duke University Press, 2007).

The fifty-year turning point, suggested in the anthology's title, has not yet elapsed, but seventeen years have passed since the book's publication. This puts the current reader in a unique position: they cannot *yet* be sure that the forecasts it signals will come true, but some already seem *more probable*. It is worth emphasizing the importance of the chosen time horizon: fifty years is a timespan within which the political map of the world can be fundamentally rearranged—as the twentieth century showed—but it is also a time that for many people is not only possible to imagine but also to live through. Jacek Dukaj was thirty years old when he edited the volume, and the predictions concerned the time when he would be eighty. For my generation—people who entered adulthood in 2004—the year 2054 will probably come at the end of their professional activity. To put it another way: the time perspective outlined here coincides with the perspective of human life. Thus, imagining Poland as it will be fifty years from now, the young generation imagines what it will experience. It is, therefore, the perspective of communicative memory.[46]

In the introduction to the volume, Dukaj mentions *Histories of the future* (*Historie przyszłości*, 1829?), written by the famous Polish poet of the Romantic era, Adam Mickiewicz (1798—1855). The work has not survived to our times, even though the poet created several drafts. However, from the fragments that were preserved, Dukaj conjectures that:

> Judging by our literature, Poland has always existed more in the past and in the future than in the present.[47]

The reference to Mickiewicz is extremely symptomatic. The most prominent Polish representative of Romanticism toiled over this never published text for several years in exile when Poland was under partitions. Strangely, this work inspired by completely different political circumstances remains a point of reference for Polish culture over 150 years later. Why is that?

Dukaj answers this question indirectly: imagining the future is not only an act of experimentation but also an attempt to take a stance towards the already undertaken efforts of anticipating the future, and towards the present, which Polish culture has the greatest difficulty with. How we imagine the future conveys very little about the actual future, but instead, it reveals a great lot about our current fears, hopes, and expectations. Even though the future is often a substitute subject for the present, all of its visions relate to the present,

---

[46] Jan Assmann, *Cultural Memory and Early Civilization: Writing, Remembrance, and Political Imagination* (Cambridge: Cambridge University Press, 2011).
[47] Jacek Dukaj, "Wstęp," in *PL + 50*, 6. All quotes from the Polish language are translated by the author of the article.

shaping our understanding of what was and what is to come. For this reason, projects such as *PL + 50* are unique texts from the point of view of literary and memory studies, as they represent with their structure the complicated relationship between the present and the future (and, which is worth mentioning, one of the few kinds of texts that allow for a clear distinction between the future as it was imagined at a certain point in time and the one which was created *ex post*).

The aforementioned anthology is comprised of works of literature, studies in political science, as well as of philosophical and sociological essays. In an attempt at categorization, two main tendencies become evident: there are the texts exploring the topic of nationhood and Polishness and the ones disregarding this theme. The second category encompasses works revealing (not only male) fear of feminism and the equal rights movement,[48] speculating on space exploration and the future of earth as a planet,[49] the possibility of manipulating the human psyche and creating human-machine hybrids, as well as scrutinizing the new forms of supranational totalitarianism curbing the freedom of expression.[50]

The questions of nationhood are taken up by Łukasz Orbitowski, who presents the possible history of a society that returns to pagan rites, banning Christianity.[51] It is worth mentioning that the history of early Slavs becomes the inspiration for new politics, as a certain future past—namely, the history of a country that never adopted Christianity—is given a new chance to be fulfilled. After 2004, this theme will become a substantial element of many alternate histories authored by Orbitowski and Ziemowit Szczerek, to name only two writers. Interestingly, a similar device was also employed by Dukaj, who, in the novel *Crux* (*Crux*), constructed a para-aristocratic universe where honor (understood in the traditional sense) is the code shaping human interactions. This anachronistic social model is slowly contested by the proletariat liberated from the necessity of work, but simultaneously completely marginalized. The joining of the past and future is best illustrated by the persona of the leader of the proletarian revolt, the titular Crux (Kruczyński):

---

[48] Bartosz Świderski, "Łabędzi śpiew ministra dźwięku," in *PL + 50*; Maja Kossakowska, "Serce wołu," in *PL + 50*.

[49] See esp. short novels of Maciej Dajnowski and Jarosław Grzędowicz in *PL + 50*.

[50] See esp. short novels of Krzysztof Maliszewski, Cezary Domarus, Bartosz Świderski, in *PL + 50*.

[51] Łukasz Orbitowski, "Władca deszczu," in *PL + 50*.

> Short cripple in an old tracksuit, all possible and impossible metals hanging from his neck, laser suns in his eyes, diamonds in his mouth.[52]

The blood of Edward Gierek, Lech Wałęsa, Andrzej Lepper, and Piotr Gliński flows in his veins. This is an exotic combination of four leaders[53] with very disparate characters, each of whom gravitates toward populist politics. It is also interesting how Dukaj manages to seamlessly join three levels in his narrative: the magical (Crux possesses supernatural powers, granting him the status of the proletarian leader), political (whose most important aspect is the neo-Sarmatian politics), and technological (it is the development of new technologies that has turned work into a privilege). The world created by Dukaj is filled with outright allusions to United Europe's extensive social policy and the first proposition of introducing guaranteed income, which is perceived as potentially dangerous, as it can lead to the marginalization of certain social classes.

The short stories described thus far painted social fears and anxieties that characterized the first years of the new millennium. However, the question of predicting the future has yet to be problematized in them. This topic is taken up in a very interesting story by Jerzy Sosnowski, titled *Auto-reversal* (*Autorewers*). The text is narrated in the first person singular, with the speaking subject unveiling his life story with noticeable effort. This is because, as it turns out, by telling the story, the protagonist also erases it. In the fictional world an auto-reverse is undertaken that is supposed to save humanity from an impending catastrophe—it is explained that this process is akin to playing a magnetic tape backward, but here the tape is made up of human consciousness:

> But if we nudge your consciousnesses to flow against the current of time, then you will relive everything, going back in time, as if the auto-reverse function of the before mentioned tape recorder was used.[54]

---

[52] Jacek Dukaj, "Crux," in *PL + 50*, 369.

[53] Edward Gierek is one of the major Polish politicians from the era of Soviet domination in Poland, Lech Wałęsa was the leader of the Solidarity movement and is a former Polish president, Andrzej Lepper was the leader of a populist party Samoobrona (Self-defense). The fact that Dukaj has included the name of Gliński, who was not a significant politician until recently (currently he is the Deputy Prime Minister of Poland), may come as a surprise. "Gliński" appears in the book without a name, but there was no other significant Polish politician (other than Piotr Gliński) active at the time.

[54] Jerzy Sosnowski, "Autorewers," in *PL + 50*, 195.

Sosnowski plays here with the perception of time in a very interesting way. History running backward, living for the second time all that which was already lived, is supposed to give hope for the survival of human consciousness, for enduring despite the catastrophe. In this case, alternate history is a history relived but with the opposite vector: from the present to the past. Deliverance from the unavoidable future is therefore found in the past, where one can find shelter from what seems bound to happen.

This brief description of the volume hopes to show that the mentioned stories share common elements and are coherent to a certain degree. They illustrate that attempts to anticipate a future beyond the shortest timespan, a simple continuation of the present, are doomed to return to the past: either the Sarmatian, the pagan, or the one which will replace the future in the act of auto-reversal. Therefore, it merits the question of whether, in the case of the projected future and alternative courses of history, the auto-reversal, as mentioned earlier (deliberate or subconscious), is not already taking place? Is it not that the pressure associated with creating a coherent vision of the future provokes the escape from thinking about what might happen and pushes us towards what once might have occurred?

AUTO-REVERSAL OF POLISH MEMORY

This research question offers new perspectives for analyzing the main trends of Polish literature and culture of the previous thirty years, especially its tendency to avoid current problems (for example, the issue of political outcomes of the 1989 transformation) and to focus on past events instead. The following section will examine a peculiar, though quite interesting book that touches upon the aforementioned matters—*Victorious republic* (*Rzeczpospolita zwycięska*, 2013) by Ziemowit Szczerek.[55]

The book managed to break free from the hermetic circle of alternate histories, securing Szczerek's position as a writer and entering into critical dialog with theoretical writing such as Jan Sowa's *The king's phantomal body* (*Fantomowe ciało króla*, 2011).[56] The book confronts the belief deeply ingrained in Polish politics of history, which has no solid factual grounding, that Second World War abruptly halted the favorable chain of events, depriving Poland of the happy future it was destined to achieve.

Szczerek based his alternative vision of history on facts while attempting to find or create a version of reality where the September campaign would not be

---

[55] Ziemowit Szczerek, *Rzeczpospolita zwycięska: Alternatywna historia Polski* (Kraków: Znak, 2013).
[56] Jan Sowa, *Fantomowe ciało króla* (Kraków: Universitas, 2011).

lost as swiftly as it was.[57] The starting point in his book is the description—completely factual, based on the analysis of historical sources—of the days directly preceding the outbreak of war and the initial days of the September campaign. What stands out the most in this account is the astonishing optimism and the belief that the war not only could be won, but will be won.

The optimism described by Szczerek is not a figment of the writer's imagination but the actual response to the first days of war. It is this optimism and the future anticipated at the time has, according to Szczerek, the greatest bearing on the later perception of the Second World War and the construction of innumerable alternative versions of Poland's history. Notwithstanding subsequent critical analyses, a gap emerged in the communal comprehension of what occurred: if the war was supposed to be won, then defeat is an incomprehensible and senseless event, which cannot be given any meaning unless through a flight into a world of phantasy. The description of this specific historical moment makes up the whole prologue to Szczerek's book. Beginning this way reveals a lot, as it lays out the affective facts that have become the cornerstones of the manufactured vision of the victorious republic—a vision that is not merely a literary fantasy but a state of affairs communicated in contemporary political debates, which in turn shape current Polish internal and external politics to a certain extent. All of this can be put into perspective with the aforementioned notion of *cruel optimism*.[58] It is fairly evident that the attitude described by Szczerek is brimming with cruel optimism, which influenced not only bad decision-making, but also the construction of the whole phantasmal structure of the possible future.

In Szczerek's narrative, the attempt to answer the question of what—besides victory—would have had to have happened for Poland to modernize is of great importance. The writer confronts the reader with Poland's possible future, one in which the country was not defeated during the war and managed to achieve exactly what is currently imagined by right-wing politicians as things that should have been done. In this vision of history, Poland—strengthened by foreign monetary aid, chosen as the regional leader

---

[57] It is worth underlining that although Poland was a part of the Allied forces and was therefore technically among the victors of the Second World War, in a common understanding, the war was lost by the Poles during the so-called September Campaign (i.e., the Polish defensive war in the first months of the conflict, which was fought between September 1, and October 6, 1939), followed by the five years of German occupation.
[58] Berlant, *Cruel Optimism*, 23.

of the Intermarium[59]—would also fall, this time not because of the war, but because of domestic problems.

Szczerek's diagnosis is particularly interesting (especially the final section, which is a short, fictional gonzo-style reportage from the alternative year 2013), as it seems to quite accurately predict the direction in which Poland is headed under current conservative rule. It is worth taking a closer look at the traces of the future past deconstructed by Szczerek that are also present in the current political landscape. For example, the concept above of Intermarium is currently perceived not as merely historical, but has become the point of reference for present-day politicians outlining the directions of Polish foreign politics in its new incarnation—the Three Seas Initiative, or Trimarium.[60] Turning to the interwar period as a source of political "inspiration" is visible even in the current fight against the coronavirus and the anticipated serious economic crisis—the currently ruling party openly declares that the spark restarting the halted economy will come from great infrastructural projects that were already under way, but now gain a new significance.[61] These projects are copies of the interwar propensity for great investment and modernization achieved through megaprojects, such as the Gdynia seaport and the Central Industrial Region. Currently, it is the Central Port of Communication that is meant to play a similar role (although it is clear that even if the Port will be built, it would not have the same positive impact on the Polish economy as the Gdynia seaport did), or the creation of a sea canal in the Vistula Spit in the exact spot first proposed five centuries ago by the Polish king Stefan Batory and afterward resurrected in 1945 by the pre-war prime minister and father of the interwar industrialization, Eugeniusz Kwiatkowski. This omnipresent "correction" of historical shortcomings seems to be more about living up to the futures presently imagined as first dreamed of in the past than anything else. A common element of actual history, the future past described by Szczerek, and the current political circumstances can be found in the specific way of envisioning modernization for contemporary

---

[59] 'Intermarium' is a concept from the interwar period relating to foreign politics that asserts a broad political alliance under Polish leadership, geopolitically determined by the confines of the Adriatic, Black, and Baltic Seas.

[60] 'Trimarium' was established in 2015 as a project to strengthen the cooperation of twelve countries in the Adriatic, Baltic and Black Sea regions. See government official website, accessed October 1, 2021, https://www.gov.pl/web/fundusze-regiony/inicjaty wa-trojmorza--przechodzimy-do-dzialania.

[61] The official government position states that "Huge investments are an impulse for the development of the national economy and ensuring its competitiveness." See government official website, accessed January 20, 2021, https://www.gov.pl/web/ aktywa-panstwowe/wielkie-inwestycje-buduja-silna-gospodarke.

society—that is, as pure economic progress dissociated from any progressive social values.

CONCLUSION

Szczerek's book can be treated as an example of the literary world dealing with the phenomenon of the self-reversal of memory: the writer confronts the reader with the fact that the version of the future past in which Poland emerged victorious from the Second World War was very unlikely. At the same time, this confrontation shows that the past future of Poland, seen in optimistic colors, is often treated by politicians as a horizon for thinking about the future: the aim of future actions is to correct past mistakes. In this situation, a complete auto-reversal takes place: the corrected past takes the place of the future, turning any conversation about the future into a discussion about the past—about what could have been, not what can still happen. This auto-reversal loop is the reason for the displacement within memory of what happened by that what could have happened but did not, due to an imagined fault of history or fate, and it tears from the field of imagination the freedom necessary to face the question of what our future should look like.

The alternative stories analyzed in this article show that the question of what could be is an active component of collective memory. Even when attempts are made to contest the vision of a lost happy future, as in Szczerek's novel, it cannot be denied that such a vision is a part of the memory framework—even if as a negative point of reference. Therefore, literature and the alternative stories created within it provide rich and often undervalued research material that explains the affective potential of the memory of specific events. In other words, the memory of particularly painful or controversial events is based not only on what happened and how the event is remembered from a contemporary perspective, but also on how the event fits into the imaginations of a once possible future—whether it is seen as a natural continuation of history or as its error. In the latter case, not only the event itself is remembered, but also the past future that could be realized if the event was eliminated from the track of history altogether. Therefore, the study of alternative histories capturing the vision of what could be is, in fact, the study of the past and present affective framework that shapes the memory of events that are particularly important for specific societies.

REFERENCES

Assmann, Aleida. *Cultural Memory and Western Civilization: Functions, Media, Archive.* Cambridge: Cambridge University Press, 2011.

Assmann, Jan. *Cultural Memory and Early Civilization: Writing, Remembrance, and Political Imagination.* Cambridge: Cambridge University Press, 2011.

Berlant, Laurent. "Intuitionists: History and the Affective Event." *American Literary History* 20, no. 4 (2008): 845–60.

Berlant, Laurent. *Cruel Optimism.* Durham, London: Duke University Press, 2011.

Boyer, Pascal, and James Wertsch, eds. *Memory in Mind and Culture.* Cambridge: Cambridge University Press, 2009.

Conway, Martin et al. "The Remembering–Imagining System." *Memory Studies* 9, no. 3 (2016): 256–65.

Crownshaw, Richard et al., eds. *The Future of Memory.* Oxford: Berghahn Books, 2010.

Czapliński, Przemysław. "Marginesy i centrum." In *Codzienne, przedmiotowe, cielesne,* edited by Hanna Gosk, 15–38. Warszawa: Świat Literacki, 2002.

Czapliński, Przemysław. "Alternowanie dziejów." *Teksty Drugie,* no. 3 (2022): 19–40.

Demandt, Alexander. *History That Never Happened: A Treatise on the Question, What Would Have Happened If...?* Translated by Colin Thomson. Jefferson: McFarland Publishing, 1993.

Dukaj, Jacek, ed. *PL+ 50: Historie przyszłości.* Kraków: WL, 2004.

Erll, Astrid. *Memory in Culture.* Translated by Sara B. Young. New York: Palgrave Macmillan, 2011.

Fukuyama, Francis. *The End of History and the Last Man.* New York: Free Press, 1992.

Gallagher, Catherine. *Telling It Like It Wasn't: The Counterfactual Imagination in History and Fiction.* Chicago: The University of Chicago Press, 2018.

Gumbrecht, Hans Ulrich. *After 1945: Latency as Origins of the Present.* Stanford: Stanford University Press, 2013.

Heise, Ursula K., ed. *Futures of Comparative Literature.* ACLA State of the Discipline Report. London: Routledge 2017.

Kobielska, Maria. *Polska kultura pamięci w XXI wieku: dominanty.* Warszawa: Wydawnictwo IBL, 2016.

Lewis, David. *Counterfactuals.* Cambridge, Mass: Harvard University Press, 1973.

Łubieński, Tomasz. *Ani tryumf, ani zgon: Szkice o Powstaniu Warszawskim.* Warszawa: Wydawnictwo Nowy Świat, 2009.

Massumi, Brian, ed. *The Politics of Everyday Fear.* Minneapolis-London: University of Minnesota Press, 1993: 3–37.

Massumi, Brian. *Ontopower: War, Powers, and the State of Perception.* Durham, London: Duke University Press, 2015.

Nijakowski, Lech. *Polska polityka pamięci.* Warszawa: WAiP, 2008.

Orbitowski, Łukasz. *Nadchodzi.* Kraków: WL, 2017.

Orbitowski, Łukasz. *Ogień*. Warszawa: NCK, 2012.

Orbitowski, Łukasz. *Widma*. Kraków: WL, 2012.

Redliński, Edward. *Krfotok, czyli stanu wojennego nie było*. Warszawa: Muza SA, 1998.

Rigney, Ann. "Remembering Hope: Transnational Activism Beyond the Traumatic." *Memory Studies* 11, no. 3 (2018): 368–80.

Rothberg, Michael. *Multidirectional Memory: Remembering the Holocaust in the Age of Decolonization*. Stanford: Stanford University Press, 2009.

Schneider-Mayerson, Matthew. "What Almost Was: The Politics of the Contemporary Alternate History Novel." *American Studies* 50, no. 3/4 (2009): 63–83.

Serwis Rzeczypospolitej Polskiej: Ministerstwo Funduszy i Polityki Regionalnej. "Inicjatywa Trójmorza – przechodzimy do działania." Accessed October 1, 2021. https://www.gov.pl/web/fundusze-regiony/inicjatywa-trojmorza--prze chodzimy-do-dzialania.

Serwis Rzeczypospolitej Polskiej: Ministerstwo Aktywów Państwowych. "Wielkie inwestycje budują silną gospodarkę." Accessed January 20, 2021. https:// www.gov.pl/web/aktywa-panstwowe/wielkie-inwestycje-buduja-silna-gosp odarke.

Sowa, Jan. *Fantomowe ciało króla*. Kraków: Universitas, 2011.

Stewart, Kathleen. *Ordinary Affects*. Durham, London: Duke University Press, 2007.

Szczerek, Ziemowit. *Rzeczpospolita zwycięska: Alternatywna historia Polski*. Kraków: Znak, 2013.

Szpunar, Karl, and Piotr Szpunar. "Collective Future Thought: Concept, Function and Implications for Collective Memory Studies." *Memory Studies* 9, no. 4 (2016): 376–89.

Topcu, Meymune, and William Hirst. "Remembering a Nation's Past to Imagine Its Future: The Role of Event Specificity, Phenomenology, Valence, and Perceived Agency." *Journal of Experimental Psychology: Learning, Memory, and Cognition* 46, no. 3 (2020): 563–79.

Wierzbiński, Maciej. *Zdobycie Gdańska*. Warszawa: Wydawnictwo Universum, 1931.

Wolski, Marcin. *Alterland*. Warszawa: WAB, 2005.

Wolski, Marcin. *Wallenrod*. Poznań: Zysk i S-ka, 2012.

Zychowicz, Piotr. *Pakt Ribbentrop-Beck czyli jak Polacy mogli u boku Trzeciej Rzeszy pokonać Związek Sowiecki*. Poznań: Dom Wydawniczy Rebis, 2012.

Chapter 2

Lies and Memories in Contemporary Russian Literature (Lyudmila Ulitskaya, Mikhail Shishkin, Andrei Gelasimov)

Jennifer Döring
University of Tübingen, Germany

Abstract: The following paper focuses on the lie as a narrative strategy to create, preserve and also delete memories in fictional, literary texts. For the permanent preservation of memories and to make them accessible, it is necessary to convey them outwards. Aside from physical practices, e.g., rites and ceremonies, this is most notably achieved by the speech (oral or written). Here, memories are selected, ordered and structured so they can be expressed as a coherent narrative. The endeavor to present a unified and coherent narrative, however, bears the danger of unconsciously or consciously filling in memory gaps or blanks. For this purpose, three texts of contemporary Russian literature are examined as examples, in which lying speech and lying narration, respectively, thematize different modes of memory: First, "forgetting" in Lyudmila Ulitskaya's *Women's Lies* (2002), secondly the "preservation of memories" in Mikhail Shishkin's *Maidenhair* (2005) and finally the lie as a generational problem in Andrei Gelasimov's *The Lying Year* (2003).

Keywords: lie, forgetting, narrative, truth, Ulitskaya, Shishkin, Gelasimov, Russian, contemporary

***

The primal scene of memory consists of bearing witness to anatrope, the plunge from life into death. It consists of the indexical act of pointing to

the dead (the ancestors) and the iconographic act of transforming the dead into a concept of what they were as living people.[1]

In her introductory chapter "Mnemotechnics and Simulacra" to the volume *Memory and Literature. Intertextuality in Russian Modernism (Gedächtnis und Literatur. Intertextualität in der Russischen Moderne,* 1990), the German Slavist and literary theorist Renate Lachmann describes the link between memory and writing about ancient mnemotechnics. By recourse to the *simulacrum*[2] as a feature inherent in every sign or image, Lachmann not only circumvents the problem of a clearly definable constitution of meaning, but also points to the fundamentally secondary, deceptive, partial, and thus fragile character of memory. The idea – that memory processes are a realistic representation of past events and experiences in the present – must therefore be fundamentally questioned. This is already pointed out by numerous works in various disciplines, such as cultural studies, sociology, and history, which reject the conception of memory as a kind of consistent and all-encompassing store or archive and understand memory work more in the sense of a horizon of experience that is constantly updated in the present.[3] With the false-memory-debate in the 1990s, the unreliability and instability of memory

---

[1] Renate Lachmann, *Memory and Literature: Intertextuality in Russian Modernism,* trans. Roy Sellars and Anthony Wall (Minneapolis, London: University of Minnesota Press, 1997), 7. See also Jan Assmann, *Das kulturelle Gedächtnis: Schrift, Erinnerung und politische Identität in frühen Hochkulturen* (München: Verlag C.H. Beck, 1992), 61.

[2] Lachmann concretizes the concept of the simulacrum (image, illusion) as follows: "Every sign, every image as a complex of signs, is inscribed in relation to an antithetical sign, a simulacrum, a 'false' or 'deceptive' sign. By presenting the identical as potentially nonidentical, the similar as potentially dissimilar, the simulacrum deprives the sign of the semantic legitimation that stabilizes it. To begin with, the simulacrum can be written into a field marked by the oppositions absent/present, false/true, invisible/visible, nonreferential/referential." Lachmann, *Memory and Literature,* 10.

[3] For example, historian Johannes Fried describes the memory process as an experience that can be actualized and modeled in the present. Johannes Fried, *Der Schleier der Erinnerung: Grundzüge einer historischen Memorik* (München: Verlag C.H. Beck, 2012), 19. See also sociologist Elena Espositio, who, with recourse to Niklas Luhmann's concepts of systems theory, understands memory not as a place to preserve past events, but as a requirement for the selective storage of events. Elena Esposito, *Soziales Vergessen. Formen und Medien des Gedächtnisses der Gesellschaft* (Frankfurt am Main: Suhrkamp Verlag, 2002), 24.

accounts became the focus of criminal and psychological discussions.[4] The memory function of literature within a culture also finds itself in constant tension between fictionality, reality and truth claims, especially regarding (auto)biographical narratives and texts.[5]

This paper attempts to approach memory practices in fictional texts of contemporary Russian literature using three selected textual examples. I am primarily concerned with how characters remember and (re)present their memory within a narrative.[6] All three texts convey the memory representation with the help of a lying and thus "false" speech as a narrative strategy. In the following, the lying representations of the characters' memories will be considered a literary motif and thus distinguished from extra-literary, reception-aesthetic questions, such as the claim to truth of literary texts in relation to the real-world context. In other words, it is not about literature as a lie, but about the characters appearing in literature who make use of lying speech.

It is necessary to delimit the concept of a lie, which can only be presented here schematically due to the manifold and interdisciplinary findings. The mentioned characteristics of consciousness and intent to deceive go back to the Augustinian definition of a lie and are also often used as a reference in more current debates.[7] This can be seen, for example, in the concept of the

---

[4] See here, for example, Hans Stoffels, "False Memory-Syndrome: Eine Herausforderung für die Psychotherapie," in *Tarnen, Täuschen, Lügen: Zwischen Lust und Last*, ed. Gunther Klosinski (Tübingen: Attempto Verlag, 2011), 101. See also the anthology edited by Paul S. Appelbaum, Lisa A. Uyehara, and Mark R. Elin, *Trauma and Memory: Clinical and Legal Controversies* (New York: Oxford University Press, 1997). Robert C. Schank and Robert P. Abelson, "Knowledge and Memory: The Real Story," in *Knowledge and Memory: The Real Story* ed. Robert S. Wyer Jr. (Hillsdale, New York: Erlbaum, 1995), 1–85.

[5] See Monika Schmitz-Emans, "Im Zwischenreich: Lügen, Fälschungen, Fiktionen, Texte und Bilder. Oder: Die Macht der Paratexte," in *Dichter Lügen*, ed. Kurt Röttgers and Monika Schmitz-Emans (Essen: Verlag die Blaue Eule, 2001),189.

[6] In their anthology *Gedächtniskonzepte der Literaturwissenschaft*, Astrid Erll and Ansgar Nünning name three basic tendencies of memory research in literature: 1) memory *of* literature 2) memory *in* literature 3) literature as a medium of memory. Astrid Erll and Ansgar Nünning, "Literaturwissenschaftliche Konzepte von Gedächtnis: Ein einführender Überblick," in *Gedächtniskonzepte der Literaturwissenschaft. Theoretische Grundlegung und Anwendungsperspektiven*, ed. Astrid Erll and Ansgar Nünning (Berlin, New York: Walter de Gruyter, 2005), 2.

[7] Augustine of Hippo (354–430) notes: "However, no one doubts that he lies who deliberately says what is false with the intention of deceiving. It is clear, then, that a lie is a false statement made with the desire to deceive." Augustinus Aurelius, "Lying," in *Treatises on Various Subjects: Saint Augustine*, ed. Roy J. Deferrari (Washington, D.C.: Catholic University of America Press, 2002), 60.

German philologist Harald Weinrich (1927—2022), in which the Augustinian notion of *duplex cogitatio* (double thinking) is replaced by the *duplex oratio* (double speech) from a linguistic perspective.[8] By this, Weinrich means that an unspoken truth-sentence is inherent in every uttered lie-sentence.[9] While Weinrich does not subject lying to any moral evaluation, Augustine, who develops his concept on the basis of the interpretation of Scripture, assumes a general prohibition of lying.[10] Independent of moral-theological evaluation, the prohibition of lying or, conversely, the imperative of truth also proves to be a stabilizing and reliable factor in practice within concrete speech situations.[11] This communication-related convention of sincerity can be concretized with Andreas-Pazifikus Alkofer's concept of "coagulated experience"[12] within a fixed and handed-down "contrast and consensus"[13] dichotomy as generationally transmitted knowledge of certain norms and rules. The premise of this 'social contract' implies that appropriate behavior is not only expected (receiver) but also observed (sender). Conversely, this also means that any violation of these rules would be tantamount to a violent transgression of the socially set normative boundaries. That this is not a rarity, especially within the political sphere, is described by Nikolai Aleksandrovich Berdyaev (1874—1948) from exile in Paris in his essay *The Paradox of the lie* (*Paradoks lzhi*, 1939). Under the impression of the Soviet regime, the philosopher of religion criticizes totalitarian states in which the quest for power prevails over the search for truth.[14] In this context, Berdyaev continues, the lie becomes a social phenomenon that, with the help of modern myths, i.e. narratives, forms the basis for and represents ordered societies:

---

[8] Augustine also uses the term *duplex cor*, which is synonymous with the concept of the *duplex cogitatio*, because according to ancient understanding, the mind was located in the heart. Augustinus Aurelius, "De mendacio," in *Augustinus Opera Werke*, ed. Johannes Brachtendorf and Volker Henning Drecoll (Paderborn: Ferdinand Schöningh, 2013), 62.

[9] Harald Weinrich, *Die Linguistik der Lüge* (München: Verlag C.H. Beck, 2016), 41.

[10] Since there are numerous examples of lies in the Bible, Augustine argues here very precisely and differentiates the lies according to their function and their degree of severity to defend the general ban on lying. See for example Augustinus, "Lying," 60.

[11] See Jörg Meibauer, "Introduction: What is lying? Towards an integrative approach," in *The Oxford Handbook of Lying*, ed. Jörg Meibauer (Oxford: Oxford University Press, 2019), 2–3.

[12] The translations are mine unless otherwise noted. Original quotation: "geronnene Erfahrung". Andreas-Pazifikus Alkofer, "'Erklär'mir Lüge, verklär' sie nicht...' Die ‚Quellen der Moralität' und die Lüge. Ein ethisch-theologischer Zwischenruf," in *Kulturen der Lüge*, ed. Mathias Mayer (Köln, Weimar: Böhlau, 2003), 45.

[13] Original quotation: "Kontrast und Konsens," Ibid.

[14] Nikolai A. Berdyaev, "Paradoks lzhi," *Sovremennaya zapiski 69* (1939): 274.

The myths deeply rooted in the mass consciousness are an expression of this lie. Through these organized myths, the lie rules the world and guards human societies. Ancient myths emerged from the collective unconscious and always had some kind of reality as their basis. Modern myths are characterized by consciously organized lies. There is no naivety in them. This may sound pessimistic, but it must be recognized that lies are at the heart of social organization.[15]

The common point of reference between memory and lie is thus the narrative. The (cultural) memory needs the coherent narrative as an outwardly directed form of representation in order to be able to provide meaning and orientation.[16] However, this requires, in case of doubt, supplementation of the gaps created by the secondary, fragmentary and fragile properties of memory. The fact that this can be done not only unconsciously, but also through deliberate misrepresentation (lying) will now be examined in more detail using three example texts from contemporary Russian literature: Lyudmila Ulitskaya's *Women's Lies* (*Skvoznaya liniya*, 2002), Mikhail Shishkin's *Maidenhair* (*Venerin volos*, 2005), and Andrei Gelasimov's *The Lying Year* (*God obmana*, 2003). The three selected texts are not so-called *ego-documents* such as memoirs, (auto)biographies or diaries, which have a special place in the debate of memory due to their particular claim to truth. Rather, these are purely fictional representations, all published in the early 2000s, in which lying speech appears as an in-text narrative strategy to present the characters' memories. Although the link between the conscious speech (lie) carried out with the intention of deception and memory as a reconstructive and meaning-giving process within a real-world context can certainly be questioned, the literary text is free to make use of such norm-bound, transgressing, repulsed or tabooed procedures.[17]

---

[15] Original quotation: "Глубоко вкорененные в массовое сознание мифы являются выражением этой лжи. Через эти организованные мифы ложь управляет миром, охраняя человеческие общества. Древние мифы возникали из коллективного бессознательного творчества, и в основании их всегда были какие-то реальности. Современным мифам свойственна сознательно организованная ложь. В них нет наивности. Это будет звучать пессимистично, но нужно признать, что ложь кладется в основание организации общества." Ibid., 273.

[16] See also Assmann, *Das kulturelle Gedächtnis*, 75.

[17] See also Astrid Erll and Ansgar Nünning, "Literatur und Erinnerungskultur: Eine narratologische und funktionsgeschichtliche Theorieskizze mit Fallbeispielen aus der britischen Literatur des 19. und 20. Jahrhunderts," in *Erinnerung, Gedächtnis, Wissen. Studien zur kulturwissenschaftlichen Gedächtnisforschung*, ed. Günter Oesterle (Göttingen: Vandenhoeck & Ruprecht, 2005), 188.

In Ulitskaya's work, lying speech is used to describe an act of forgetting, which will be examined in more detail in the first chapter using Aleida Assmann's theory on the forms of forgetting. Unlike Ulitskaya, in Shishkin's work, it is the preservation of memory in the form of a coherent narrative at the center of the novel's plot, which can be seen more closely in Donald P. Spence's psychoanalytic approach, *Narrative Truth and Historical Truth*. In Gelasimov's *The Lying Year*, lying speech appears as a generational problem, a legacy that cannot be escaped.

LYUDMILA ULITSKAYA'S *WOMEN'S LIES (SKVOZNAYA LINIYA,* 2002)[18]

And yet the fibbing of woman, unlike the pragmatic lying of man, is a highly rewarding topic. Women do everything differently: alternative thinking, feeling, suffering — and lying. And God in heaven, how they lie! [...] En passant, unintentionally, purposelessly, passionately, suddenly, surreptitiously, irrationally, desperately, and simply for no reason at all. [...] The lying of woman is as much a natural phenomenon as milk, or a birch tree, or a bumblebee.[19]

Lyudmila Evgen'evna Ulitskaya is probably one of the best-known voices in contemporary Russian literature. It is not only the major historical events such as the Stalinist past, war or the collapse of the Soviet Union to which the author devotes herself in her work, but equally the small, rather inconspicuous stories and fates at the center of which are often female protagonists.[20] This is also the case in *Women's Lies* from 2002, a text composed of five individual episodes, which deals with the lies of women, who, according to the author in her preface, do this in a very special way and, above all, differently from men. The lies in Ulitskaya's text are neither productive nor power-politically oriented. Rather, the descriptions are fictitious memories, i.e., supposedly experienced stories of life and suffering,

---

[18] The original text comprises a total of five stories. An English translation exists only for the story "Diana" and "End of story," whereby the latter is part of the German translation, but not of the original Russian text.

[19] Lyudmila Ulitskaya, "Women's Lies," in *Nine of Russia's foremost women writers*, trans. Arch Tait, ed. Svetlana Aleksievich (Moskva: Glas. Publ., 2003), 239–40.

[20] For example: *Medea and her children (Medeya I ee deti)* (1996), *Lyalin dom* (1999) or *Lyudi nashego tsarya* (2005). Lyudmila Ulitskaya was born in 1943 in Bashkiria and grew up in Moscow. After graduating, she worked as a geneticist before achieving a literary breakthrough in the early 1990s with her first novel *Sonechka* (1992). Since then, Ulitskaya has not only received numerous awards, but is also active as an activist against the Putin government.

which are exposed as untruths in the course of the narratives and thus cover up the actual memories or events of the characters.

The originators of the tall tales in the individual episodes, and their stories, vary and are held together only by the main character Zhenya, who appears as a constant link between the individual chapters throughout the entire plot period from the late 1970s to the 1990s. For the most part, she acts as a passive listener – initially in private, and later in her function as an employee at a television station. Only in the fourth episode, "Natural phenomenon"[21] the young girl Masha takes Zhenya's place, although in the end, it is the main character who exposes the lying descriptions of the former literature professor Anna Venianimovna to Masha. In addition to the literature professor, the narrators of the tall tales are various women, such as Zhenya's accidental vacation acquaintance Irene, little Nadya, Zhenya's thirteen-year-old niece Lyalya, and the prostitutes Tamar, Lada, and Lyuda. While the stories of the women dominate the individual episodes, the reader learns only fragments about Zhenya, for example, her planned dissertation as a literary scholar, which she later abandons for a job at the TV station. This fragmentary information about the main heroine is communicated with the help of a distanced, non-diegetic narrator[22] and stands in clear distinction to the internal narratives of the lying women, described from the respective first-person perspective. Ulitskaya thus makes use of a quasi-('as if')-autobiographical narrative style, i.e., a preferred form of representation for the credible communication of memories.[23] Christiane Solte-Gresser, professor of comparative studies, also refers to this in her study of Ulitskaya's *Women's Lies*, identifying the interior narratives as "small literary narratives within the fictional world"[24] and elaborating on the reception-aesthetic significance of Zhenya as a listener. She attests to the protagonist's dynamic development in dealing with the respective tall tales, within which she gradually moves into the center of the action.[25] This tendency is confirmed in the course of the text by the less sensitive reactions of the listener Zhenya to the women's tall tales. While the first story "Diana" becomes a downright traumatic experience for

---

[21] In original: "Yavlenie prirody."
[22] I am using the categories according to Wolf Schmid, *Narratology: An introduction* (Berlin, New York: Walter de Gruyter, 2010), 68; 105.
[23] See Michael Basseler and Dorothee Birke, "Mimesis des Erinnerns," in *Gedächtniskonzepte der Literaturwissenschaft*, ed. Astrid Erll and Ansgar Nünning (Berlin, New York: Walter de Gruyter, 2005), 234.
[24] Original quotation: "kleine literarische Erzählungen innerhalb der fiktionalen Welt." Christiane Solte-Gresser, "Begabte Schwindlerinnen: Über die Inszenierungen der Lüge bei Ljudmila Ulickaja," *Cahiers d'Études*, 68, Vol. 2 (2015): 192.
[25] Ibid., 193.

Zhenya, her reaction to the lies of the prostitutes, described in the last chapter, is far more rational.

Ulitskaya's text resembles a palimpsest in that the individual lying stories are overwritten with the help of new narrative texts, and only the form of the lying speech remains recognizable as a trace. The latter thus appears as a constantly repeating narrative strategy of staging feigned memories, while the event remembered is hidden, repressed, and made unrecognizable by the women such that it can ultimately be forgotten. If memory is understood as a process of reconstruction of past events updated in the present, it would be obvious to describe forgetting as a deconstructive activity and thus an antipode to memory. Aleida Assmann rejects this assessment and describes the acts of remembering and forgetting as a mutually dependent and intertwined phenomenon.[26] She argues that any remembering as a process of reconstructing events experienced or witnessed in the past that takes place in the present includes an, at least temporary, forgetting that is an absence within consciousness.[27] In other words, forgetting is the precondition for remembering at all. Assmann distinguishes nine different techniques of forgetting as they occur in the practical reality of life, two of which seem particularly relevant with regard to Ulitskaya's text: First, *covering-up*, which Assmann understands as the deliberate exclusion of an event from a communicative situation, following Avishai Margalit's reconciliation model.[28] And secondly, the *overwriting* in *Women's Lies* occurs in two ways. On the one hand, the lying women 'overwrite' their past metaphorically by making up new and more spectacular narrations. On the other hand, the individual stories in Ulitskaya's entire text are overwritten by the ever more new (lying) stories of the other women.[29]

I would now like to consider the first aspect of overwriting in the first chapter "Diana." The story is about Irene, who, along with her demented mother, Susan Yakovlevna and their well-behaved son Donald, accidentally meets Zhenya and her son Sasha in the late 1970s. The fact that Irene is a red-haired, polyglot Englishwoman with Dutch-Russian roots is emphasized several times and is already perceived by Zhenya at the beginning in the form of an "exotic"

---

[26] Aleida Assmann, *Formen des Vergessens* (Bonn: bpb, Bundeszentrale für Politische Bildung, 2018), 13.

[27] Ibid., 16.

[28] Ibid., 21. Avishai Margalit is an Israeli professor emeritus in philosophy at the Hebrew University of Jerusalem. Furthermore: Avishai Margalit, *The Ethics of Memory* (Cambridge: Harvard University Press, 2021), 188.

[29] The other techniques Assmann mentions are: 1) Delete 2) Hiding and Repression 3) Silence 4) Ignoring 5) Neutralization 6) Denial and 7) Losing. Assmann, *Formen des Vergessens*, 21–26.

appearance. So Irene's foreign origin and subsequent foreign language, in contrast to Russian, can be seen as the first indication of the Englishwoman's later false or different speech. A similar picture is painted by the last story ("Schastlivyj sluchaj"), which deals with the Ukrainian and Russian prostitutes Lada, Tamar and Lyuda, respectively, who work in Switzerland, for they, too, are foreigners and stand on the fringes of Swiss society.

The location of the events surrounding Irene is a small vacation resort in the Crimea, whose architecture resembles a "theater set"[30] and thus provides the appropriate setting for the impressively staged appearance of the main character. Although Zhenya initially shies away from contact and prefers to read *Anna Karenina* to learn more about "the real drama of a real woman,"[31] the Englishwoman persuades her to join her for an evening drink. What follows far surpasses the events surrounding Tolstoy's main character. Irene devotes the first evening to a detailed rendering of an impressive family history, ranging from the communist youth of her Dutch-born mother Susan to the Soviet espionage activities of her British father. Zehnya "got more and more drunk, but by now not from the port, [...] but from admiration and delight at her new acquaintance,"[32] and therefore, she initiates another meeting the following day. The following get-together begins with Irene's remark that she had never told anyone the following story before, despite her chattiness:

'Zhenya, you must realise by now what a chatterbox I am. I tell people everything about myself. I'm no good at keeping secrets. Mine or anybody else's. Don't say you haven't been warned. There is one thing, though, that I've never told to a soul. You shall be the first. For some reason I suddenly want to.'[33]

Irene not only clearly marks the beginning of the following story-within-the-story, but also points out to Zhenya her exclusive privilege as a listener. This is followed by the spectacular descriptions of Irene's past, which include the death of a total of four children, as well as the great love of the Englishwoman. Especially the stories about the second-born Diana, who is said to be distinguished by her long black hair and equally long legs right after her birth and who already starts to speak her first words at the age of four months, for example, by saying "Thank you"[34] to her mother after breastfeeding, capture

---

[30] Ulitskaya, *Women's Lies*, 242.
[31] Ibid., 243.
[32] Ibid., 245.
[33] Ibid., 248.
[34] Ibid., 254.

Zhenya's attention. The tragic story about Diana ends with Irene's confession that she had caused her daughter's death by an erroneously administered dose of medication. A few days later, when their mutual acquaintance Vera[35] appears at the resort, she reveals to Zhenya the true story of the Englishwoman's life:

> 'Listen, Zhenya, I am going to have to upset you. Or gladden you. The point is, all the tenants of our house in Pechatnikov were rehoused ten years ago, in 1968. At that time Irene was twentyfive. To my knowledge, she had got through an army of lovers, had, I should guess, a dozen or so abortions, but there were absolutely no children. I swear! Or husbands, for that matter.'[36]

The techniques of forgetting mentioned at the beginning – *covering up* and *overwriting* – are evident from this passage at the end of the narrative. Irene's true past, with its numerous love affairs and abortions, is covered up, made invisible, and overwritten with a new text by the remarkable stories of lies. The positive images of self and others can thus not only be maintained, but are also intensified as Irene stylizes herself as the victim of a multitude of traumatic events.

MIKHAIL SHISHKIN'S[37] *MAIDENHAIR* (*VENERIN VOLOS*, 2005)

While in Ulitskaya's work, the fictitious memory moves within an intimate, familial space, in Mikhail Shishkin's novel *Maidenhair*, it is the collective trauma[38] of victims of war and violent events that the characters in a Swiss immigration office, hoping for asylum, take up in their narratives.[39]

The novel is divided into a total of four storylines, which in turn represent four different levels of memory: The first level, which is largely structured as a

---

[35] The name Vera translated from Russian means faith and implies a truth claim for which no logical or factual evidence is needed.

[36] Ulitskaya, *Women's Lies*, 267.

[37] Mikhail Pavlovich Shishkin was born in Moscow in 1961 but has lived in Switzerland with his family since the mid-1990s. He has received numerous awards for his work, including the Russian Booker Prize in 2000, and writes his texts, such as *Taking Izmail* (*Vzyatie Izmaila*, 1999), *Maidenhair* (*Venerin Volos*, 2005), and *Pis'movnik* (2010) in Russian.

[38] I use the term 'collective trauma' here because the applicants in *Maidenhair* appear as a largely homogeneous and nameless group in which the traumatic event is not tied to the individual subject but circulates within the group.

[39] On the collective trauma in Shishkin's *Maidenhair*, see also Helena Goscilo, "Narrating trauma," in *Russian literature since 1991*, ed. Evgeny Dobrenko and Mark Lipovetsky (Cambridge: Cambridge University Press, 2015), 167–87.

question-and-answer dialog, tells of the everyday life of an unnamed translator who works in a Swiss immigration office together with Peter, the "master of fates,"[40] where they decide on the asylum applications of the so-called "Gesuchsteller" (GS).[41] The second plot line is formed by the translator's private memories, which revolve around his failed marriage to Isolde, who is still attached to her first husband, Tristan, who has already died. One day, the translator is commissioned to write a biography of the famous singer and actress Isabella Dmitrievna (Bella), and he comes across her diary, the reception of which marks the beginning of the third of the four storylines. The last level comprises the numerous interpolations from Greek and Egyptian mythology as well as the intertextual references to literary works by authors such as Aleksandr Blok, Pushkin, but also Arthur Conan Doyle. In addition to texts by other authors, Shishkin also refers to his own work. Thus, the collage-like structure of the text, interspersed with mythological stories, resembles his novel *Taking Izmail* (*Vzyatie Izmaila*, 1999).[42] Another similarity can be seen in the auto-biographical references interspersed by the author. While in *Taking Izmail*, a fictional author named Mikhail Shishkin is given the chance to speak, in *Maidenhair* it is the "paradise"[43] Switzerland, the adopted country of the real author Mikhail Shishkin, to which the applicants would like to gain entrance. While the translator's private reminiscences and Bella's diary entries are individually marked memories, the mythological and intertextual interpolations and quotations can be understood in the sense of a memory of literature.[44] The interviews with the applicants, on the other hand, represent a

---

[40] Mikhail Shishkin, *Maidenhair*, trans. Marian Schwartz (Rochester: Open Letter. Literary translations from the university of Rochester, 2012), 7. In the Christian tradition of the New Testament, the apostle Peter is regarded as the representative of Jesus Christ, who controls the entrance to the Kingdom of Heaven.

[41] The word "Gesuchsteller" is written in German in the original Russian text and in the English translation.

[42] Shishkins *Maidenhair* not only resembles its predecessor in terms of narrative structure, but also quotes it. So it says: "'And Izmail? You must have sailed past Izmail!'." Shishkin, *Maidenhair*, 231. Shishkin also takes up the theme of writing or telling stories in order to survive, as described in *Maidenhair*, in his novel *Pis'movnik*, published in 2010. There, it is the correspondence between the two lovers Sasha and Volodya, that keeps the soldier Volodya alive beyond the limits and time of this world.

[43] Shishkin, *Maidenhair*, 21.

[44] See also Renate Lachmann, "Intertextuality and Dialogism," in *Memory and Literature: Intertextuality in Russian Modernism*, trans. Roy Sellars and Anthony Wall (Minneapolis, London: University of Minnesota Press, 1997), 49. Furthermore Oliver Scheiding, "Intertextualität," in *Gedächtniskonzepte der Literaturwissenschaft*, ed. Astrid Erll and Ansgar Nünning (Berlin, NewYork: Walter de Gruyter, 2005), 55.

common and literally understood collective memory[45]. It is not the truthfulness of the individual stories that decides whether the asylum application is approved, but merely the quality of the narratives. Thus it is said:

> Those speaking may be fictitious, but what they say is real. Truth lies only where it is concealed. Fine, the people aren't real but the stories, oh, the stories are! It's just that they raped someone else at that orphanage, not fat-lips. And the guy from Lithuania heard the story about the brother who burned up and the murdered mother from someone else. What difference does it make who it happened to? It's always a sure thing. The people here are irrelevant. It's the stories that can be authentic or not. [...] We become what gets written in the transcript. The words. You have to understand.[46]

Experiences of war and violence, as well as their subsequent memories, are not understood here as subject-bound events, but circulate as shared memories or narratives within the group of inquirers. The incessant and repeated question-answer passages between the translator and the mostly nameless inquirers resemble a conversation between psychoanalyst and patient, listener and narrator. The American psychoanalyst Donald Pond Spence (1926—2007) refers to this connection as a "narrative tradition"[47] established by Sigmund Freud. He distinguishes between "narrative truth," the goal of which is to establish a coherent narrative, and "historical truth," i.e., what is actually experienced:

> Narrative truth can be defined as the criterion we use to decide when a certain experience has been captured to our satisfaction; it depends on continuity and closure and the extent to which the fit of the pieces takes on an aesthetic finality. Narrative truth is what we have in mind when we

---

[45] The concept of collective memory goes back to Maurice Halbwachs. He assumes, that memory is always socially shaped. Maurice Halbwachs, *On Collective Memory* ed. and trans. Lewis A. Coser (Chicago, London: University of Chicago Press, 1992), 43; 54.

[46] Shishkin, *Maidenhair*, 24.

[47] Donald P. Spence, *Narrative Truth and Historical Truth.* (New York, London: W.W. Norton & Company, 1982), 25. Spence draws an analogy between the psychoanalytic and the narrative tradition and recognizes the psychoanalyst as listener and the patient as narrator. Here, the narrative tradition influences not only the psychoanalyst in his judgment, but also the patient, who is involuntarily anxious to tell a coherent story. Further, Spence points out that the clinical records are perceived as "quasi-literature," whose form is as important as its content. Ibid., 23.

say that such and such is a good story, that a given explanation carries conviction, that *one* solution to a mystery must be true.[48]

Spence criticizes the Freudian notion of the patient's free association, but also the highly interpretative procedure called "narrative listening,"[49] which the psychoanalyst carries out as "quasi-literary"[50] with the help of medical documents. The "literary quality,"[51] and thus also the aesthetic quality, take on such a large role in Freud, Spence continues, that a separation between historical and narrative (narrated) truth is hardly possible anymore.[52] The problem of translating an experienced event in the past into the reconstructive memory process of the present is aggravated by the fact that the memory images, in order to be able to represent them, have to be translated into words, which, together with the interpretation and documentation by the psychoanalyst, can also lead to distortions.[53] In *Maidenhair*, the memory images of the applicants undergo a double translation, on the one hand, in that they have to be transcribed as best-possible narratives, on the other hand, through the translation of the translator. The latter documents and records the descriptions, which becomes of existential importance for the applicants. Thus it is said:

> *Answer.* Tell me, why do you write down what I say if nothing's going to come of it anyway? They're going to say, you heard the bells, now clear out! I know that's what they tell everyone.
>
> *Question:* So at least something remains of you.
>
> *Answer.* You mean what you write about me will remain after I'm gone?
>
> *Question:* Yes.
>
> *Answer.* And what you don't will disappear with me? And nothing will remain?
>
> *Question:* No. Nothing.[54]

---

[48] Ibid., 31.
[49] Ibid., 29.
[50] Ibid., 23.
[51] Ibid., 22.
[52] Ibid., 27.
[53] The exact wording is: "we can think of his memories as being the result of an earlier translation from reality. His experience has been transformed into a series of discrete visual images that correspond to real life in the way a manifest dream corresponds to dream thought." Ibid., 59.
[54] Shishkin, *Maidenhair*, 271.

The historical truth loses its meaning. Only words recorded in the official protocol are maintained and secure the applicant's existence beyond this world. Jan Assmann describes in his fundamental work on memory *Das kulturelle Gedächtnis*[55] the issue of writing by distinguishing between ritual and textual coherence. Written cultures, or as the anthropologist Claude Lévi-Strauss calls them, "hot societies,"[56] leave ritual coherence behind and shift their cultural memory to the level of the text. While ritual coherence is based on constant repetition with as little variation as possible, the textual principle, as it is anchored in the present, allows for constant variation of content. The collective trauma in Shishkin's case and the equally collective attempt of the GS to obtain asylum in Switzerland encompass both techniques described by Assmann, that of the ritual and that of the text. The ritual coherence is not only evident in the constantly repeating question-answer constellation, but is revealed in the initiation rituals of the immigration office, which are always the same:

> All is the same as ever there. What could be new in the interpreting service? Everything follows a well-beaten path. Everything goes according to the form approved in the upper echelons. Each question according to the established model; likewise each answer. Peter doesn't even waste his voice on the standard greeting; he lets the interpreter read it off the page to the intimidated GS.[57]

After the interview, Peter signs the protocol and marks almost every document with the stamp "Prioritätsfall,"[58] with which a rejection of the asylum application is probable, and the questioning at the end is pending. The protocol, as the written result of the oral interviews, thus acts as an official repository for the statements contained therein, regardless of whether they are true or untrue.[59]

---

[55] Assmann, *Das kulturelle Gedächtnis: Schrift, Erinnerung und politische Identität in frühen Hochkulturen*, 87–88.

[56] Original quotation: "*les sociétés chaudes.*" Claude Lévi-Strauss, *La pensée sauvage* (Paris: Plon, 1962), 309.

[57] Shishkin, *Maidenhair*, 20.

[58] The word "Prioritätsfall" is written in German in the original Russian text and in the English translation. It means a fast process due to an obvious rejection. Ibid., 16.

[59] At this point, one should also think of the interrogation practice during the Stalinist era, in which confessions were often forced and had no relation to actual events.

ANDREI GELASIMOV'S[60] *THE LYING YEAR (GOD OBMANA,* 2003)

After that, I would get away episodically on less convincing grounds, but one way or another I always had to tell some lie. Lying had become an inalienable part of my life once again. What other choice did I have?[61]

The 1990s in Russia were characterized by a spirit of departure and new beginnings. The reforms initiated by Mikhail Gorbachev beginning in the mid-1980s under the slogan of transformation (*perestroika*) and transparency (*glasnost*) led to the disintegration of the hitherto strictly centralized Soviet Union in 1991. While a small part of the Russian population benefited from the liberalization tendencies and the transformation processes of the market (*oligarchiya*), the majority of Russians were confronted with a new but politically unstable system promoting corruption. The instability of the market economy and monetary policy led the Russian state under Boris Yeltsin's leadership into a financial crisis (*defolt*) in 1998, which resulted in the state insolvency, numerous bankruptcies of major banking institutions and a massive burden on the Russian population.

The plot of Andrei Gelasimov's novel *The Lying Year* (2003) is set in this period of instability and chaos. Unemployed Mikhail Vorob'ev receives an order from his former boss Pavel Pavlovich, a self-made businessman, to make his son Sergei into a man: "In short, he wanted me to teach him to drink. He wanted me to teach him to fight. He wanted me to teach him to chase women."[62] Meanwhile, Pavel plans to marry his son to the daughter of an Italian investor to boost his business. A partnership of convenience develops between Mikhail and Sergei: Sergei pretends to go on drinking binges and visits to prostitutes, while Mikhail keeps quiet about the secret relationship between Sergei and Marina, but later begins a love affair with his protégé's girlfriend. Marina lives together with her little brother Misha and their father Il'ya Semenovich in rather poor circumstances and sees in Sergei, about whose wealthy father she is secretly aware, only a lucrative marriage candidate. Sergei has no idea of this and tells Marina that he lives with his

---

[60] Andrei Valer'evich Gelasimov was born in 1965 in Irkutsk. With his novels *Thirst* (*Zhazhda,* 2002), which tells the story of a veteran of the Chechen war, and *Gods of the Steppe* (*Stepnye bogi*), published in 2008, the author achieved a breakthrough beyond the country's borders. Andrei Gelasimov writes in Russian, but his texts have been translated into numerous other languages.

[61] Gelasimov, *The Lying Year,* 184.

[62] Ibid., 11.

mother – who has run away to Switzerland with an artist – in a small apartment southwest of Moscow, in Kaluga.

The mesh of lies that unfolds around the two main characters, Mikhail and Sergei, within a year (1998—1999) can be read as a symptom of the social conditions in Russia in the 1990s. Crime, corruption and predatory capitalism are the themes Gelasimov's text deals with in four main chapters. These are named according to the seasons (spring, summer, fall and winter), suggesting a natural and recurring cycle. This cyclical concept forms the pattern for the action dimensions of the characters in Gelasimov's text, in that the lie permeates as a leitmotif.

This is particularly evident in the generational conflict between Pavel and his son Sergei. While the first one does everything he can to marry off his son to the daughter of a wealthy Italian investor with the help of an arranged marriage, Sergei tries to rebel against his father, who is driven by wealth and power. Instead of conforming to paternal, typically "masculine" behaviors, Sergei secretly takes piano lessons, watches old Audrey Hepburn movies, and reads Oscar Wilde. However, here the cyclical form of the narrative is revealed by the generationally determined pattern of action, the son does not manage to completely escape his father's influences, as is evident from a letter from his mother, Lena:

> Then you became more and more like him. That's something I hadn't expected. I became upset because I thought you were yourself [...]. Later, I thought, you would be free. Of me and your father. Of any obligations to resemble either one of us. [...]. But you started to look like him. [...] Sometimes I get the feeling that he treats you the way a photographer does a successful shot – he was lucky with the light and sitter, and the film developed excellently. [...] Then your endless enthusiasms began that never led anywhere. Your father encouraged them, but apparently even he eventually grew irritated. He was afraid nothing serious would ever come of you. That's what he wanted, seriousness. He didn't just want to have a son. A son was never enough. You had to excel. Which meant you had to become someone like him. A fine delusion of grandeur. [...] On top of the Adam's apple and hairy covering on the face. Men want not just sons. They need a big mirror. And no one had better prevent them from gazing into it endlessly.[63]

---

[63] Ibid., 116–17.

Lies and deceit are the common denominators with which father and son try to approach their respective goals: the former wants to accumulate and secure wealth, the latter wants to win Marina's sympathies. Without any critical examination of himself or his environment, Sergei remains in the role he has been led to play. The stagnation of the main character corresponds to the rest of the characters, none of whom undergo any significant development to break the recurring cycle. This is also illustrated by the example of Mikhail, who, by his own admission, is tired of his lying narratives, but cannot rid himself of them.

Despite the overall cyclical form, the text does not move linearly, but is repeatedly interrupted by different narrative techniques and voices. Thus, the first-person narrator Mikhail dominates "Spring" (Chapter 1) and "Autumn" (Chapter 3), while the chapters "Summer" and "Winter" are composed collage-like from the various voices of the other characters and are conveyed either in letter form, as a message on an answering machine, but also in the form of diary entries.

This narrative instability, together with the numerous lie constructs, can be read as an expression of the political and social situation in Russia in the 1990s and reveals a hopeless outlook on the future:

> Prices were rising every day at lightning speed. There were demons on the loose in the government. In Moscow and Petersburg, politicians were being shot, one after another. [...] The entire country had been declared bankrupt. In this situation, only a cretin could have any hopes. Russia was going down the tubes and taking us all with it. I had the feeling we had only a few months left. But the country as a fucking whole didn't get me too worked up.[64]

The lies and dishonest machinations in Gelasimov's text are a generational product, a burdensome legacy that fathers pass on to sons.

CONCLUSION

What conclusions can now be drawn from the textual examples considered above, in which the theme of memory occurs together with, or is conveyed by, lying speech?

Memories in a real-world context do not represent an exact reproduction of events experienced or witnessed in the past. With the exception of consciously controlled falsification of memory and history due to ideological efforts, an

---

[64] Ibid., 206.

erroneous reconstruction of memories can mostly be traced back to unconsciously occurring processes as well as internal and external influences. Despite the knowledge of the fragility and, to a certain extent, the unreliability of memory, the topic is of great importance in the social discourse of the late twentieth and early twenty-first century, which is already evident from the numerous works on memory studies. Memories, such as those described by contemporaries and eyewitnesses, not only serve as instruments against forgetting, but also make the past tangible, enlightening and explanatory for subsequent generations and thus have a forward-looking effect.

The three textual examples from contemporary Russian literature open up a new perspective on the fragility of memories by bringing together the reconstructive and sense-making process of remembering with the deliberately deceptive and meaningless lie.

In Ulitskaya's *Women's Lies*, the women's mendacious narratives function as a means of forgetting by covering and overwriting the actual events and their memories with new stories. In this process, the made-up narratives are socially accepted variations of the history experienced and remembered.

The situation is different in Shishkin's *Maidenhair*, in which the plot's focus is not on forgetting, but on the writing down of orally transmitted narratives and their subsequent preservation and conservation. The individual stories are not tied to a single individual, but circulate between the characters. The focus here is not on the truthfulness of an individual story, but merely on the quality of the telling, which determines its entry into the record or archive. The lying accounts of memory in Ulitskaya's and Shishkin's novels, moreover, are delineable internal narratives conveyed as quasi-autobiographical accounts, thus suggesting a fundamental instability and unreliability of (auto)biographical accounts of memory, although here they are fictional and untrue to the reader.

In Gelasimov's text *The Lying Year*, it is not only individual groups, such as women or applicants to Ulitskaya or Shishkin, who lie. Rather, the lie is revealed here as an overall social phenomenon passed on from generation to generation, from fathers to sons.

All these aspects – forgetting, unreliability, instability, and lack of truthfulness – are often tabooed varieties of memory, which can be expressed precisely in the literary text, as shown above.

REFERENCES

Alkofer, Andreas P. "'Erklär' mir Lüge, verklär' sie nicht...' Die ,Quellen der Moralität' und die Lüge. Ein ethisch-theologischer Zwischenruf." In *Kulturen der Lüge*, edited by Mathias Mayer, 35-68. Köln, Weimar: Böhlau, 2003.

Appelbaum, Paul S., Lisa A. Uyehara, and Mark R. Elin, eds. *Trauma and Memory: Clinical and Legal Controversies.* New York: Oxford University Press, 1997.

Assmann, Aleida. *Formen des Vergessens.* Bonn: bpb, Bundeszentrale für Politische Bildung, 2018.

Assmann, Jan. *Das kulturelle Gedächtnis: Schrift, Erinnerung und politische Identität in frühen Hochkulturen.* München: Verlag C.H. Beck, 1992.

Aurelius, Augustinus. "De mendacio." In *Augustinus Opera Werke*, edited by Johannes Brachtendorf and Volker Henning Drecoll, 59–149. Paderborn: Ferdinand Schöningh, 2013.

Aurelius, Augustinus "Lying." In *Treatises on Various Subjects: Saint Augustine*, edited by Roy J. Deferrari, 47-112. Washington, D.C.: Catholic University of America Press, 2002.

Basseler, Michael and Dorothee Birke. "Mimesis des Erinnerns." In *Gedächtniskonzepte der Literaturwissenschaft*, edited by Astrid Erll and Ansgar Nünning, 123–48. Berlin, New York: Walter de Gruyter, 2005.

Berdyaev, Nikolai. "Paradoks lzhi." *Sovremennaya zapiski* 69 (1939): 272–79.

Erll, Astrid and Ansgar Nünning. "Literatur und Erinnerungskultur: Eine narratologische und funktionsgeschichtliche Theorieskizze mit Fallbeispielen aus der britischen Literatur des 19. und 20. Jahrhunderts." In *Erinnerung, Gedächtnis, Wissen: Studien zur kulturwissenschaftlichen Gedächtnisforschung*, edited by Günter Oesterle, 185–210. Göttingen: Vandenhoeck & Ruprecht, 2005.

Erll, Astrid and Ansgar Nünning. "Literaturwissenschaftliche Konzepte von Gedächtnis: Ein einführender Überblick." In *Gedächtniskonzepte der Literaturwissenschaft. Theoretische Grundlegung und Anwendungsperspektiven*, edited by Astrid Erll and Ansgar Nünning, 1-10. Berlin, New York: Walter de Gruyter, 2005.

Esposito, Elena. *Soziales Vergessen: Formen und Medien des Gedächtnisses der Gesellschaft.* Frankfurt am Main: Suhrkamp Verlag, 2002.

Fried, Johannes. *Der Schleier der Erinnerung: Grundzüge einer historischen Memorik.* München: Verlag C.H. Beck, 2012.

Gelasimov, Andrei. *The Lying Year.* Translated by Marian Schwartz. Las Vegas: Amazon Crossing, 2013.

Goscilo, Helena. "Narrating trauma." In *Russian literature since 1991*, edited by Evgeny Dobrenko and Mark Lipovetsky,167–87. Cambridge: Cambridge University Press, 2015.

Halbwachs, Maurice. *On Collective Memory.* Edited and translated by Lewis A. Coser. Chicago, London: University of Chicago Press, 1992.

Lachmann, Renate. *Memory and Literature: Intertextuality in Russian Modernism.* Translated by Roy Sellars and Anthony Wall. Minneapolis, London: University of Minnesota Press, 1997.

Lévi-Strauss, Claude. *La pensée sauvage.* Paris: Plon, 1962.

Margalit, Avishai. *The Ethics of Memory*. Cambridge: Harvard University Press, 2021.

Meibauer, Jörg. "Introduction: What is lying? Towards an integrative approach." In *The Oxford Handbook of Lying*, edited by Jörg Meibauer, 1–12. Oxford: Oxford University Press, 2019.

Schank, Robert C. and Abelson, Robert P. "Knowledge and Memory: The Real Story." In *Knowledge and Memory: The Real Story* edited by Robert S. Wyer Jr., 1-85. Hillsdale, New York: Erlbaum, 1995.

Scheiding, Oliver. "Intertextualität." In *Gedächtniskonzepte der Literaturwissenschaft*, edited by Astrid Erll and Ansgar Nünning, 53–72. Berlin, New York: Walter de Gruyter, 2005.

Schmid, Wolf. *Narratology: An introduction*. Berlin, New York: Walter de Gruyter, 2010.

Schmitz-Emans, Monika. "Im Zwischenreich: Lügen, Fälschungen, Fiktionen, Texte und Bilder. Oder: Die Macht der Paratexte." In *Dichter Lügen*, edited by Kurt Röttgers and Monika Schmitz-Emans, 187–212. Essen: Verlag die Blaue Eule, 2001.

Shishkin, Mikhail. *Maidenhair*. Translated by Marian Schwartz. Rochester: Open Letter. Literary translations from the university of Rochester, 2012.

Solte-Gresser, Christiane. "Begabte Schwindlerinnen: Über die Inszenierungen der Lüge bei Ljudmila Ulickaja," *Cahiers d'Études*, 68, Vol. 2 (2015): 191–205.

Spence, Donald P. *Narrative Truth and Historical Truth*. New York, London: W.W. Norton & Company, 1982.

Stoffels, Hans. "False Memory-Syndrome: Eine Herausforderung für die Psychotherapie." In *Tarnen, Täuschen, Lügen: Zwischen Lust und Last*, edited by Gunther Klosinski, 97–118. Tübingen: Attempto Verlag, 2011.

Ulitskaya, Lyudmila. *Skvoznaya linya*. Moskva: Eksmo, 2003.

Ulitskaya, Lyudmila. "Women's Lies." In *Nine of Russia's Foremost Women Writers*. Translated by Arch Tait and edited by Svetlana Aleksievich, 238–79. Moskva: Glas. Publ., 2003.

Weinrich, Harald. *Die Linguistik der Lüge*. München: Verlag C.H. Beck, 2016.

Chapter 3

Embodied Memory: Post-Communist Scenes of Writing in Novels by Kéthévane Davrichewy, Kateřina Tučková, and Lyudmila Ulitskaya

Alena Heinritz

University of Innsbruck, Austria

Abstract: Post-communist literature can be defined by its active engagement with the communist past and the attempt to create new narratives. This paper asks how post-communist literature establishes transtemporal networks, connecting the 'post-communist condition' (Groys) with the communist past. For an approach to an answer to this question, I compare three post-communist novels that were published in the 2010s in French, Russian and Czech: *The Black Sea* (*La mer noire*, 2010) by Kéthévane Davrichewy, *Jacob's Ladder* (*Lestnitsa Yakova*, 2015) by Lyudmila Ulitskaya, and *The Žítková Goddesses* (*Žítkovské bohyně*, 2012) by Kateřina Tučková. The analysis focuses on the role that figurations of writing processes play. In these novels, writing is described as a synthesis between body, material, and discourse. All three novels have in common both artifacts of writing and the discussion of writing processes bridging the gap between generations combining individual memories and the realization that the present is inextricably linked to the past.

Keywords: post-communist literature; scenes of writing; Kéthévane Davrichewy; Kateřina Tučková; Lyudmila Ulitskaya

***

EMBODIED MEMORY IN THE "POST-COMMUNIST CONDITION"

I argue that 'embodied memory' as a central form of postmemory plays an important role in transtemporal post-communist literature, reflecting on the past and imagining new structures of knowledge. As post-communist literature, I understand, firstly, literature published after 1990, and secondly, literature dealing with communism from a position beyond communism, but nevertheless closely related to it, seeking to reveal its traces in the present and new forms for its representation.[1] I am following here Boris Groys' concept of the post-communist condition: as a situation in which a society (or at least parts of it) consciously turns to reflect on the "historical event of communism" and reveal its traces in the present:

> to speak of the post-communist condition means giving serious consideration to the historical event that communism was and earnestly inquiring what traces still remain of communism and to what degree the experience of communism still marks our own present reality [...].[2]

The fact that this is done insufficiently in many former state socialist countries is described, for example, by cultural studies researcher Alexander Etkind in his book *Warped Mourning. Stories of the Undead in the Land of the Unburied* (2013). In literary texts dealing with this task, those born afterward often feel a responsibility to their ancestors to bring untold stories to light. In the sense of Walter Benjamin's "weak messianic power," they feel – often unconsciously – connected and obliged to their ancestors.[3] To conceptualize this phenomenon, the notion of embodied memory is pertinent. Second, I refer to Piret Peiker's definition of the "post" in post-communism in parallel with post-colonialism as "denoting a space or position beyond colonialism, yet inextricably linked to it."[4]

Post-communist literature is thus fundamentally hybrid in that it unites two completely different temporal orders: the communist and the post-communist.

---

[1] Alena Heinritz, *Postkommunistische Schreibweisen: Formen der Darstellung des Kommunismus in Romanen zu Beginn des 21. Jahrhunderts* (Heidelberg: Winter, 2021), 43.

[2] Boris Groys, "The Post-Communist Condition," Becoming Former West, trans. Matthew Partridge, accessed August 30, 2021, http://becoming-former.tumblr.com/post/262880375/the-post-communist-condition-boris-groys-the.

[3] Walter Benjamin, "On the Concept of History," in *Selected Writings Vol. 4: 1938–1940*, eds. Howard Eiland and Michael W. Jennings, trans. Edmund Jephcott et al. (Cambridge, London: The Belknap Press of Harvard University Press, 2003), 390; see Sigrid Weigel, *Genea-Logik: Generation, Tradition und Evolution zwischen Kultur- und Naturwissenschaften* (München: Fink, 2006), 138; and in the context of postcommunist literature Alena Heinritz, "Burying the Undead: Coming to Terms with the Soviet Past in Novels by Slavnikova and Lebedev," *Acta Universitatis Carolinae – Studia Territorialia* 17, no. 2 (2017): 61.

[4] Piret Peiker, "Post-Communist Literatures: A Postcolonial Perspective," *Eurozine*, March 28, 2006, accessed December 20, 2021, https://www.eurozine.com/post-communist-literatures-a-postcolonial-perspective/?pdf.

The interactions of these different temporal orders manifest themselves aesthetically. This interaction of two temporal orders can best be studied by looking at texts that were written after the collapse of communism and whose narrative perspective is post-communist, but whose narrating protagonists at the same time feel a strong corporeal and affective connection with the temporal order of communism. This is the case in novels representing so-called "embodied memory."

The idea of embodied memory is based on the proposition that knowledge and the remembering engagement with the past are situated within the bodies of actors who deal with materialities and discourses. The term "embodied memory" is used repeatedly in cognitive and memory research. For example, Sutton and Williamson's definition of embodied memory focuses on the idea of experience being actively embodied in practices.[5] The cultural sociological theory of practice plays an important role here because it considers practices and discourses as "two coupled aggregate states of the material existence of cultural knowledge orders."[6] In this sense, Thomas Fuchs understands "embodied memory" as

> implicit 'body memory' that underlies our everyday habits and skills, without necessarily being made explicit [...]. This embodied knowledge is realized in suitable situations through habitual action or through overarching volitional acts. It then connects body and environment through ongoing cycles of perception and action that are based on earlier experiences.[7]

I understand "embodied memory" in the context of post-communist literature as a form of postmemory, following Marianne Hirsch's understanding of "postmemory" as "a *structure* of inter- and trans-generational transmission of

---

5 John Sutton and Kellie Williamson, "Embodied Remembering," in *The Routledge Handbook of Embodied Cognition*, ed. Lawrence Shapiro (London: Routledge, 2014), 315–25. From a different, psychoanalytic perspective, Culbertson uses the term "embodied memory" for repressed traumatic memories of violations of the body, Roberta Culbertson, "Embodied Memory, Transcendence, and Telling: Recounting Trauma, Re-Establishing the Self," *New Literary History* 26, no. 1 (1995): 169–95.

6 Andreas Reckwitz, "Praktiken und Diskurse: Zur Logik von Praxis-/Diskursformationen," in *Kreativität und soziale Praxis: Studien zur Sozial- und Gesellschaftstheorie* (Bielefeld: transcript, 2016), 61, trans. A.H.

7 Thomas Fuchs, "Embodied Knowledge – Embodied Memory," in *Analytic and Continental Philosophy: Methods and Perspectives: Proceedings of the 37th International Wittgenstein Symposium*, ed. Sonja Rinofner-Kreidl and Harald A. Wiltsche (Berlin, Boston: De Gruyter, 2016), 217–18.

traumatic knowledge and experience."[8] The idea of postmemory (Hirsch, Weigel) assumes that memory – especially that of traumatic events – is passed on intergenerationally through kinship.[9] Those born later feel an embodied memory in themselves. Developed in the context of her research on Holocaust memories, Hirsch's concept "postmemory" is based on the notion that familial togetherness and family "as a space of transmission" is a central factor in remembering traumatic events affectively:

> Postmemory describes the relationship that the generation after those who witnessed cultural or collective trauma bears to the experiences of those who came before, experiences that they 'remember' only by means of the stories, images, and behaviors among which they grew up. But these experiences were transmitted to them so deeply and affectively as to seem to constitute memories in their own right. Postmemory's connection to the past is thus not actually mediated by recall but by imaginative investment, projection, and creation.[10]

By presenting various forms of embodied memory, the three novels show the close entanglement between past and present in the post-communist condition.

The concept of the writing scene, as the interplay of instrument, body and discourse in writing, offers a methodological key to making post-communist embodied memory evident in literary texts. The term 'scene of writing' (Campe, Stingelin, Zanetti), referring to representations of writing processes whose product is the writing itself, allows us to scrutinize the ensemble of discursivity, materiality, and corporeality in post-communist fiction. A writing scene (*Schreibszene*) denotes

> the constellation of writing, which varies historically and individually from author to author, that takes place within the framework formed jointly by language (semantics of writing), instrumentality (technology of writing), and gesture (physicality of writing), without these factors themselves becoming problematic as counter- or resistance [...].[11]

---

[8] Marianne Hirsch, "The Generation of Postmemory," *Poetics Today* 29, no. 1 (2008): 106, italics in the original.

[9] For the concept of intergenerational memory, see Astrid Erll, *Kollektives Gedächtnis und Erinnerungskulturen: Eine Einführung* (Stuttgart: Metzler, 2017), 14.

[10] Hirsch, "The Generation of Postmemory," 106–7.

[11] Martin Stingelin, "‚Schreiben'. Einleitung," in *‚Mir ekelt vor diesem tintenklecksenden Säkulum': Schreibszenen im Zeitalter der Manuskripte*, ed. Martin Stingelin (München: Fink, 2004), 15, trans. A.H.

All three novels I am looking at deal with writing and its materiality represented in the form of letters and archival documents. Astrid Erll describes those as "semiosis-enabled communication tools for externalizing memory-relevant information" (e.g., writing), "media technologies for disseminating and transmitting memory content," and "cultural objectifications" (e.g., letters and archival documents).[12] These objectifications create so-called "postal relations" (Derrida, Weigel) with the protagonists and the readers: a form of precarious and warped communication over time.[13] Mnemonic actors – in this case, the novels' protagonists – deal with these objectifications, and in reading, according to Jean-Luc Nancy, the bodies of writers and readers touch – albeit through temporal, spatial, and material detours.[14] I assume that in the three novels compared, transtemporal networks manifest themselves in three points: transtemporal "postal relations," metahistoriography, and the imagination of writing.

EMBODIED MEMORY IN NOVELS BY KÉTHÉVANE DAVRICHEWY, KATEŘINA TUČKOVÁ, AND LYUDMILA ULITSKAYA

Kéthévane Davrichewy tells in *The Black Sea* (*La mer noire*, 2010) the story of a Georgian family that, fleeing bolshevism, emigrated to France in 1918. The experience of immigration is partly autobiographical: Kéthévane Davrichewy (born in 1965 in Paris) is a French writer whose grandparents emigrated to France in 1905. The writer, literature and theater scholar, journalist, and children's book author Davrichewy deals in her work, among other things, with the communist past of Georgia and with Georgian emigration to France. In the novel, the young woman Tamouna loses her lover Tamaz after her emigration. She writes letters to Tamaz, but never sends them written not on loose paper, but in a notebook.[15] In her old age, Tamouna imagines retrospectively a life with Tamaz and reflects on what it means to write down one's story. She has thus led two alternative lives: with and without Tamaz. *La mer noire* tells the story of Tamouna and her love to Tamaz in three different narrative modes: The first one is the internal focalized narrative in the third person singular of Tamouna's

---

[12] Erll, *Kollektives Gedächtnis und Erinnerungskulturen*, 143–44, translation A.H.

[13] Weigel renders Derrida's idea of the "postal principle" as follows: "The figure of absence and the difference of space and time that accompany every postal transmission establish a specific form of 'postal différance'. Addressing, circulation, and the uncertainty of reception are thereby tied to the simultaneity of public delivery and intimate or secret sending." (Weigel, *Genea-Logik*, 170, translation A.H.).

[14] Jean-Luc Nancy, *Corpus* (Paris: Éditions Métailié, 2000), 47, see Sandro Zanetti, "Einleitung," in *Schreiben als Kulturtechnik: Grundlagentexte*, ed. Sandro Zanetti (Berlin: Suhrkamp, 2012), 16.

[15] Kéthévane Davrichewy, *La mer Noire* (Paris: Wespieser, 2010), 93, 174–75.

ninetieth Birthday. The second mode is Tamouna's first-person narrative about her life, beginning with her early youth in Georgia, her summer vacations, emigration to Paris, and her life as a wife and mother, interrupted by a few meetings with Tamaz. The third narrative level consists of the letters, Tamouna writes in emigration to her teenage love, Tamaz, but never sends. These letters are italicized and inserted into Tamouna's first-person narrative. While the three narrative modes allow for different perspectives on Tamouna's life, they are restricted to Tamouna's unreliable internal view. This focus shows that reality and Tamouna's imagination cannot be clearly separated. Until the end, it remains open whether the meetings between Tamouna and Tamaz described in the novel from Tamouna's internal point of view take place or are just Tamouna's wishful thinking.

Jacob's Ladder (*Lestnitsa Yakova*, 2015) likewise deals with the conditions for writing a life story. Lyudmila Ulitskaya, born in 1943, is one of the most prominent figures of contemporary Russian literature and has received great international attention. In her novels, she has repeatedly dealt with Russian-Soviet family stories. In *Lestnitsa Yakova*, the stage designer Nora reads the letters of her grandparents Yakov and Marusya that they exchanged between 1911 and 1954, many years of which Yakov spent in Siberian exile. Nora's grandfather, Yakov Osetskii, was a Jewish economist who was first drawn into military service and then exiled several times for many years by the Soviet regime and had to spend most of his life in harsh conditions in remote places, separated from his family. With the help of these letters, Nora approaches the history of her family against the backdrop of late Tsarist Russia and the Soviet Union. In 2011, Nora contextualizes these letters anew when the records of her grandparents in KGB archives become accessible and finally decides to make a book out of the letters. The narrative is divided into three narrative modes: firstly, the personal focalized narrative in the third person tells Nora's story (from her birth in 1943 to the birth of her grandson Yakov in 2011). At the end of the book, a chapter about Nora also includes the reproduction of archival documents about Yakov Osetskii, which Nora reads and transcribes in the KGB archives. Secondly, a multiple-focalized narrative in the third person tells Nora's family history from 1905 onwards, and thirdly, a narrative headlined "from the chest" contains letters and diaries of Nora's grandparents Yakov Osetskii and Mariya (called Marusya) Kern. According to a note by the author, these documents are oriented to the materials on the author's grandfather, Yakov Ulitskii.[16]

---

[16] Lyudmila Ulitskaya, *Lestnitsa Yakova* (Moskva: AST, 2015), 725. For parallels with Ulitskaya's family history, see, for example, her memoir *Svyashchennyi musor* (2012, published in English translation under the title *Discarded Relics*).

Archival research also plays a central role in Kateřina Tučková's novel. Kateřina Tučková (born in 1980 in Brno) holds Ph.D. in literature and art studies, worked as a curator and debuted as a writer in 2006. Her novels have been awarded the highest Czech literary prizes and have been translated into several languages. In these texts, she deals with Czech and Czechoslovak history between documents and fiction. This is also the case for her novel *The Goddesses of Žítkov* (*Žítkovské bohyně*, 2012). The novel tells the story of the Czech ethnologist Dora, who, after the archives have been opened, begins to research the history of her female ancestors, the so-called "goddesses" in the Moravian area of Kopanice.[17] These "goddesses" are nature-knowledgeable women with magical abilities – good or bad – who heal and prophesize. The documents she finds about the goddesses during the time of the Protectorate and state socialist ČSSR, as well as excerpts of research literature, newspaper articles and Dora's thesis, are reproduced within the novel.[18] Dora's writing process becomes an image of embodied postmemory that links Dora corporeally to her ancestors. In the end, Dora is murdered before being able to publish her book. The novel suggests that by killing Dora, an old family curse placed on Dora's female family line is being fulfilled, again highlighting the transgenerational connection between Dora and her ancestresses.

TRANSTEMPORAL "POSTAL RELATIONS"

The three novels compared have in common the description of both artifacts of writing and embodied writing processes bridging the gap between generations and combining individual memories and representations of post-communist memory politics. It is the bodies of ancestors and descendants, or in Davrichewy's novel, the bodies of alternative lives of a woman, that are related to each other. It is in writing scenes and pieces of writing in all three novels that these legacies manifest themselves. In the case of Davrichewy's and Ulitskaya's novel, these manifestations are letters and the narrator's characters writing about these letters. In *Lestnitsa Yakova*, Yakov and Marusya's letters connect the generations:

> This was the first letter of that long correspondence that continued for twenty-five years—the correspondence, carefully tied up in a bundle,

---

[17] The genealogical tree of the female line of Dora's family is an important detailed described scriptural artifact in the text that illustrates Dora's inclusiveness in the gender of the goddesses (e.g., Kateřina Tučková, *Žítkovské bohyně* (Brno: Host, 2012), 116–17).

[18] Archive documents are typographically highlighted in the text by using Courier New font thus creating a facsimile effect; newspaper articles are reproduced as facsimiles (e.g., Ibid., 158).

that had lain on the bottom of the willow chest in the communal apartment on Povarskaya Street until Marusya's death, and had then migrated to Nikitsky Boulevard, to the home of her granddaughter, Nora, where it waited to be read.[19]

Due to Ulitskaya's interest in the moment of intergenerational memory passed on through biological kinship in her novel,[20] Makaryan understands the "epicist as a kind of geneticist from literature. The need to trace the genesis of the present is Ulitskaya's principal attitude."[21] This is similarly described by Sutcliffe, according to whom *Lestnitsa Yakova* "uses the flesh to portray the trauma of Russia's bloody twentieth century through the lives of grandparents Yakov and Mariia Osetskii and granddaughter Nora" with the idea that "the flesh connects the living and commemorates the dead."[22] The idea of *telesnost'* – "corpereality" is here central: according to Sutcliffe that *Lestnitsa Yakova* "examines history through blood ties, uncovering how *telesnost'* reveals the past molding different generations."[23] Mind and body are presented as an indivisible whole.[24] This whole manifests itself in *Lestnitsa Yakova* in the discourse on writing. Text and writing here take on a

---

[19] Ludmila Ulitskaya, *Jacob's Ladder*, trans. Polly Gannon (New York: Farrar, Straus and Giroux, 2019), 135. The original reads: "Это было первое из писем той обширной переписки, которая длилась двадцать пять лет, а потом в тщательно упакованном свертке пролежала в ивовом сундуке в коммуналке на Поварской до смерти Маруси, переехала на Никитский бульвар и лежала у ее внучки Норы, ожидая прочтения." (Ulitskaya 2015, 188).

[20] On the genre of the family novel from a psychoanalytic perspective and its significance for intergenerational memory, see Weigel, *Genea-Logik*, 76–80.

[21] Ol'ga Markaryan, "'Lestnitsa Yakova'. Roman o proshlom" (2016). Accessed August 30, 2021, http://rara-rara.ru/menu-texts/lestnica_yakova_roman_o_proshlom., translation A.H. Of course, the fact that Ulitskaya is a trained biologist and geneticist underlies this comparison.

[22] Benjamin Sutcliffe, "Commemoration and Connection: Liudmila Ulitskaia and the Universe of the Body in Jacob's Ladder," *The Slavonic and East European Review* 97, no. 3 (2019): 451–52.

[23] Ibid., 455. For an overview of the concept of "telesnost'" in Ulitskaya's oeuvre, in which Sutcliffe disagrees with a reduction of her texts to "women's prose," see Ibid., esp. 453–54. Knurowska however had identified before Ulitskaya's use of "corporeality [telesnost'] as artistic material" as "feminine writing" and she states "Ulitskaya's protagonists are corporeal, biological" (Monika Knurowska, "Telesnost' v rasskazakh Lyudmily Ulitskoi," *Acta Universitatis Wratislaviensis* 152, no. 3251 (2010): 68, 69, 78, translation A.H.). "Telesnost'" is defined by Knurowska as the description of processes of the body ("sexuality physiology, birth, menstruation, initiation and especially disease") (Ibid., 68).

[24] Sutcliffe, "Commemoration and Connection," 452.

metaphysical meaning.[25] This is particularly evident in the ideas of Grisha, a Jewish scientist who is friends with Nora's ex-husband. He assumes that every human being is a text, with DNA understood as the alphabet of all creation.[26] In addition, human consciousness also can generate new text (and thus new life) and is therefore equal to God. Text is an existential form of information; the is creator immortal because he can bring forth new information, thus, new life.[27] Against the background of this idea, it is no surprise that the novel can be read as a story about writing. All the characters are introduced through their relationship to writing: grandfather Yakov, who writes diaries, letters, scientific, and literary texts throughout his life and in the most adverse circumstances;[28] grandmother Marusya, who writes ideological articles;[29] Nora's mother Amaliya, a technical draftswoman from whom Nora inherited the practices of holding a pencil;[30] her father Genrikh sticking till the end of his life to a stiff professional style of writing,[31] and Nora's son Yurik, whose physical writing problems and his illegible handwriting are a recurring theme.[32] While Nora initially only draws designs for stage sets[33] and uses drawing as a practice to process important events in her life,[34] she begins to write more and more as the novel progresses.[35] In this process, she is encouraged by her lover Tengiz, who points out to her the fundamentally corporeal-material aspect of writing:

> "Now get some paper and start writing."
> "Are you crazy? [...]"
> "Write, Nora, write!" Tengiz said. [...]
> "I'm not a writer," Nora said.
> "How do you know? Have you ever tried it? A writer is someone who takes up a pencil and writes."[36]

---

[25] Yakov, e.g., compares heaven to a book that one must know how to read, much older than the first letter writings (Ulitskaya, *Lestnitsa Yakova*, 559).

[26] Ibid., 302, 659.

[27] Ibid., 660–62. For an intellectual-historical contextualization of these thoughts, see e.g. Weigel, *Genea-Logik*, 246–53 and Sutcliffe "Commemoration and Connection," 462.

[28] E.g., Ulitskaya, *Lestnitsa Yakova*, 71, 104, 539–40.

[29] Ibid., 515, 518.

[30] Ibid., 377.

[31] Ibid., 382–83.

[32] Ibid., 233; 252.

[33] Ibid., 205.

[34] Ibid., 41, 130.

[35] Ibid., 310–11.

[36] Ulitskaya, *Jacob's Ladder*, 227–28. The original reads:
"— А теперь бери бумагу, пиши.
— С ума сошел? [...]

The embodied process of writing then becomes Nora's way to discover her corporeal and affective transtemporal connection with her ancestors.

In the case of Tučková, it is writing from a synthesis of ethnography and kinship. The protagonist Dora realizes that it is her kinship relationship with former Goddesses that allows her to physically experience an event that took place more than three hundred years ago. Her historical research on the persecution of the first historically proven goddess in the seventeenth century, Kateřina Shánělká, makes her physically witness the torturing of the so-called "witch" who turns to her for help.[37] Later she realizes that it is her kinship relationship with Shánělká that allows her to physically experience an event that took place more than three hundred years ago.[38] From this realization, Dora derives her task to write about the goddesses:

> The moment she thought of it, she felt as if she had found the key to a door that had been locked for years. And no sooner had it opened than her true role also emerged before her, and suddenly she had a sense of what was being asked of her, what she was to contribute. She, the only one standing on the border between such different worlds, with one foot in scholarship, yet deeply rooted in the essence of the life of the goddesses. Her task, she told herself, was to find the fate of all the women of their lineage, to retrieve their stories from the darkness of the past, and most importantly, to inform the world of their extraordinary art, which their enemies had tried for ages to erase from the face of Kopanice. She was the one who would prevent their legacy from fading away.[39]

— Пиши, Нора! Пиши! – настаивал Тенгиз. [...]

— Я не писатель, — сопротивлялась Нора.

— Откуда ты знаешь? [...] Ты что, пробовала? Писатель тот, кто берет в руки карандаш." (Ulitskaya, *Lestnitsa Yakova*, 310–11).

[37] Tučková, *Žítkovské bohyně*, 82–83.

[38] Ibid., 118.

[39] All translations from Davrichewy's and Tučková's novels A.H. The original reads: "V tu chvíli, kdy ji to napadlo, měla pocit, jako by našla klíč k léta zamčeným dveřím. A sotva se otevřely, vyvstala před ní také její skutečná role, a najednou tušila, co se po ní chce, čím má přispět. Ona, která jediná stojí na hranici mezi těmi tak odlišnými světy, jednou nohou ve vědě, a přitom hluboce vkořeněná do podstaty života bohyní. Jejím úkolem, říkala si, je nalézt osudy všech žen z jejich rodu, vydobýt jejich příběhy z temna minulosti, a hlavně zpravit svět o jejich neobyčejném umění, které se jejich nepřátelé po věky snažili vymazat z tváře Kopanic. To ona měla zabránit tomu, aby se jejich odkaz vytratil." (Tučková, *Žítkovské bohyně*, 118).

By combining her function as a scholar and as part of the goddess lineage, the protagonist, Dora, accesses embodied memory and writes about it. The knowledge she gathers during her research is not gained purely cognitively, but it is often an intuitive knowledge she experiences through her transgenerational connection with her ancestresses. All three of the novels analyzed are postmnemonic texts that depict the survival of the socialist legacy in an embodiment: the person of the narrator's character after the end of communism carries the legacy of communism into the post-communist era through his own experiences and those of his ancestors. In all three novels, letters and documents are reproduced within the text, and these objectifications of memory establish transtemporal constellations or 'postal relations'.

Metahistoriography

The three novels share a metahistorical approach: the protagonists Nora (Ulitskaya) and Dora (Tučková) are both actively involved in the reconstruction of past events, they receive sources that are directly reproduced in the text, and they research the archives of state security in post-communist Russia and the Czech Republic, respectively.[40] Both protagonists, however, have a strong awareness of their familial embeddedness in history: they feel themselves linked to the generational sequence and sense the heritage of their ancestors within them.[41] Their writing therefore arises from a synthesis of, on the one hand, knowledge obtained from their intense study of historical documents. On the other hand, it is itself conditioned by their family affiliation and the heritage they assume within themselves. The protagonists, Nora (Ulitskaya) and Dora (Tučková) feel a responsibility for their ancestors that is primarily physical and manifests itself in writing. Through the description of writing

---

[40] Tippner terms this genre "research novels" ("Rechercheromane") (Anja Tippner, "Familiengeschichten als Gegengeschichten: Jüdische Identität in zeitgenössischer russischer Literatur," *Osteuropa* 69, no. 9–11 (2019): 203). Fulda and Jaeger describe the boom in this genre of "generational narrative in which people of the present go in search of the historical experiences of older family members" since the 2000s (Daniel Fulda and Stephan Jaeger, "Einleitung: Romanhaftes Geschichtserzählen in einer erlebnisorientierten, enthierarchisierten und hybriden Geschichtskultur," in *Romanhaftes Erzählen von Geschichte. Vergegenwärtigte Vergangenheiten im beginnenden 21. Jahrhundert*, ed. Daniel Fulda and Stephan Jaeger (Berlin, Boston: de Gruyter, 2019), 9, 13, translation A.H.).

[41] Cf. Tippner on postcatastrophic writing on Holocaust and ethnic cleansing, which applies here as well: "In extending plot lines into the present and focusing on children and grandchildren, they stress the latency and continuing effects of these experiences" (Anja Tippner, "Postcatastrophic Entanglement? Contemporary Czech Writers Remember the Holocaust and Post-war Ethnic Cleansing," *Memory Studies* 14, no. 1 (2021): 89).

scenes, the processes of physical kinship and responsibility to remember and writing to fulfill this responsibility can be represented and reflected upon.

Tamouna (Davrichewy) reflects at the end of her life, on autobiographical writing and compares two alternative versions of narrating the story of her life, which both seem true to her. She realizes that she should have taken notes to gain certainty about facts and dates because her memory and the letters she wrote to Tamaz are unreliable:

> She should have taken notes [...] at least write down the facts, be able to say what really happened, when. Their story remains only in shreds in her flickering memory. She hid things from Tamaz, omitted details. She probably doesn't know everything either.[42]

In the end, though, in her imagination "her multiple lives form a whole":

> She has often preferred immobility. [...] Sometimes, reality and imagination, past and present merge in this immobile world. It is what she always wished. That her multiple lives form a whole. [43]

Tamouna has lived two alternative lives. For the reader, it remains undecidable whether Tamouna actually meets Tamaz or whether she only imagines these encounters; the unreliability of the narrative perspective leaves this open until the end. Semi-consciously, she decides against writing in the notebooks brought to her by her granddaughter, worried that manifesting them in writing would cause her to lose the relationship with Tamaz that she had imagined all her life in her fictitious letters – even at the price that her story will disappear with her death. Instead, in physical immobility, she imagines the writing scene as she narrates her life as a whole, and physical and imaginary spheres unite. The novel realizes what Tamouna desires: the narrative design of *La mer noire* leaves ambivalences without resolving them.

---

[42] The original reads: "Elle aurait dû prendre des notes, [...] noter au moins les faits, pouvoir dire ce qui s'est réellement passé, à quel moment. Leur histoire ne subsiste que par lambeaux dans sa mémoire vacillante. Elle a caché des choses à Tamaz, omis des détails. Elle ne sait sûrement pas tout non plus." (Davrichewy, *La mer Noire*, 43).

[43] The original reads: "Elle a souvent préféré l'immobilité. [...] Parfois, la réalité et l'imaginaire, le passé et le présent se confondent dans ce monde immobile. C'est ce qu'elle a toujours souhaité. Que ses vies multiples forment un tout." (Davrichewy, *La mer Noire*, 131–32).

Imagination of Writing

All three novels are also about the *imagination* of writing: texts are drafted in the mind, but the writing is disrupted. In *La mer noire*, ninety-year-old Tamouna receives notebooks from her granddaughter Tsiala who encourages her to write her story, but Tamouna cannot bring herself to write. Instead, she describes telling her story for her descendants as "stolen from her memory":

> The notebooks that Tsiala gave her are still in their packaging. Tsiala pushes her to write, violates her a little [...]. She would like to please her, to tell her story, but she can't. [...] When she speaks sometimes – stories stolen from her memory – Tsiala says: This is better than nothing. It's important to us, to me anyway.[44]

Instead of writing, she imagines a life that integrates imagined alternative life paths without the detours of history.

In *Žítkovské bohyně*, Dora retrospectively reflects on how she could have written her thesis better. In this imagining of a writing scene, the implicit knowledge of academic writing conventions in the ČSSR and the contradiction to the mission Dora feels to carry out, the legacy of the goddesses becomes evident. In her mind, she makes plans for the structure of her text, as she would have liked to introduce it, namely with a description of the landscape of Kopanice, where the goddesses worked for generations. But because of the political observation to which her writing was subjected during state socialism, such an introduction was impossible. The imagined introduction about Kopanice then develops from these thoughts about the structure of the text, and from the negation emerges a vivid description of the place:

> When it was possible then, she would begin her work with a description of the place. [...] [The following is the description of the place, AH] That's how Dora would have liked to start then. [...] An academic text cannot begin with a description of a crisp mountain summer, which in an instant can turn into a hellish storm that envelops the ridges in dark, impenetrable clouds [...]. On the pages of such a work, one cannot draw a huge round moon, with shreds of night clouds skimming over the tops of the huddled hills, or write that when

---

[44] The original reads: "Les carnets que lui a offerts Tsiala sont encore dans leur emballage. Tsiala la pousse à écrire, la violente un peu [...]. Elle aimerait lui faire plaisir, raconter, mais elle n'y parvient pas. [...] Quand elle parle parfois – des histoires volées à sa mémoire – Tsiala dit : C'est mieux que rien. C'est important pour nous, pour moi en tout cas." (Davrichewy, *La mer Noire*, 32).

the night is cloudless, one can see the paths on the slopes almost as well as in the daytime. [...] The real beginning of her thesis was supposed to be just that – it was supposed to illuminate what a magical place Kopanice is on the slopes of the White Carpathians and that only in such a place could something special be born and develop its power. A *goddess*. But nothing like that belongs in an academic text bound by the strict rules of zero aesthetics.[45]

Dora then imagines how the reviewers would have reacted to such a text, followed by a reproduction of the text that initiated her work at the time, including footnotes.[46] In the excerpt quoted above, it becomes clear that from the meta-perspective on writing, here arises ex negativo very immediate vivid descriptions of a place whose magic is directly revealed to the reader. This development of the immediate from the meta-perspective on writing, the fluid transitions between imagined writing scene, the reflection of the standards for academic work in the ČSSR and description, is a lucid way to stylistically reflect on embodied memory. At the end of the novel, the protagonist, Dora's almost completed book, is mentioned. However, her murder makes the completion and publication impossible.

The imagination of writing also plays a central role in Ulitskaya's novel. In the very end, the protagonist Nora expresses her intention to write the book that her grandfather was unable to write, focusing on the transtemporal connection between generations:

> Perhaps she would arrange [the, A.H.] old letters and write a book, the sort of book that either her grandfather had not had time to write, or, if it had been written, had been burned in the Internal Prison of the Lubyanka.

---

[45] The original reads: "Kdy to tehdy bylo možné, začala by svou práci popisem toho místa. [...] [The following is the description of the place, A.H.] Tím by Dora tehdy ráda začala. [...] Vědecký text nelze začít popisem svěžího horského léta, které se v jediném okamžiku může změnit v pekelnou smršť bouře, jež zahalí hřebeny do temných, neprostupných mračen [...]. Na stránky takové práce nelze vykreslovat obrovský kulatý měsíc, který nad špičkami semknutých kopců šlemují cáry nočních oblak, nebo psát, že když je noc bez mráčku, je vidět na cesty po svazích skoro stejně jako v dne. [...] Skutečný začátek její diplomové práce měl být právě takový — měl osvětlit, jakým magickým místem jsou Kopanice na svazích Bílých Karpat a že právě jen v takovém místě se mohlo zrodit a rozvinout svou sílu něco zvláštního. *Bohyně*. Jenže nic takového do vědeckého textu svázaného přísnými pravidly nulové estetiky nepatří." (Tučková, *Žítkovské bohyně*, 105–7).
[46] Ibid., 107, 108–10.

But who is he, my protagonist? Jacob? Marusya? Genrikh? Me? Yurik? No. No one, in fact, who is conscious of an individual existence, of birth and an anticipated, and unavoidable, death.

[...] It is more likely an essence that belongs neither to being or nonbeing. It wanders through generations, from person to person, and creates the very illusion of personality.[47]

In all three novels, it seems reasonable to assume that the respective novel itself is the result of the imagined writing scenes of the three protagonists. Metaleptically, the unfinished texts do reach the public. In the three novels, however, the focus is not on the result, but on the process of the material or imagined writing scenes.

The writing scenes described centrally in the novels illustrate this synthesis. All three novels show, through various forms of embodied memory in writing, the temporal entanglement between past and present in the post-communist condition.[48] As the previous analyses have shown, the confrontation with written material from the past and writing in confrontation with it not only has a preserving character, but also always restructures knowledge. The imagination of writing, finally, mirrors the works of postcommunist literature on finding new narratives of the past.

REFERENCES

Benjamin, Walter. "On the Concept of History." In *Selected Writings. Vol. 4: 1938–1940*, edited by Howard Eiland and Michael W. Jennings, translated by Edmund Jephcott, 389–400. Cambridge, London: The Belknap Press of Harvard University Press, 2003.

Culbertson, Roberta. "Embodied Memory, Transcendence, and Telling: Recounting Trauma, Re-Establishing the Self." *New Literary History* 26, no. 1 (1995): 169–95.

---

[47] Ulitskaya, *Jacob's Ladder*, 539–40. The original reads: "А, может, разложит старые письма и напишет книжку… Такую книжку… которую дед то ли не успел написать, то ли ее сожгли во внутреннем дворе Внутренней тюрьмы на Лубянке…

Но кто он, мой главный герой? Яков? Маруся? Генрих? Я? Юрик? Нет, нет! Вообще ни одно из существ, осознающих свое индивидуальное существование, рождение и предполагаемую и неминуемую смерть.

[...] Скорее сущность, не принадлежащая ни бытию, ни не-бытию. То, что блуждает в поколениях, из личности в личность, что создает самую иллюзию личности." (Ulitskaya 2015, 721).

[48] Cf. Tippner, "Postcatastrophic Entanglement," 87–89 about "Entanglement of the past and present – love and family ties."

Davrichewy, Kéthévane. *La mer Noire*. Paris: Wespieser, 2010.

Erll, Astrid. *Kollektives Gedächtnis und Erinnerungskulturen: Eine Einführung*. Stuttgart: Metzler, 2017.

Etkind, Alexander. *Warped Mourning: Stories of the Undead in the Land of the Unburied*. Stanford: Stanford University Press, 2013.

Fuchs, Thomas. "Embodied Knowledge – Embodied Memory." In *Analytic and Continental Philosophy: Methods and Perspectives. Proceedings of the 37th International Wittgenstein Symposium*, edited by Sonja Rinofner-Kreidl and Harald A. Wiltsche, 215–30. Berlin, Boston: De Gruyter, 2016.

Fulda, Daniel, and Stephan Jaeger. "Einleitung: Romanhaftes Geschichtserzählen in einer erlebnisorientierten, enthierarchisierten und hybriden Geschichtskultur." In *Romanhaftes Erzählen von Geschichte: Vergegenwärtigte Vergangenheiten im beginnenden 21. Jahrhundert*, Eeited by Daniel Fulda and Stephan Jaeger, 1–53. Berlin, Boston: de Gruyter, 2019.

Groys, Boris. "The Post-Communist Condition" (2009). Translated by Matthew Partridge. Accessed August 30, 2021. http://becoming-former.tumblr.com/post/262880375/the-post-communist-condition-boris-groys-the.

Heinritz, Alena. "Burying the Undead: Coming to Terms with the Soviet Past in Novels by Slavnikova and Lebedev." *Acta Universitatis Carolinae – Studia Territorialia* 17, no. 2 (2017): 59–78.

Heinritz, Alena. *Postkommunistische Schreibweisen: Formen der Darstellung des Kommunismus in Romanen zu Beginn des 21. Jahrhunderts*. Heidelberg: Winter, 2021.

Hirsch, Marianne. "The Generation of Postmemory." *Poetics Today* 29, no. 1 (2008): 103–28.

Knurowska, Monika. "Telesnost' v rasskazakh Lyudmily Ulitskoĭ." *Acta Universitatis Wratislaviensis* 152, no. 3251 (2010): 67–79.

Markaryan, Ol'ga. "'Lestnitsa Yakova'. Roman o proshlom" (2016). Accessed August 30, 2021. http://rara-rara.ru/menu-texts/lestnica_yakova_roman_o_proshlom.

Nancy, Jean-Luc. *Corpus*. Paris: Éditions Métailié, 2000.

Peiker, Piret. "Post-Communist Literatures: A Postcolonial Perspective." *Eurozine* (March 28, 2006): 1–8. Accessed December 20, 2021. https://www.eurozine.com/post-communist-literatures-a-postcolonial-perspective/?pdf.

Reckwitz, Andreas. "Praktiken und Diskurse: Zur Logik von Praxis-/Diskursformationen." In *Kreativität und soziale Praxis. Studien zur Sozial- und Gesellschaftstheorie*, 49–66. Bielefeld: transcript, 2016.

Stingelin, Martin. "'Schreiben': Einleitung." In *'Mir ekelt vor diesem tintenklecksenden Säkulum': Schreibszenen im Zeitalter der Manuskripte*, edited by Martin Stingelin, 7–21. München: Fink, 2004.

Sutcliffe, Benjamin. "Commemoration and Connection: Liudmila Ulitskaia and the Universe of the Body in *Jacob's Ladder*." *The Slavonic and East European Review* 97, no. 3 (2019): 451–70.

Sutton, John, and Kellie Williamson. "Embodied Remembering." In *The Routledge Handbook of Embodied Cognition*, edited by Lawrence Shapiro, 315–25. London: Routledge, 2014.

Tippner, Anja. "Familiengeschichten als Gegengeschichten: Jüdische Identität in zeitgenössischer russischer Literatur." *Osteuropa* 69, no. 9–11 (2019): 203–22.

Tippner, Anja. "Postcatastrophic Entanglement? Contemporary Czech Writers Remember the Holocaust and Post-war Ethnic Cleansing." *Memory Studies* 14, no. 1 (2021): 80–94.

Tučková, Kateřina. *Žítkovské bohyně*. Brno: Host, 2012.

Ulitskaya, Ludmila. *Jacob's Ladder*. Translated by Polly Gannon. New York: Farrar, Straus and Giroux, 2019.

Ulitskaya, Lyudmila. *Lestnitsa Yakova*. Moskva: AST, 2015.

Ulitskaya, Lyudmila. *Svyashchennyi musor*. Moskva: Astrel', 2012.

Weigel, Sigrid. *Genea-Logik: Generation, Tradition und Evolution zwischen Kultur- und Naturwissenschaften*. München: Fink, 2006.

Zanetti, Sandro. "Einleitung." In *Schreiben als Kulturtechnik: Grundlagentexte*, edited by Sandro Zanetti, 7–34. Berlin: Suhrkamp, 2012.

PART II.
CONFLICTING IDENTITY

Chapter 4

Poland's False Symmetry: How Szczepan Twardoch's Jakub Szapiro Knocks Out the Myth of Polish-Jewish Conflict

Karolina Kołpak
Yale University, USA

Abstract: This chapter examines aspects of the story of Jakub Szapiro in Szczepan Twardoch's *The King of Warsaw* and *The Kingdom* to demonstrate the persistence as well as failure of an interpretive framework which treats the subject of Polish-Jewish relations as a Polish-Jewish "conflict" characterized by a "symmetry" of strength. The narrative of a "symmetrical" Polish-Jewish "conflict" within the broader discourse on Polish-Jewish relations dominates in Poland. This has prevented reviewers of Twardoch's work from finding that his duology actually dismantles the Polish-Jewish dichotomy and alleged rivalry of equals, presenting the Polish readers with the opposite of what they (would like to) see. Poles and Jews were never equals; there was no Polish-Jewish conflict because there was no symmetry between the two groups. Twardoch presents his readers with a vivid picture of this false symmetry accentuated throughout the story of the Jewish boxer and gangster, Jakub Szapiro.

Keywords: Szczepan Twardoch, Warsaw, interwar Poland, Polish-Jewish relations, antisemitism, conflict, symmetry

***

Szczepan Twardoch's *The King of Warsaw* (*Król*) came out in Poland in 2016, becoming a bestseller with over a hundred thousand copies sold nationwide.[1]

---

[1] This is no small number considering the low readership in Poland. According to annual studies conducted by the Polish National Library, between 2016 and 2017, less than 40% of Poles (37% and 38% respectively) ages 15 and up have read at least a single book per year. See: Izabela Koryś et al., eds. *Stan czytelnictwa w Polsce w 2017 roku*

In 2017, *The King of Warsaw* was nominated for the Gdynia Literary Prize, and in 2021, it received the EBRD Literature Prize for the novel's English translation.[2] The English translation, available since April 2020, generated much positive noise abroad. London's daily, *The Times*, named *The King of Warsaw* one of its picks for the April 2020 historical fiction of the month; meanwhile, *The New York Times* included it among over two hundred books worldwide coming out in English in 2020. The novel's cover boasted positive reviews from *Die Welt*, *Rolling Stone* (Germany) and *World Literature Today*. Meanwhile, others joined the chorus of thumbs up, endorsing the literary product of "one of Poland's emerging literary stars."[3] On May 18, 2018, *The King of Warsaw* made it onto the stage of the Polish Theater in Warsaw, becoming something of a sensation and stirring some unrest: instances of destruction of event posters and antisemitic reactions. The performance, however, was quite successful and received fairly positive reviews.[4] More successful was the television series *The King* (*Król*), directed by the acclaimed

---

(Warszawa: Biblioteka Narodowa, 2018), https://polona.pl/item/stan-czytelnictwa-w-polsce-w-2017-roku,MTIzODA1MzI2/0/#info:metadata.

[2] European Bank for Reconstruction and Development Literature Prize; the English translator is Sean Gasper Bye. See: "Szczepan Twardoch," accessed November 15, 2021, http://szczepantwardoch.pl/en/home/.

[3] Quote from "The King of Warsaw," *Kirkus Reviews*, January 27, 2020, https://www.kirkusreviews.com/book-reviews/szczepan-twardoch/the-king-of-warsaw/; See also: Eddy Portnoy, "The Yiddish-Speaking Hitmen's Union," *Jewish Review of Books*, Winter 2021, https://jewishreviewofbooks.com/articles/9547/the-yiddish-speaking-hitmens-union/; Clea Simon, "'The King of Warsaw' is a Holocaust Novel with a Twist," *The Boston Globe*, April 16, 2020, https://www.bostonglobe.com/2020/04/16/arts/king-warsaw-is-holocaust-novel-with-twist/; Fran Hawthorne, "The King of Warsaw: A Novel," *New York Journal of Books*, https://www.nyjournalofbooks.com/book-review/king-warsaw-novel; Gray Beltran, Rebecca Lieberman, and Tammy Tarng, "Globetrotting," *The New York Times*, September 8, 2020, https://www.nytimes.com/interactive/2020/01/08/books/new-books-international.html?searchResultPosition=2; Antonia Senior, "The best new historical fiction for April 2020 – Family Dramas, from Galilee to Restoration England," *The Times*, April 7, 2020, https://www.thetimes.co.uk/article/the-best-new-historical-fiction-for-april-2020-family-dramas-from-galilee-to-restoration-england-9b5g58dtq.

[4] "Plakaty teatralne, które wywołały kontrowersje," eWejściówki.pl, August 19, 2021, https://ewejsciowki.pl/poradnik/plakaty-teatralne-ktore-wywolaly-kontrowersje/#Wroclawski_Teatr_Lalek_Z_dociekow_nad_zyciem_plciowem; Jakub Krasny, "Niech żyje 'Król' – adaptacja powieści Twardocha w Teatrze Polskim," Czytaj PL, June 16, 2018, https://czytajpl.pl/2018/06/16/niech-zyje-krol-adaptacja-powiesci-twardocha-w-teatrze-polskim/; Dominik Gac, "Kapiszonowy Król," Teatralny.pl, July 11, 2018, https://teatralny.pl/recenzje/kapiszonowy-krol,2429.html.

Jan P. Matuszyński[5], which premiered in November 2020 on the Canal+ network. Szczepan Twardoch was closely involved in creating the series, making an appearance on the screen himself. *The King* received the Polish Film Award *Orły* for the Best Feature Series in 2021.[6]

The King of Warsaw was not the first of Twardoch's novels to become a national bestseller. Before it, *Morphine* (*Morfina*, 2012) and *Drach* (2014) became literary successes collecting multiple prizes and nominations.[7] The last of Twardoch's bestsellers was *The King of Warsaw*'s sequel, *The Kingdom* (*Królestwo*), which appeared in Poland in 2018 and gained a nomination for the Nike Literary Prize in 2019.[8] While much less has been happening around it since publication – no theater performances or screen adaptations – the book received positive reviews, and many appreciated the change in tone, style, and point of view which Twardoch employed in *The Kingdom*.[9] The sequel was "explicitly about the Holocaust," told no longer from the perspective of the main protagonist of both novels – Jewish boxer and gangster, Jakub Szapiro – but his son, Dawid, and former lover, Ryfka Kij.[10]

---

[5] Natalia Mętrak, "Jan P. Matuszyński," Culture.pl, last modified September 2021, https://culture.pl/pl/tworca/jan-p-matuszynski.

[6] "Polskie Nagrody Filmowe Orły 2021 rozdane!" Polskie Nagrody Filmowe, accessed November 15, 2021, http://pnf.pl/polskie-nagrody-filmowe-orly-2021-rozdane/; Janusz R. Kowalczyk and Natalia Sajewicz, "Szczepan Twardoch," Culture.pl, last modified June 2021, https://culture.pl/pl/tworca/szczepan-twardoch.

[7] "Szczepan Twardoch," accessed November 15, 2021, http://szczepantwardoch.pl/en/home/; Kowalczyk and Sajewicz, "Szczepan Twardoch."

[8] "Szczepan Twardoch," accessed November 15, 2021, http://szczepantwardoch.pl/en/home/.

[9] Justyna Sobolewska, "Recenzja książki: Szczepan Twardoch, 'Królestwo.' Bez znieczulenia," *Polityka*, October 28, 2018, https://www.polityka.pl/tygodnikpolityka/kultura/ksiazki/1769468,1,recenzja-ksiazki-szczepan-twardoch-krolestwo.read; Martyna Gancarczyk, "Upadek króla, czyli 'Królestwo' Szczepan Twardoch," Czytaj PL, November 10, 2018, https://czytajpl.pl/2018/11/10/upadek-krola-czylikrolestwo-szczepan-twardoch/; Paweł Majewski, "Pokrętna afektywność historii. O 'Królestwie' Szczepana Twardocha," *Kultura Liberalna*, November 13, 2018, https://kulturaliberalna.pl/2018/11/13/pawel-majewski-recenzja-krolestwo-szczepan-twardoch/. A negative review: Kinga Dunin, "Okrucieństwo, sentymentalizm, cynizm...," *Krytyka Polityczna*, January 4, 2019, https://krytykapolityczna.pl/kultura/czytaj-dalej/kinga-dunin-czyta/okruciens two-sentymentalizm-cynizm/.

[10] Twardoch confessed that *The King of Warsaw* was also a book about the Holocaust, just not explicitly. "The whole idea for *The Kingdom* resulted a bit from the fact that having written a fragment of *The King of Warsaw*, I was proud of myself; I was so fucken pleased with myself that, you know, I am just so artistically talented and intelligent, that I succeeded in writing a book about the Holocaust in which there is not a word about the Holocaust." See: Emilia Padoł, "Szczepan Twardoch: dobrze się robi literaturę o tym,

What could only be inferred from the ending of *The King of Warsaw* – the coming of the Second World War and the Holocaust – was openly narrated in *The Kingdom*.[11] In this sense, the two parts constitute a complete whole and reinforce each other. Twardoch himself highlighted the relationship between the "sensationalist narrative" of *The King of Warsaw*, which "[got] the attention of the reader," and *The Kingdom*, which the same readers would perhaps grab out of curiosity and consequently "confront" its story.[12]

In *The King of Warsaw* and *The Kingdom*, Twardoch treated the question of identity, particularly ethnonational, with consideration for the complexity of the issue.[13] Yet, in Poland, the leading reading of the story of Jakub Szapiro – concentrated, to a large extent, on the first part of the duology – has been quite simplistic. Assessments of it have employed a popular interpretative framework that reduces the story to a purported Polish-Jewish conflict – one characterized by a "symmetry" of strength – in which Poles and Jews confronted each other as equals, not unlike two opponents meeting in a boxing ring. The boxing ring was, after all, a space where Jakub Szapiro and Andrzej Ziembiński, a Jew and a Pole, met for the first time, and this encounter has been accepted as a lens through which all *The King of Warsaw* can and should or, less often, can but should not, be read.

In this chapter, I will illustrate how the Polish-Jewish "conflict" and its "symmetrization"[14] has manifested itself in the interpretations (and even the physical presentation) of *The King of Warsaw* and the story of Jakub Szapiro in Poland. The employment of the narrative of a "symmetrical" Polish-Jewish "conflict" within the broader discourse on Polish-Jewish relations in Poland has not gone unnoticed by scholars. According to Piotr Forecki and Anna

---

o czym ludzie nie chcą słuchać [WYWIAD]," *Onet Kultura*, November 6, 2018, https://kultura.onet.pl/wywiady-i-artykuly/szczepan-twardoch-dobrze-sie-robi-literature-o-tym-o-czym-ludzie-nie-chca-sluchac/h53k58m.

[11] Szczepan Twardoch, *Król* (Kraków: Wydawnictwo Literackie, 2016), 426–29.

[12] Emilia Padoł, "Szczepan Twardoch: dobrze się robi literature o tym, o czym ludzie nie chcą słuchać [WYWIAD]."

[13] Szczepan Twardoch creates in the Polish language, but he identifies with Silesia (and calls himself a Silesian), a southwestern region in Poland with a complex history – a place where he was born and lives today. His relationship with Poland and Polishness is not at all straightforward as he himself admits. See: Konrad Chwast, "'Moja książka, od kiedy ją wydałem, nie należy do mnie.' Rozmawiamy ze Szczepanem Twardochem," *Rozrywka.Blog*, November 7, 2020, https://spidersweb.pl/rozrywka/2020/11/07/szczepan-twardoch-wywiad-krol-serial; Kowalczyk and Sajewicz, "Szczepan Twardoch."

[14] Term borrowed from Piotr Forecki and Anna Zawadzka, "Reguła złotego środka: Kilka uwag na temat współczesnego dominującego dyskursu o 'stosunkach polsko-żydowskich'," *Zagłada Żydów. Studia i Materiały*, no. 11 (2015): 415, 426.

Zawadzka, "[i]n the Polish discursive practice, symmetry serves, above all, the invalidation of antisemitism. To present it [antisemitism] as a Polish reaction to the wrong [encountered] from the Jewish side;" it serves to "improve Polish self-esteem."[15] The term 'conflict', as Forecki observes, suggests the equality and proportionality of means possessed by two opposing sides:

> The word 'conflict' gives rise to a false sense of symmetry as if it was also Jews who called for an economic boycott, broke windows in Polish stores, introduced ghetto benches for Poles at the universities, their parties had hatred toward the Poles written into their programs, and forces in this alleged conflict were even. The acceptance of such perspective marginalizes the violence of the dominant group towards the subordinate minority.[16]

Put more precisely, "due to symmetrization, the structurally determined majority-minority relationship, with its entire dynamic, and above all with the power, domination and violence inscribed in it, disappears from sight."[17] Such conceptualization of the Polish-Jewish past reinforces the "ethnically understood conception of the nation," which perceives the Jews as "a foreign body, competitors or simply opponents of the Polish state."[18] As such, Polish-Jewish "conflict" and its purported symmetry constitute one of the components of one of the most persistent Polish national myths: the "heroico-martyrological narrative."[19] This component sustains an imagined Polish-Jewish "balance of wrongs;"[20] any disruption of this "balance" threatens the

---

[15] Forecki and Zawadzka, "Reguła złotego środka," 415, 425.

[16] Piotr Forecki, *Po Jedwabnem: Anatomia pamięci funkcjonalnej* (Warszawa: Instytut Badań Literackich PAN, 2018), 243–44.

[17] Forecki and Zawadzka, "Reguła złotego środka," 415.

[18] Forecki, *Po Jedwabnem*, 243–44.

[19] The term is used by Elżbieta Janicka as well as Forecki. See: Elżbieta Janicka, "Pamięć i tożsamość w przestrzeni dawnego getta warszawskiego/Memory and Identity in the Former Warsaw Ghetto Area," *Herito: dziedzictwo, kultura, współczesność/heritage, culture & the present*, no. 13 (April 2013): 68. On the idea of myth as a conceptual tool used by me to better understand the functioning of the narrative of a "symmetrical" Polish-Jewish "conflict," see: Aleida Assmann, "Transformations between History and Memory," *Social Research: An International Quarterly* 75, no. 1 (Spring 2008): 66–70. According to Assmann, "myth" in memory studies "may refer to an idea, an event, a person, a narrative that has acquired a symbolic value and is engraved and transmitted in memory [...] it is used to distinguish between the object of historical knowledge on the one hand and collectively remembered events on the other [...]. Myth in this sense of 'collectively remembered history' is meant as a neutral description." Ibid., 68.

[20] Forecki, *Po Jedwabnem*, 188.

whole myth, putting into question the Poles' dominant perception of themselves as both heroes and victims.

The utilization of the above-mentioned Polish-Jewish "conflict" in the reading of Twardoch's duology was present in various reviews, regardless of whether the reviewer used it as a lens through which to then criticize Twardoch's work or to praise it. Polish commentators saw in the story of Jakub Szapiro a depiction of two worlds at odds with each other, ready to throw punches with equal force. Yet, as I will show, Twardoch's duology can be read differently, and it should. The story of Jakub Szapiro – far from reinforcing it – dismantles the Polish-Jewish dichotomy and alleged rivalry of equals, presenting the Polish readers with the opposite of what they (would like to) see. In Twardoch's literary universe, Poles and Jews are never equals; they could not be. Prewar Poland belonged to ethnic (mostly Catholic) Poles, and Jews could never be more than guests (at best) or aliens (at worst). There was no Polish-Jewish "conflict" because there was no equality between the two groups. Thus, the critics' employment of the framework of Polish-Jewish "symmetry"– whether to praise or criticize Twardoch's work– in fact repeats the established discourse of false symmetry and endorses the mythical understanding of Polish nationhood ("wishful history" to use Forecki's term).[21]

SZAPIRO AND ZIEMBIŃSKI MEET IN THE RING: A TALE OF TWO WARSAWS, JEWS VERSUS POLES, AND A RIVALRY OF EQUALS

The King of Warsaw opens with a boxing match between Jakub Szapiro and Andrzej Ziembiński. Szapiro is a Jew, representing the Jewish Zionist sports club Makabi Warsaw while Ziembiński is a Pole, entering the ring for the Polish Legia Warsaw. Their fight is part of a larger event: the faceoff between Makabi and Legia for the capital city's team championship.[22] Before the reader opens Twardoch's book, the cover of the Polish edition of *The King of Warsaw* already prepares him for the first scene. On the front cover, below the title, one can read: "Warsaw. Turbulent thirties of the XX century. Multicultural, divided world on the brink of the second war, torn by national, political, social, and religious conflicts. Plot twists, romances, rape, chopping up of bodies, extortions, coups – everyday life of the capital lined with violence." And just below: "A suspenseful novel in which the author collides two perspectives of Poland of the thirties: Jewish and Polish." In a similar vein, facilitating the framework for reading the story at hand, the back cover continues: "Two Warsaw's, speaking two languages, living in separate worlds,

---

[21] Forecki, *Po Jedwabnem*, 247.
[22] Szczepan Twardoch, *Król* (Kraków: Wydawnictwo Literackie, 2016), 7–22.

showing each other indifference, sometimes burning with hatred. And a man, who in 1937 is on everyone's lips..." Right below, in a smaller font, is a much-abridged excerpt of the first scene of *The King of Warsaw*, with Jakub Szapiro and Andrzej Ziembiński standing opposite each other in the boxing ring, each emanating a different kind of beauty and strength observed by young Bernsztajn.[23] Szapiro and Ziembiński are thus rivals in sport, but as the cover suggests, their confrontation spills over the confines of the ring, alluding to a broader Polish-Jewish "conflict" to be encountered by the reader on the pages of the novel.

Interestingly, the book cover of the English translation of *The King of Warsaw* lacks the kind of metaphoric language of "two Warsaw's," "divided world", and "separate worlds" found in the original. There is no mention of Andrzej Ziembiński, a Polish boxer, as Szapiro's ultimate rival or even a general "conflict" between Poles and Jews or a Polish versus Jewish perspective of 1930s Poland. Instead, the cover presents a much more general "specter of violence" looming over Poland, which is "about to catch fire" (within the context of "Hitler is rising. Fascism is escalating."). Meanwhile, whereas "[i]n the boxing ring, Jakub Szapiro commands respect, revered as a hero by the Jewish community," that same Jewish community of interwar Poland is "marginalized and vilified."[24] The attention here is given to Poland's radicalization in the context of 1930s Europe and to Poles' antisemitism; two allegedly opposing forces – Polish and Jewish – are not even hinted at. Yet the way in which the Polish edition of the *King of Warsaw* presents the story to a potential reader, utilizing the moment a Jewish and a Polish boxer compete in the ring – incidentally, the very first scene of the actual novel – has evidently resonated with a certain reading and interpreting of this book in Poland.

---

[23] Translations from the original cover of Szczepan Twardoch, *Król*. All translations in the text are my own.

[24] For the cover of the book see: Szczepan Twardoch, *The King of Warsaw*, trans. Sean Gasper Bye (Seattle: Amazon Crossing, 2020), https://www.amazon.pl/King-Warsaw-Novel-Szczepan-Twardoch/dp/1542044448. As a sidenote, the book cover of the German translation of *The King of Warsaw* also lacks the original's metaphors of Polish-Jewish conflict in a divided city (and the English cover's specter of impending doom). Instead, the focus is on Szapiro the gangster once Kum Kaplica's arrest shakes the underworld. "It's the troubled thirties, everything is uncertain" – including Szapiro's place as the potential Godfather of the city. There is no mention of the fact that Szapiro is a Jew. See: Szczepan Twardoch, *Der Boxer*, trans. Olaf Kühl (Berlin: Rowohlt, 2019), https://www.amazon.com/Boxer-Szczepan-Twardoch/dp/3499291479. English reviews of *The King of Warsaw* (cited in the introduction) also lack the Polish-Jewish "conflict" as an interpretive concept.

The most sophisticated and perhaps the most popular representation of this variant of interpreting *The King of Warsaw* belongs to an established Polish poet, prose writer and translator, Jacek Dehnel, recipient of the 2005 Kościelski Foundation Prize and the 2006 Paszport "Polityki" Prize.[25] The interpretation presented by Dehnel in two Facebook posts was, in fact, a critique of Twardoch's novel, and the author of the two biting reviews openly admitted, "I criticized *The King of Warsaw* because you [Twardoch] simply did a bad job."[26] Dehnel remarked on a few errors and liberties Twardoch took in his writing, but it is not this nit-picky part of his review which deserves further scrutiny. Most interesting and revealing was Dehnel's underlying reading of *The King of Warsaw*, which found an echo in several other assessments of the book.

In the first Facebook post, Dehnel's main critique was somewhat constrained but nonetheless quite clear.

The whole book is based on the cult of strength and violence, on the metaphor of a fight in the ring...Therefore, on one side are Jews, workers, PPS [Polish Socialist Party], and at the forefront – cruel but just and, essentially, benevolent Kum Kaplica as well as his adjutant Szapiro...and on the other side – Poles, intellectuals, fascists (including pederasts, and in general impotent men...). In order to satisfy this dichotomy, in the narrative of *The King of Warsaw*, prewar Warsaw is strictly divided into Polish and Jewish, into Polish, intellectual, wealthy

---

[25] Paweł Kozioł, "Jacek Dehnel," Culture.pl, last modified October 2020, https://culture.pl/pl/tworca/jacek-dehnel. For some media noise regarding the Dehnel versus Twardoch polemic see: Marcin Andrzejewski, "Shitstorm o literaturę – 'Król' Szczepana Twardocha, *Art Galeria Sng*, February 4, 2018, http://sngkultura.pl/2018/02/shitstorm-o-literature-krol-szczepana-twardocha/; Łukasz Jadaś, "Cud na Facebooku. Wybuchła pierwsza gównoburza, którą czyta się bez zażenowania," *Asz Dziennik*, November 24, 2017, https://aszdziennik.pl/121729,cud-na-polskim-facebooku-wybuchla-pierwsza-gownoburza-ktora-czyta-sie-bez-zazenowania. The polemic between the two authors: Jacek Dehnel, "Przez pare ostatnich dni poczytywałem sobie 'Króla' (spoilers will follow)," Facebook, October 18, 2016, https://www.facebook.com/jacek.dehnel/posts/10154662445229914; Szczepan Twardoch, "Kto skrytykuje krytyków?," Onet Kultura, November 23, 2017, https://kultura.onet.pl/ksiazki/kto-skrytykuje-krytykow/frl12pp?utm_source=kultura.onet.pl_viasg_kultura&utm_medium=referal&utm_author=null&utm_campaign=leo_automatic&srcc=ucs&utm_v=2; Jacek Dehnel, "Drogi Szczepanie, kryminały, które piszę sobie z Piotrem (nie sam), traktuję jako literaturę bez większych literackich ambicji, rodzaj żartu, którym bawimy się wspólnie z czytelnikami," Facebook, November 23, 2017, https://www.facebook.com/jacek.dehnel/posts/10155996870819914.

[26] Dehnel, "Drogi Szczepanie."

and paved districts as well as Jewish, working-class, poor and with cobblestone or mud.[27]

Here, the critic found issue with Twardoch's allegedly rigid division of Warsaw into a Polish sphere and a Jewish sphere, which neglected any "mixing" between the two "communities."[28] In his short depiction above, the asserted dichotomy falls somewhat apart; the first "side" mentioned by Dehnel (Jews, workers, the Polish Socialist Party, Kaplica and Szapiro) makes for quite a diverse group. Yet pushing aside this inconsistency, Dehnel's second post – a response to Twardoch's article – unveiled the heart of the matter much more clearly even if also more vehemently.

> You lied [about] the history of Polish-Jewish Warsaw, and in a country where history is mucked up and falsified at will, you performed unforgivable – for me – shifts in the history of a city, which I consider my own. There was no symmetry between Polish and Jewish Warsaw, and Jewish militias did not beat professors at the university. In contrast to endecja's [militias; endecja is a commonly used term for the nationalist National Democratic Party] ...It is true that Polish and Jewish boxers (as well as their fans) competed with each other in Warsaw, but the fact that you sketched out a false image of a Polish and Jewish Warsaw "standing in the ring," separated districts, etc. is simply an instrumental and untrue treatment of the history of my city.[29]

Thus, according to Dehnel's interpretation, *The King of Warsaw* not only divided Warsaw into two distinct parts – Polish and Jewish – but it employed the "metaphor of a fight in the ring" and of "standing in the ring" to establish an underlying backdrop of Polish-Jewish "conflict" based on symmetry: two opponents with equal chances at victory and equally binding rules of the game. This metaphor, as perceived by Dehnel, expanded beyond the actual ring where Szapiro and Ziembiński fight – which is why the novel proved so problematic for him. Because *The King of Warsaw*, read in this way, presents a wishful story about an even Polish and Jewish rivalry over a city which belongs to both (although ownership here is clearly divided between districts), a rivalry between two groups of balanced strength, power, and force.

Jacek Dehnel was not alone in his interpretation of Twardoch's *The King of Warsaw*; reviewers picked up the Polish-Jewish dichotomy and symmetry in

---

[27] Dehnel, "Przez pare ostatnich dni poczytywałem sobie 'Króla' (spoilers will follow)."
[28] Ibid.
[29] Dehnel, "Drogi Szczepanie."

"conflict" presumably constructed by the author of the novel. Some embraced it quite straightforwardly, giving it explicit expression:

> The action of the novel takes place in the thirties of the XX century in Warsaw, which was, at the time, a multicultural and multinational melting-pot...[T]here begin to appear the increasingly noticeable tensions between hitherto amicably coexisting Poles and Jews...Jewish militias stand opposite fascist militias on equal terms...Jews are full-fledged gangsters, who – just like their rivals – will stop at nothing to get their way.[30]

> [Twardoch] faithfully captured Polish-Jewish relations if we look from the Jewish side...Jews are undoubtedly the biggest and most tragic victim of the second war. In light of this fact, how can Poles – the prewar rivals of Jews – be assessed? Automatically, they stand in the position of a negative hero. Because were prewar Jews and Poles each other's friends and brothers? Maybe nominally because, in fact, these were two nations in one country competing with each other...Yet the ascertainment on the back, advertisement cover of the *King of Warsaw*, that prewar Jews and Poles constituted two completely separate worlds, is not fully accurate.[31]

Others used it unconsciously, almost automatically, as if what they perceived to be Twardoch's literary construction was a sort of (historical) given. Here, in the perception of the authors, the Polish-Jewish "symmetry" of experience became especially pronounced and the playing field evened out with the coming of the Second World War.

> At the beginning of the novel, Szapiro and a Polish nationalist stand against each other in the ring, masculine strength against masculine strength. In a few years, both will lose or die, and those who defeated them will die. A black, castrating despair will remain.[32]

> In the background of the novel, we have...a rivalry, at times brutal, between militias – ONR [National Radical Camp], Jewish, socialist...Twardoch plots all of this with volubility, skillfully distributing

---

[30] Piotr Młynarski, "Szczepan Twardoch Król," Instytut Książki: Literatura, 2017, https://instytutksiazki.pl/literatura,8,recenzje,25,klubowiczow,1,krol,63.html.

[31] Andrzejewski, "Shitstorm o literaturę – 'Król' Szczepana Twardocha."

[32] Kinga Dunin, "Król i królowa," *Krytyka Polityczna*, October 19, 2016, https://krytyka polityczna.pl/kultura/czytaj-dalej/kinga-dunin-czyta/krol-i-krolowa/.

the accents... [E]veryone is marked by Evil: this is not an easy lesson about Polish antisemitism, Jewish anti-Polonism or simple fascination with aggression. It is a much deeper vivisection of the evil growing inside a person...And when the reader thinks he has come to know everything that is the worst, Twardoch suggests that this is, after all, just the beginning because at any moment now, Germans will come here and only they will arrange a real festival of Evil, against which the gangsters of the Second Polish Republic are pleasant little angels.[33]

Twardoch shows a Warsaw divided, just like an audience of boxing matches. A better, Polish, elegant Warsaw as well as a worse, Jewish [one]...These two worlds are also represented by Jakub's women: Ryfka – madame, and earlier a Jewish mistress of Kum Kaplica, and on the other side – Anna, not only a Polish woman but also a daughter of a fascist-leaning prosecutor...He [Szapiro] did not know...what is approaching. But we also see the future which the protagonists do not know – the horribleness, which sweeps away everyone: it puts fascists in Auschwitz or treats them to trials after the war, it destroys those on the left and the right alike.[34]

Finally, a voice most akin to Dehnel. Here, the author similarly applied the metaphor of a fight in the ring and read *The King of Warsaw* as a set of conflicts, which ultimately took away from the gravity of real Polish antisemitism in interwar Poland. The criticism of Twardoch's alleged distortion and simplification of history echoed Dehnel's as well.

[H]istory of Polish antisemitism of the interwar period is reduced to a conflict between strong personalities: between a Jewish and a Polish boxer; between a PPS gangster and a right-wing cynic (in this role

---

[33] Marcin Fijołek, "'Król' – zanurzenie w rzece Zła przed uderzeniem wodospadu. Nowa powieść Twardocha to kawał mocnej lektury [RECENZJA]," *wPolityce*, October 8, 2016, https://wpolityce.pl/kultura/311242-krol-czyli-zanurzenie-w-rzece-zla-przed-atakiem-prawdziwego-wodospadu-nowa-powiesc-twardocha-to-kawal-mocnej-lektury.

[34] Justyna Sobolewska, "Dawna Warszawa według Twardocha," *Polityka*, October 4, 2016, https://www.polityka.pl/tygodnikpolityka/kultura/1677624,1,dawna-warszawa-wedlug-twardocha.read. World War II seems to create a space where the concept of Polish-Jewish dichotomy breaks down as an interpretive tool; now *everyone* suffers at the hands of a third party. "Symmetry" of suffering replaces here the "symmetry" of strength. On the multiple variants of Polish-Jewish symmetry in Polish discourse see: Forecki and Zawadzka, "Reguła złotego środka," 416.

Bolesław Piasecki)…Because the world of *The King of Warsaw* is ruled by strength (physical one and political one), and who does not have it, must fall out of this world. And there's nothing to be surprised at, this is, after all, a novel about a boxer – and when you look at society like at a boxing match, everything becomes simple.[35]

Yet what if the reduction, simplification, dichotomy, symmetry of a boxing match, etc., perceived by the reviewers is not Twardoch's creation? What if the story of Jakub Szapiro tells us something entirely different? Namely, it exposes the persistence of the prevailing interpretative framework of Polish-Jewish "conflict" and "symmetry" when the subject of Polish-Jewish history emerges; it also highlights this framework's uselessness in any attempts at rethinking and deconstructing the subject. The myth is so well-established in Polish discourse that even those who oppose it and see fault in it are unable to recognize that Twardoch's work actually dismantles it, vividly illustrating the false symmetry underlining the entire story of Jakub Szapiro.

THE REIGN THAT NEVER WAS: "HOW MUCH IS THIS VICTORY OF YOURS WORTH, JAKUB?"[36]

The moment Szapiro and Ziembiński met in the ring, they met not only as opponents in a heavyweight bout but also – and perhaps more importantly – as bearers of universally recognized *unequal statuses* in the capital city of a country, the Second Polish Republic, which was their common home. The boxing match between these two men naturally roused the spectators in the stands, eager to see which of them would hold the victorious title. Jakub, Jankiew Szapiro belonged to the Jewish crowd, although his Yiddish name, just like the Yiddish language more generally, were used rarely and only by people closest to him. Szapiro and Emilia, his wife, never spoke Yiddish with their sons, Dawid and Daniel. When Dawid asked his father "why they speak Polish at home if he heard how he [Szapiro] and mom say about Poles 'they' and not 'we'," Szapiro responded: "[S]ince we live among Poles, then – without forgetting our language [Yiddish] – we must speak Polish even better than Poles. We must be smarter than them, stronger, and better educated, more handy, more intelligent and more cunning."[37]

---

[35] Maciej Jakubowiak, "Przyjdzie bokser i nas zbawi," *Dwutygonik,* September 2016, https://www.dwutygodnik.com/artykul/6780-przyjdzie-bokser-i-nas-zbawi.html.
[36] Szczepan Twardoch, *Królestwo* (Kraków: Wydawnictwo Literackie, 2018), 128. Quote from Jakub Szapiro's wife, Emilia, a few months before the start of the Second World War.
[37] Twardoch, *Królestwo,* 126–27.

His opponent, Andrzej Ziembiński, belonged to the Poles. He did not have a second language or name; he did not have to worry about surpassing Poles in everything because he was a Pole by origin and conviction – an ethnic nationalist radical, who did not have to prove anything. He led counter-manifestations aimed at demonstrations of united socialist parties and workers; he stood at the head of the student militia in charge of segregating Jewish students from their Polish peers at the university; and "he took part in the whole fuss with shooting at the headquarters of the [Jewish] Bund."[38] Ziembiński manifested the extreme and lawless violence as well as exclusionary practices aimed specifically at the Jews. Important member of ONR-"Falanga" – an ultranationalist and fascist splinter group of the National Radical Camp, "organized paramilitarily and directed in an authoritarian manner,"[39] functioning illegally for most of its existence – he came into contact with the underworld of Jakub Szapiro. Yet by the late 1930s, when Ziembiński met Szapiro in the ring, the existing nationalist mainstream was not far from the position exemplified by Ziembiński's – at least regarding Jews. The foundations for it erupted in full force as early as 1922, with the election and assassination of President Gabriel Narutowicz: the "Jewish president." This was the moment when Polish nationalists realized the potential and strength of antisemitism as a mobilizing tool; this was when the Doctrine of the Polish Majority – ethnic Poles alone should decide the fate of Poland and participate in its affairs – was established and accepted by nearly all political parties, not to mention the general Polish public.[40] Falangist Ziembiński was just the embodiment of the most total and dedicated heir of Polish integral nationalism.

And yet, it was Szapiro who won the fight. He defeated Ziembiński in less than two minutes, and he did so with great skill, precision, and confidence.

The audience hollers, gets up from their chairs in crowd emotion as of yet unchanneled, flowing solely from surprise, excitement of the fight...a second later, the enthusiasm is being channeled, everyone already knows what happened, Jewish fans explode with joy as if it was they themselves who had just knocked down every Pole who ever

---

[38] Twardoch, *Król*, 57, 166-75, 222.

[39] Jan Józef Lipski, *Idea Katolickiego Państwa Narodu Polskiego: Zarys ideologii ONR "Falanga"* (Warszawa: Wydawnictwo Krytyki Politycznej, 2015), 15.

[40] Paul Brykczyński, *Primed for Violence: Murder, Antisemitism, and Democratic Politics in Interwar Poland* (Madison: University of Wisconsin Press, 2016). Reference to "Jewish president" on page 24.

frowned upon them; the Christian audience boos, outraged, that the proper order of things has been disrupted.[41]

As if acknowledging the enthusiasm of his Jewish fans and understanding the meaning they attached to his spectacular knockout of Ziembiński – "very tall, with long albeit muscular limbs as well as a long torso of a swimmer; very light, almost white hair, shaven on the sides and longer on top, combed with a part; and pale-blue eyes and angular jaw, art déco...like from photographs and drawings of German athletes, Aryan half-gods..."[42] – Szapiro decided to give them more. He offered a gesture.

Before Ziembiński regained consciousness and just after his body stopped trembling on the floor of the ring, Szapiro's cornerman "[took] out a cigarette case from the pocket, [lit] the cigarette and [put] it straight into the boxer's mouth. Szapiro [took] a few drags, lean[ed] over the ring ropes, the cornerman [took] the cigarette out of his mouth and [put] it out."[43] Everyone present, including Mojżesz Bernsztajn, the narrator of *The King of Warsaw*, watched Szapiro in his display of strength – "Szapiro blows out a huge cloud of blue smoke, which, in the light of the spotlights, arranges into arabesques as if into some alphabet of male strength" – and "lordly arrogance," something rarely witnessed in a Jew.[44] This type of behavior, deemed inappropriate by convention, made an impression on the seventeen-year-old Mojżesz, "a skinny little Jew from Nalewki [one of the main streets of the old Jewish district]," a "nobody,"[45] for whom the entire fight and Szapiro's chance at victory appeared surreal – "an impossibility." After all,

---

[41] Twardoch, *Król*, 17.

[42] Ibid., 10.

[43] Ibid., 18.

[44] Ibid., 18, 20.

[45] Ibid., 7, 146. Mojżesz Bernstajn, the narrator of most of *The King of Warsaw*, was killed by Szapiro shortly after Szapiro killed the boy's father, Naum Bernsztajn, who could not pay back his debt. Towards the end of the book, the reader finds out that Mojżesz the narrator was in fact the old, post-war Szapiro, who believed to be Mojżesz Bernsztajn, presumably as a coping mechanism for his guilt (page 396–401). Throughout the book, Mojżesz-Szapiro used these and other similar self-characterizations, which defined his existence in relation to Jakub Szapiro at his prime. The tension between "old Mojżesz" and "new Mojżesz" was, in fact, the tension between "old Szapiro" and "new Szapiro." See, for example, "little Jew with sidelocks" (page 19); "Before, throughout my whole short life, I was invisible. Such an ordinary, little, skinny Jew from Nalewki. One out of thousands of little, skinny Jews from Nalewki" (page 31) versus; "I was Szapiro's boy. First time in my life I was somebody" (page 138); "In my dark grey suit from Zaremba, I was no longer a skinny Jew from Nalewki; I was a slim, elegant young man of Semitic beauty" (page 144).

Ziembiński appears to tower over him [Szapiro] not only physically, not only in the reach of his arms and height, but also in that Ziembiński is at home here, he belongs to the class of owners and administrators of this country...As a fair-haired giant with the coat of arms of Legia on his chest, he will always be someone better than a Jewish boxer in a Makabi shirt.[46]

But Szapiro did win, and he openly and unapologetically owned his space and his victory, disregarding conventions, expectations, and – most importantly – slighting his opponent, a Pole, by extension, his Polish audience, and symbolically, Poles in general: the owners of Poland.

***

In the final scene of the *King of Warsaw*, the reader learns that the whole Szapiro family could have left Poland in 1937, but they did not. After much protest, Jakub did, in the end, purchase plane tickets to Palestine. He boarded the plane with his wife and children, and the plane did lift off from the ground. But they did not make it to Palestine. "I'm looking," Jakub narrated,

> I see Tłomackie [Street]. I see Kercelak [a marketplace square]. Lines of streets, Leszno, Chłodna, Miła, I do not know, which one is which, but I know that they are there, I know everyone who walks on their pavement, and everyone certainly knows me, on those streets I am Jakub Szapiro, policemen bow to me, girls smile, devout Jews, indignant, turn their gaze away, fascists and stallholders fear me, I am Jakub Szapiro.

> Be the king of this city...Be the king of this city. This is your kingdom.

> 'We are turning around,' I whisper.[47]

Jakub turned the plane around, and he and his family remained in Warsaw. He could not let go of what he knew, of who he was – or rather, of whom he became: the most fearsome and powerful gangster of the city's underworld, a proud successor of Kum Kaplica – the veteran of the Polish Socialist Party (PPS), revolutionary and independence fighter, a "short, cheerful and terrifying

---

[46] Twardoch, *Król*, 16.
[47] Ibid., 426.

goy"[48] known by all of Warsaw. Kaplica chose him; this was the victory he earned through years of unfaltering loyalty and hard, brutal work. Thus, aboard the plane, he rationalized: "I am Jakub Szapiro. It's not time to abdicate yet. I am the king of this city...I am staying to reign, and my reign will last twenty-three months, and then," he remembered, as a survivor of the Second World War, "I will lose everything."[49] A fragile ascendance to power.

Szapiro lost everything shortly after his participation in the futile September 1939 campaign, something he chose to partake in himself. This was not his first time enlisting in the Polish army. He did so years earlier, in 1919, to fight the Bolsheviks, only to be interned in the Jabłonna camp along with other Jewish officers and soldiers (including volunteers) from units outside the front a year and a half after fighting for the reemerging Poland in the Polish-Soviet War (1919—1921). The camp was set up by order of the Minister of Military Affairs, General Sosnkowski, during the decisive Battle of Warsaw (1920). The camp caused an uproar abroad and inside the country, and it was shut down after twenty-five days of existence thanks to the efforts of socialist politicians (PPS) and leading progressive intellectuals. All the same, it radically confirmed that independent Poland did not trust its Jewish citizens, linking them to the threat of Bolshevism and thus feeding on and reinforcing the myth of *żydokomuna* (Judeo-Communism), which continued to operate throughout the interwar period and beyond.[50] According to Jakub's son, Dawid, "during his whole life between the two wars, he [Szapiro] claimed that he will never forgive Poland for this, that he stuck out his neck for her, but Poland locked him up in a camp when he wanted to fight for her." Yet, "at the end of August 1939, he again wanted to go fight for this Poland" despite his former degradation and Poland's great insult to every citizen of Jewish background who fought on her behalf.[51] Despite what Dawid recalled about his father in mid-September 1939:

---

[48] Twardoch, *Król*, 22-23. The character of Kum Kaplica is based on Łukasz Siemiątkowski known as Tata Tasiemka, a Polish gangster, PPS activist, involved in the Polish underground during the Second World War. See: Emilia Padoł, "Szczepan Twardoch: nie mamy pojęcia czym jesteśmy," *Onet Kultura*, October 12, 2016, https://kultura.onet.pl/wywiady-i-artykuly/szczepan-twardoch-nie-mamy-pojecia-czym-jestesmy/cyk1s4l.

[49] Twardoch, *Król*, 428.

[50] Jacek Walicki, "Położenie Żydów polskich podczas kampanii 1920 r.," *Acta Universitatis Lodziensis. Folia Historica*, no. 52 (1995): 121–22; *Polski Słownik Judaistyczny*, s.v. "Obóz dla internowanych w Jabłonnie," accessed September 1, 2021, https://delet.jhi.pl/pl/psj?articleId=16617; Aleksander Hertz, *Żydzi w kulturze polskiej* (Warszawa: Biblioteka "Więzi," 2014), 223-25.

[51] Twardoch, *Królestwo*, 62.

Poland did not want him, Poland pushed him away as a Jew, who did not intend on making every effort to be worthy of the honorable title of a Pole. Such a Jew, who wanted to be a Pole, who dreamed of Polishness, who strived to be a Pole and was ready to fiercely defend his fresh, new Polishness, still remained, of course, a conditional Pole, remained suspicious – let alone a Jew who believed that in Warsaw he is at home but being a Pole did not interest him. In the eyes of the Poles, the proper attitude of a Jew was to try to get rid of one's own Jewishness like of a sickness, wash it off oneself...Some, like the poet Tuwim, aspired to Polishness impudently...and this irritated many; yet even more irritating, much more irritating was a Jew, a Varsovian Jew, who in Warsaw was, after all, at home because where else was he to be at home if he was never anywhere, and yet despite this, he did not at all even try, he did not want to be a Pole, he defended himself from Polishness.[52]

In the summer of 1937, just two years before he decided to stick out his neck for Poland, which did not want him, boxer Szapiro flaunted his unwillingness to accept and play by its rules, "especially irritating and arousing anxiety" of Polish spectators because he so defiantly "reject[ed] the traditional [Jewish] type of 'kike' and 'little jew'." His physical appearance of emanating strength, as well as his confidence and cool "outrage[d]" those who saw in this bearing a "Jewish arrogance," an "undermining of the traditional social hierarchy," a very clear "stepping outside of a social role."[53] Szapiro, a "tall, handsome Jew with wide shoulders and a massive back of a Maccabean boxer,"[54] a thirty-seven-year-old rich gangster, feared and respected, loved and desired by all women – Christian and Jewish – married to a beautiful and intelligent Emilia, father of two twin boys, Dawid and Daniel, was a "different Jew, just as good as Christian gentlemen."[55] As good as a Pole. This emanated from the ring – leaving the Jewish audience awestruck and the Polish outraged – and manifested itself everywhere Szapiro went. Even in places which belonged to Warsaw's wealthy Polish elite, Szapiro showed no sign of discomfort, fear or "being out of place."[56] No one would tell him where he did or did not belong. That was up to him to decide, and he had his fists and his gun to back this up.

---

[52] Twardoch, *Królestwo*, 126.
[53] Hertz, *Żydzi w kulturze polskiej*, 240-43.
[54] Twardoch, *Król*, 7.
[55] Ibid., 13, 20, 60.
[56] Ibid., 150–51.

Nonetheless, it was the working-class streets of Wola and "the northern district, in [his] old homeland"[57] where Szapiro felt truly at home. Despite his wealth – or perhaps because of it – he *chose* to live on Nalewki Street, the heart of the Jewish district.

> He could have, of course, just moved out and lived in one of the beautiful, modern residential areas of Żoliborz…but he did not want to. The Northern District – with the stench of gutters flowing through its streets, with the smell of cholent on Friday, and its indisputable dirt – was the only homeland he had, and he could not abandon this homeland…He did not want to assimilate…

> Jakub did not want to wash anything off himself. There was something ostentatious and insolent in how he paraded down Nalewki in the most expensive suits from Zaremba; how he jumped over puddles in shoes shinier than the jackboots of a Polish calvary captain; how he drove around the Northern District in his Buick. People, our people, the Jewish poor, did not look at him with distaste, which they had for Polish gentlemen…In some measure, Jakub Szapiro wore these suits and drove a Buick in their name because Jakub Szapiro remained one of them.[58]

Not that Szapiro was a Jewish nationalist – Zionist or otherwise. As Dawid recalled,

> My father spoke Polish because although for him it was a second language, Polish was nevertheless the first language of his city, and he himself also did not experience his Jewishness too intensely on a daily basis. A Jew awoke in my father only when he faced antisemitism, my father always became a Jew when someone hated Jews, whereas when he was not hated, he effectively forgot about his Jewishness. He was not proud of the fact that he is a Jew, nor was he ashamed of it, and he did not allow for anyone to force him to feel pride – therefore, as I remember, he constantly fought with uncle Moryc – nor, all the more, shame.[59]

He stayed in the Northern District because this was his domain. He chose to live on Nalewki to demonstrate to Poles that despite his wealth and success,

---

[57] Twardoch, *Królestwo*, 244.
[58] Twardoch, *Król*, 121–22.
[59] Twardoch, *Królestwo*, 134–35.

he had no aspiration of becoming one of them (unlike assimilated or assimilating Jews) and of living on the fancier streets of Warsaw. He remained on Nalewki to stand out among the Jewish masses, proving to them that one could have it all yet remain a Jew. In reality, however, he was proving more to himself than to Poles or Jews. Because the Northern District made him feel superior, this was where he could *feel* like a real gentleman, a respected and admired citizen. No wealth and power would replicate this feeling on the Polish street. So he stayed and paraded his wealth instead.

***

"You were the king of Warsaw. Two years," Ryfka Kij, his former lover, reminded him after the war when he no longer wanted to remember.[60] In the winter of 1944, when this past boxer, soldier, and fearsome gangster lost all will to live, when, in the ashes of Warsaw, Ryfka would not grant Szapiro the relief of death, she recalled the combination of vanity and self-loathing, which made him a particularly vulnerable king before the war.

> He once loved himself, he loved all of those little bibelots of his, his little guns, pocketknives and suits, he loved expensive leather shoes and automobiles with which he gussied up because he wanted to be someone more than another little Jew from Warsaw, little Jew-nobody, shit, human manure…And Jakub wanted to be something more than manure, that is why he boxed, shot, gussied up, spread the peacock tail, bred sons, strolled around, paraded, promenaded from Tłomackie to the Kercelak, lifted his hat, smiled, bowed to whomever necessary, tooted, flirted, a little male, a little bull, a beast, and then what happened, happened and Jakub no longer loved himself; therefore, he no longer loved anyone, and he lies here now, in a sack of rags, duvets, and coats, in a sack by the wall, thin, unshaven, covered with tatters, for a week he hadn't said a single word in any human language, instead he wanted to scream…[61]

When his kingdom fell, and he became a policeman of the Jewish Ghetto Police, Szapiro had no aspirations to reign. "Perhaps he realized that even if he was the king of the ghetto – mightier than all these ghetto caciques – still any

---

[60] Twardoch, *Król*, 399.
[61] Twardoch, *Królestwo*, 9.

German could always shoot him in a moment of irritation or, what's worse, punch him in the face or beat with a whip or a riding crop."[62]

Emilia kicked him out of the house; he left and never came back – not even when his wife and children were taken to the Umschlagplatz and crammed into a train to Treblinka. Emilia "would have forgiven him the armband and the hat if from this whole collection of matters to be forgiven she could subtract at least one. But she could not."[63] So he left his family, became "nothing more" than just an ordinary "policeman in the first district;" then, after the Grossaktion, he made brushes for a ticket to live, a "shadow of his own legend and everyone knew that."[64] It was the end of the famous, handsome, all-powerful Jakub Szapiro. The escape from the ghetto in March 1943 was planned entirely by Ryfka, who simply informed him that "[w]e are leaving. That they have a hiding place for us on the Aryan side. That they will hide us until the war ends. That they don't even want money…Jakub just shrugged his shoulders."[65] Szapiro did not care, although "he was not yet as lethargic, he was not as deep in darkness as later" when Ryfka took care of him amid the ruins of Warsaw in 1944.[66]

In March 1943, when they made it to their hiding spot on the Aryan side of the city, Szapiro "came alive" one last time. Their host was Andrzej Ziembiński's sister, Anna Ziembińska, "the worst of all of Jakub's loves," this "Polish whore of his, who locked us up in the apartment like in a cage and looked after us like little house pets."[67] Jakub and Anna met before the war, shortly after Szapiro's boxing match with her brother. What started as a transaction in favors turned into a short but steamy love affair between a Polish beauty from a "good family"[68] and a handsome Jewish bandit. Jakub believed that Anna was dead – shot by her brother, Andrzej, upon his learning of their relationship. But when "she rose as if from the dead," allegedly returning from London, Jakub became "revived all of a sudden; he thought and analyzed like before, as if he forgot for a while about the lawyer's daughter [Emilia] and the boys he begot with her. Next to her, next to this Polish whore, he always readily forgot about everything."[69]

---

[62] Twardoch, *Królestwo*, 318.
[63] Ibid., 296.
[64] Ibid., 94, 318.
[65] Ibid., 100–101.
[66] Ibid., 101.
[67] Ibid., 102, 227.
[68] Twardoch, *Król*, 324.
[69] Twardoch, *Królestwo*, 227.

His revival did not last long, and ultimately Anna died at his hands – or rather at Ryfka's hands because she alone knew how to manipulate Szapiro's pride, which was always his defining feature but became more vulnerable in the dark closet where Anna forced him to hide. Ryfka knew that. She knew that "Jakub Szapiro's pride resulted from his fear, from the horror that anyone could consider him as someone worse, while its effect was the constant necessity of proving to everyone his significance."[70] And so, when Anna Ziembińska was having sex with a German after a conversation which smelled of collaboration, Jakub shot both. "'She deserved it, she buddied up with Germans...' said Szapiro," but Ryfka knew this was just an excuse, a justification for firing the pistol.[71] Ryfka wanted Anna dead not because she was, quite likely, a collaborator. "Of course, I was disgusted by Germans, and I hated Germans," explained Ryfka, "but I was disgusted by Poles and hated them equally. For something else and differently, but these disputes of theirs, accusations regarding the extent to which good Poles could cooperate with Germans, in which spheres of life it was proper and in which it wasn't proper, did not interest me at all."[72] She wanted Anna dead because "in her eyes I saw that I am no longer human, that I am only a Jewess;" because "she thought that she was better than me in everything...For this I wanted to punish her and in principle all those like her, and I did."[73]

Ryfka's ultimate triumph was the final blow to Jakub Szapiro. They were alive, but "Jakub was teetering on the brink of life and death, and after he shot Ziembińska, in this balance he clearly tilted towards death – not biological, but internal."[74] Nothing was left of the Maccabean body and strength, of the spirit and confidence, which amazed and infuriated those who encountered Mr. Szapiro before the war. Ryfka witnessed Szapiro's fall first-hand: in the ghetto, on the Aryan side, in hiding. She saw it after the war. Yet she detected its roots even when Szapiro was at the height of his career and power in 1937. So did Emilia.

> 'Do you see, Jakub, how they arrange your life? How you dance to their music?'... 'Poles...All of them. That you do everything to spite them, that your whole life is proving to them that you are better than them in everything. You have already won everything that was to be won, Jakub, but still you are so tense inside, taut, like you were ten years

---

[70] Twardoch, *Królestwo*, 270.
[71] Ibid., 272.
[72] Ibid., 268.
[73] Ibid., 103, 273.
[74] Ibid., 280.

ago…Shouldn't the goal of victory be that you no longer have to fight, to cease fighting? You only think that you won, Jakub, you think that you triumphed. But in reality, you are unable to win because you can't stop fighting. That's what victory is about, Jakub. That you win and don't have to keep fighting.[75]

The illusory nature of Szapiro's triumph in the final years of the Second Polish Republic slipped away entirely during the Nazi occupation. His kingdom was annihilated, and he was powerless to do anything about it, pushed to the brink of sane existence. Yet it was Anna Ziembińska's humiliating rejection and the link to the pre-war world that she embodied, which ultimately knocked Szapiro out. Warsaw was never truly his because it could never be his; it was a mere fantasy shattered by the Nazi occupier and confirmed by most of Polish society. He might have defeated Andrzej Ziembiński once, but the Makabi club lost the championship. Szapiro might have defeated one Pole in the ring, but, as a Jew, he never really stood a chance at winning Warsaw.

REFERENCES

Andrzejewski, Marcin. "Shitstorm o literaturę – 'Król' Szczepana Twardocha." *Art Galeria Sng*, February 4, 2018. http://sngkultura.pl/2018/02/shitstorm-o-literature-krol-szczepana-twardocha/.

Assmann, Aleida. "Transformations between History and Memory." *Social Research: An International Quarterly* 75, no. 1 (Spring 2008): 49–72. https://muse.jhu.edu/article/527984.

Beltran, Gray, Rebecca Lieberman, and Tammy Tarng. "Globetrotting." *New York Times*, September 8, 2020. https://www.nytimes.com/interactive/2020/01/08/books/new-books-international.html?searchResultPosition=2.

Brykczyński, Paul. *Primed for Violence: Murder, Antisemitism, and Democratic Politics in Interwar Poland*. Madison: University of Wisconsin Press, 2016.

Chwast, Konrad. "'Moja książka, od kiedy ją wydałem, nie należy do mnie.' Rozmawiamy ze Szczepanem Twardochem." *Rozrywka.Blog*, November 7, 2020. https://spidersweb.pl/rozrywka/2020/11/07/szczepan-twardoch-wywiad-krol-serial.

Dehnel, Jacek. "Drogi Szczepanie, kryminały, które piszę sobie z Piotrem (nie sam), traktuję jako literaturę bez większych literackich ambicji, rodzaj żartu, którym bawimy się wspólnie z czytelnikami." Facebook, November 23, 2017. https://www.facebook.com/jacek.dehnel/posts/10155996870819914.

Dehnel, Jacek. "Przez parę ostatnich dni poczytywałem sobie 'Króla' (spoilers will follow)." Facebook, October 18, 2016. https://www.facebook.com/jacek.dehnel/posts/10154662445229914.

---

[75] Twardoch, *Królestwo*, 127–28.

Dunin, Kinga. "Król i królowa." *Krytyka Polityczna*, October 19, 2016. https://krytykapolityczna.pl/kultura/czytaj-dalej/kinga-dunin-czyta/krol-i-krolowa/.

Dunin, Kinga. "Okrucieństwo, sentymentalizm, cynizm…" *Krytyka Polityczna*, January 4, 2019. https://krytykapolityczna.pl/kultura/czytaj-dalej/kinga-dunin-czyta/okrucienstwo-sentymentalizm-cynizm/.

Fijołek, Marcin. "'Król' – zanurzenie w rzece Zła przed uderzeniem wodospadu. Nowa powieść Twardocha to kawał mocnej lektury [RECENZJA]." *wPolityce.pl*, October 8, 2016. https://wpolityce.pl/kultura/311242-krol-czyli-zanurzeni e-w-rzece-zla-przed-atakiem-prawdziwego-wodospadu-nowa-powiesc-tw ardocha-to-kawal-mocnej-lektury.

Forecki, Piotr. *Po Jedwabnem: Anatomia pamięci funkcjonalnej*. Warszawa: Instytut Badań Literackich Pan, 2018.

Forecki, Piotr and Anna Zawadzka. "Reguła złotego środka. Kilka uwag na temat współczesnego dominującego dyskursu o 'stosunkach polsko-żydowskich'." *Zagłada Żydów: Studia i Materiały*, no. 11 (2015): 408–28. https://www.zagladazydow.pl/index.php/zz/article/view/478/498.

Gac, Dominik. "Kapiszonowy Król." Teatralny.pl, July 11, 2018. https://teatral ny.pl/recenzje/kapiszonowy-krol,2429.html.

Gancarczyk, Martyna. "Upadek króla, czyli 'Królestwo' Szczepana Twardocha." Czytaj PL, November 10, 2018. https://czytajpl.pl/2018/11/10/upadek-kr ola-czylikrolestwo-szczepan-twardoch/.

Hawthorne, Fran. "The King of Warsaw: A Novel." *New York Journal of Books*. https://www.nyjournalofbooks.com/book-review/king-warsaw-novel.

Hertz, Aleksander. *Żydzi w kulturze polskiej*. Warszawa: Biblioteka "Więzi," 2014.

Jadaś, Łukasz. "Cud na Facebooku. Wybuchła pierwsza gównoburza, którą czyta się bez zażenowania." *Asz Dziennik*, November 24, 2017. https://asz dziennik.pl/121729,cud-na-polskim-facebooku-wybuchla-pierwsza-gowno burza-ktora-czyta-sie-bez-zazenowania.

Jakubowiak, Maciej. "Przyjdzie bokser i nas zbawi." *Dwutygodnik*, September 2016. https://www.dwutygodnik.com/artykul/6780-przyjdzie-bokser-i-nas-zbawi.html.

Janicka, Elżbieta. "Pamięć i tożsamość w przestrzeni dawnego getta warszawskiego/Memory and Identity in the Former Warsaw Ghetto Area." *Herito: dziedzictwo, kultura, współczesność/heritage, culture & the present*, no. 13 (April 2013): 66–81.

Koryś, Izabela, Dominika Michalak, Zofia Zasacka, and Roman Chymkowski, eds. *Stan czytelnictwa w Polsce w 2017 roku*. Warszawa: Biblioteka Narodowa, 2018. https://www.bn.org.pl/raporty-bn/stan-czytelnictwa-w-polsce/stan-czytelnictwa-w-polsce-w-2017-r.

Kowalczyk, Janusz R., and Natalia Sajewicz. "Szczepan Twardoch." Culture.pl. Last modified June 2021. https://culture.pl/pl/tworca/szczepan-twardoch.

Kozioł, Paweł. "Jacek Dehnel." Culture.pl. Last modified October 2020. https://culture.pl/pl/tworca/jacek-dehnel.

Krasny, Jakub, "Niech żyje 'Król' – adaptacja powieści Twardocha w Teatrze Polskim." Czytaj PL, June 16, 2018. https://czytajpl.pl/2018/06/16/niech-zyje-krol-adaptacja-powiesci-twardocha-w-teatrze-polskim/.

Krzywiec, Grzegorz. "O faszyzmie w wersji polskiej i jego nieoczywistych dziejach raz jeszcze (na marginesie książki Szymona Rudnickiego *Falanga: Ruch Narodowo-Radykalny)*." *Zagłada Żydów. Studia i Materiały*, no. 15 (2019): 633–52. https://www.zagladazydow.pl/index.php/zz/article/view/37/30.

Lipski, Jan Józef. *Idea Katolickiego Państwa Narodu Polskiego: Zarys ideologii ONR "Falanga."* Warszawa: Wydawnictwo Krytyki Politycznej, 2015.

Majewski, Paweł. "Pokrętna afektywność historii: O 'Królestwie' Szczepana Twardocha." *Kultura Liberalna*, November 13, 2018. https://kulturaliberaln a.pl/2018/11/13/pawel- majewski-recenzja-krolestwo-szczepan-twardoch/.

Mętrak, Natalia. "Jan P. Matuszyński." Culture.pl. Last modified September 2021. https://culture.pl/pl/tworca/jan-p-matuszynski.

Młynarski, Piotr. "Szczepan Twardoch Król." Instytut Książki: Literatura, 2017. https://instytutksiazki.pl/literatura,8,recenzje,25,klubowiczow,1,krol,63.html.

Padoł, Emilia. "Szczepan Twardoch: dobrze się robi literaturę o tym, o czym ludzie nie chcą słuchać [WYWIAD]." *Onet Kultura*, November 6, 2018. https://kultura.onet.pl/wywiady-i-artykuly/szczepan-twardoch-dobrze-si e-robi-literature-o-tym-o-czym-ludzie-nie-chca-sluchac/h53k58m.

Padoł, Emilia. "Szczepan Twardoch: nie mamy pojęcia czym jesteśmy." *Onet Kultura*, October 12, 2016. https://kultura.onet.pl/wywiady-i-artykuly/szcz epan-twardoch-nie-mamy-pojecia-czym-jestesmy/cyk1s4l.

"Plakaty teatralne, które wywołały kontrowersje." eWejściówki.pl, August 19, 2021. https://ewejsciowki.pl/poradnik/plakaty-teatralne-ktore-wywolaly-ko ntrowersje/#Wroclawski_Teatr_Lalek_Z_dociekow_nad_zyciem_plciowem.

Polski Słownik Judaistyczny. Accessed September 1, 2021. https://delet.jhi.pl/pl/psj?articleId=16617.

"Polskie Nagrody Filmowe Orły 2021 rozdane!" Polskie Nagrody Filmowe. Accessed November 15, 2021. http://pnf.pl/polskie-nagrody-filmowe-orly-2021-rozdane/.

Portnoy, Eddy. "The Yiddish-Speaking Hitmen's Union." *Jewish Review of Books*, Winter 2021. https://jewishreviewofbooks.com/articles/9547/the-yiddish-spe aking-hitmens-union/.

Rudnicki, Szymon. *Falanga: Ruch Narodowo-Radykalny*. Warszawa: Oficyna Wydawnicza ASPRA-JR, 2018.

Senior, Antonina. "The Best New Historical Fiction for April 2020 – Family Dramas, From Galilee to Restoration England." *The Times*, April 7, 2020. https://www.thetimes.co.uk/article/the-best-new-historical-fiction-for-apri l-2020-family-dramas-from-galilee-to-restoration-england-9b5g58dtq.

Simon, Clea. "'The King of Warsaw' is a Holocaust Novel with a Twist." *The Boston Globe*, April 16, 2020. https://www.bostonglobe.com/2020/04/16/ar ts/king-warsaw-is-holocaust-novel-with-twist/.

Sobolewska, Justyna. "Dawna Warszawa według Twardocha." *Polityka*, October 4, 2016. https://www.polityka.pl/tygodnikpolityka/kultura/167762 4,1,dawna-warszawa-wedlug-twardocha.read.

Sobolewska, Justyna. "Recenzja książki: Szczepan Twardoch 'Królestwo.' Bez znieczulenia." *Polityka*, October 28, 2018. https://www.polityka.pl/tygodni

kpolityka/kultura/ksiazki/1769468,1,recenzja-ksiazki-szczepan-twardoch-k
rolestwo.read.

"Szczepan Twardoch." Accessed November 15, 2021. http://szczepantwardoc
h.pl/en/home/.

"The King of Warsaw." *Kirkus Reviews*, January 27, 2020. https://www.kirkusr
eviews.com/book-reviews/szczepan-twardoch/the-king-of-warsaw/.

Twardoch, Szczepan. *Der Boxer.* Translated by Olaf Kühl. Berlin: Rowohlt, 2019.
https://www.amazon.com/Boxer-Szczepan-Twardoch/dp/3499291479.

Twardoch, Szczepan. *Król.* Kraków: Wydawnictwo Literackie, 2016.

Twardoch, Szczepan. *Królestwo.* Kraków: Wydawnictwo Literackie, 2018.

Twardoch, Szczepan. "Kto skrytykuje krytyków?" *Onet Kultura*, November 23,
2017. https://kultura.onet.pl/ksiazki/kto-skrytykuje-krytykow/frl12pp?utm_
source=kultura.onet.pl_viasg_kultura&utm_medium=referal&utm_author=
null&utm_campaign=leo_automatic&srcc=ucs&utm_v=2.

Twardoch, Szczepan. *The King of Warsaw.* Translated by Sean Gasper Bye.
Seattle: Amazon Crossing, 2020. https://www.amazon.pl/King-Warsaw-
Novel-Szczepan-Twardoch/dp/1542044448.

Walicki, Jacek. "Położenie Żydów polskich podczas kampanii 1920 r." *Acta
Universitatis Lodziensis. Folia Historica*, no. 52 (1995): 113–25.

Chapter 5

Why Didn't You Tell? Identifying Silencing as a Memory Event of the Previous Generation About the Cold War Period (Péter György, György Száraz Miklós, Márta Mészáros)

Melinda Harlov-Csortán

Apor Vilmos Catholic College in Vác, Hungary

Abstract: Silencing as a social practice common among others in the Central and Eastern European context of and about the previous political period (and the events regarding World War II) is investigated in this chapter by focusing on two novels (Péter György's *Instead of my father* [*Apám helyett*] and György Száraz Miklós' *My father in Pieces* [*Apám darabokban*]) and one movie (Márta Mészáros' *Aurora Borealis*) from and about Hungary. The plots are taken place in approximately the same period (early 2000s) and all have the main theme: the realization of the parent's silencing act by the child. The analysis looks at the represented characters and the depicted memory techniques through which the personal memories and the collective memory of the previous political area clash and form a new understanding retrospectively. The chapter also identifies the analyzed art pieces as possible techniques of turning personal memories into community ones by the "in-between" generation in a post-socialist context.

Keywords: silencing, Hungary, post-socialist context, representation of parent-child relation, personal memory, community memory, novels and film

***

INTRODUCTION

The events of the twentieth century increased the importance of memory and the identification of guilt and innocence. Specialists name this intensive increase of projects 'memory boom.'[1] The notion of the past and the elements that refer to it motivate the process of remembering. As Kurt Forster (1935), the Swiss professor of history and theory of art and architecture, described, there is no objective past but only a continual refraction of the absent in the memory of the present.[2] Sociological research projects show that memories of communism[3] often diverge from the attempts to come to terms with communist crimes on the one hand and idealizations of state socialism on the other.[4] However, it is also possible to reject the process of remembering by not communicating or transforming the past. Among many reasons, for example, Ralf Dahrendorf, German sociologist and philosopher (1929—2009), pointed out that people's "habits of the heart" (such as the way of understanding and behaving) adapt to system transformation slower than the actual historical events, and such persistence to the former way of life and not-remembering is one key barrier for change.[5] Three contemporary Hungarian examples of such silencing are analyzed in this chapter through the poetics adopted by the authors, represented characters and based on the interviews the authors gave.

Hungary was allied with Nazi Germany in the Second World War and was part of the Eastern bloc for numerous decades. Central and Eastern European countries had different memories of the communist past due to the different historical events within the individual countries and their relations with the

---

[1] Jay Winter, "The Generation of Memory: Reflections on the 'Memory Boom' in Contemporary Historical Studies," *Bulletin of the German Historical Institute* 27 (2000): 69–92.

[2] Kurt Forster, "Introduction," in *The Renewal of Pagan Antiquity*, Aby Warburg (Los Angeles: Getty Research Institute, 1999) 52.

[3] As Western historiography often uses the terms 'socialist' and 'communist' as synonyms for the same ideological and political system that was widespread in the discussed territories of Europe just after Second World War. This text uses the terms as synonyms as well.

[4] Ulf Brunnbauer and Stefan Troebst, eds., *Zwischen Amnesie und Nostalgie: die Erinnerung an den Kommunismus in Südosteuropa* (Köln, Weimar, Wien: Bohlau, 2007); Stefan Troebst, ed., *Postdiktatorische Geschichtskulturen im Süden und Osten Europas: Bestandsaufnahme und Forschungsperspektiven* (Göttingen: Wallstein-Verlag, 2010).

[5] Ralf Dahrendorf, *Reflections on the Revolution in Europe* (London: Chatto and Windus, 1990).

Soviet Union.[6] For instance, in Hungary, between the 1960s and 1980s, a less autocratic and oppressive system operated. Accordingly, it was named the 'happiest barrack,' but it still experienced a lack of democracy and distance from the rest of the World. For example, the 1956 revolution and freedom fight, when Hungarians stood up against the one-party system, and what the Soviet military presence brutally oppressed, was misinterpreted as counter-revolution up until 1989. The truth could not be communicated, and personal memories were also silenced. As Katherine Verdery, the American anthropologist (1948), pointed out, the post-socialist transformation involved "a reordering of people's entire meaningful worlds,"[7] and this open-ended process entailed rewriting history, forming new political arenas, and rearranging physical places. These processes were even reinforced during the preparation for and at the realization of EU accession, which happened in 2004 in the case of Hungary.

Regarding Hungarian central commemorations, textbooks, and the central narrative about the previous political system and the Second World War, the main focus is still on uprisings and resistance, rather than everyday life or the local participation in the oppressive systems of the twentieth century. Moreover, the revolutionary events of 1956 and 1989, when the democratic changes happened, were and are symbolically linked. They are seen as decisive moments in Hungarian history when people had to defend the sovereignty and territorial integrity of their country.[8] On the other hand, those studies which help to understand cultures and the past via, for instance, biographical or monographic works serve another aim.[9] Different actors might want to hush up memories about certain periods, or they might strive to restore an era prior to the represented one.[10] Artistic representation of remembering the recent past (mainly literature, theater, and films) seem to be the only medium that reaches a wide range of audiences and addresses alternative relations, and an understanding of the recent past, such as silencing, even among family circles.[11] These unique examples do not investigate the actual former events, but rather focus on those aspects that

---

[6] Maria Todorova, Augusta Dimou, and Stefan Troebst, eds., *Remembering Communism: Private and Public Recollections of Lived Experience in Southeast Europe* (Budapest: Central European University Press, 2014), 150.

[7] Katherine Verdery, *The Political Lives of Dead Bodies: Reburial and Postsocialist Change* (New York: Columbia University Press, 1999), 35.

[8] László Eörsi, "A Corvin közi emléktáblák," *História* 31, no. 9 (2009): 60–62.

[9] Alan S. Milward, "Bad Memories," *Times Literary Supplement*, April 14, 2000.

[10] Katalin Sinkó, "Oh, Amnézia úrnő (ne) jöjj el! (Gondolatok a szobordöntögetésről)," *Magyar Narancs*, May 3, 1990, 10.

[11] For example, Majgull Axelsson, *My name is not Miriam* (Stockholm: Brombergs, 2014).

individuals experienced, and the unchanging viewpoints and habits at the time of transition.[12]

The chapter focuses on three Hungarian artistic representations (two books and one film) of not telling certain segments of personal past during the previous political system to the next generation, namely to the son and daughter. The narrators or side figures of the presented pieces are the children who realize their parents' silencing act decades after the political change at the time of or after the parents' death. The investigation first introduces the three storylines and the authors of the analyzed literary pieces, then describes the main analytical perspectives: remembering and silencing, based on which the comparative critical analysis takes place. The investigation examines the personal and community-level remembering processes in the chosen analyzed examples and discusses the silencing act from the different characters' perspectives. It identifies those techniques with which both remembering and silencing are presented. The analysis also looks at the depicted memory techniques, through which personal memories and collective memory of the previous political area (the socialist time of Hungary) clash with the unleashed information, and start to form a new understanding retrospectively. These examples draw attention to the personal level of the system transition in post-socialist society regarding the interpretation of lived memory and the formation of identity. In conclusion, the analyzed art pieces are identified as possible techniques for transforming personal memory elements into collective memory.

ESSAYS, LETTERS AND A MOTION PICTURE ON SILENCING

The two analyzed publications (Péter György's *Instead of My Father [Apám helyett]* (2011) and György Száraz Miklós' *My Father in Pieces [Apám darabokban]* (2016)) elaborate silencing realized between sons and fathers, while one of the latest movies by Márta Mészáros (titled *Aurora Borealis – Northern light [Aurora Borealis – Északi fény]* (2017)) represents the issue of silencing in a daughter – mother relationship. Péter György (born in 1954) is an aesthetician and university professor of the twentieth century, as well as contemporary art and media. He is the author of numerous interdisciplinary scholarly publications concerning various topics (such as critical analysis of museum narration techniques and memory politics with public art examples). The analyzed book of essays describes the socialist period of the country, but also has a very personal aspect. The author provides a detailed analysis of the ideological, institutional and artistic life of the previous political period via

---

[12] Harry Eckstein, "A Culturalist Theory of Political Change," *American Political Science Review*, no. 3 (1988): 789–804.

compact and self-standing chapters. However, the explicit aim of the entire investigation is to find justification for the standpoints and acts of his belated father and to solve their separation and constant disputes retrospectively. His father had Jewish background and survived a forced labor camp at the end of the Second World War in Bor, today's Serbia. He had silenced his Jewishness during the previous political period and did not acknowledge it even after the political change that – among others – resulted in several quarrels and finally, decades-long separation from his son, the author.

György Száraz Miklós is four years younger than Péter György and is an author of novels and short stories, editor and photographer. His works focus on the correlation of people and places through time via surrealistic representation. The analyzed love story speaks about the first two years of his parents' relationship (between 1956 and 1958), but it is also a family story of many generations (going back to the nineteenth century) presented through letters and other sources. Its timeline is not chronological, and the narrator (the son) only appears in some comments and a handful of actual scenes. Accordingly, the structure can be connected to Péter György's text which has various intertextual allusions to numerous other publications and artistic representations, and montage-like photos, which suit the author's often-adapted surrealistic approach. The author's father, György Száraz, who can be directly connected to the main character of the analyzed text, was an autodidact playwright and aesthetician. He had been born but deported from present day Slovakia during the population change after the Second World War. He was imprisoned in the early 1950s for political reasons that challenged him and his family's life. These life events were for long decades silenced and could be identified only after his death due to thorough scientific research of the son, the narrator.

Márta Mészáros, the internationally well-known director and screenwriter,[13] is a member of an earlier generation (born in 1931) who lived through most of the previous political period as an adult. In her numerous films, she mainly discusses the topics of identity search and the fate of women. She also has personal experience with the twentieth century totalitarian systems by losing his father, an acknowledged sculptor, due to the terror of the Stalin era. The plot of *Aurora Borealis* is not personally connected to the director but focuses on an otherwise unrepresented and very personal aspect of the 1956 revolution and freedom fight: the atrocities against women by (the occupying Soviet) soldiers and the numerous children born out of these attacks. Just like

---

[13] Her productions were awarded among others at Berlinale, the Chicago International Film Festival and at the Cannes Film Festival. In 2021, she received the Lifetime Achievement Award of the European Film Academy.

György Száraz Miklós' work, the film does not tell the life story of the leading female character chronologically, but segments of the past appear through memories and hallucinations. The plot of the film and György Száraz Miklós' text have a focal point at and after the 1956 historical events. At this time, the main heroin of the film, a young girl called Mária Pogány, loses her love on the way to escape from the country, gets raped by Soviet soldiers, and has to establish a life alone, pregnant in a new country, Austria. Throughout the film, we get to know Mária's eventful youth, how she finds her future husband, gives up her child to protect her friend's daughter, and raises her as her own. The saved daughter, Olga, searches her mother's and her own past with the same emotional intensity as the narrator of Péter György's book.

In all three analyzed stories, both the historical contexts and the personal storylines are expressed. The plots occur approximately at the same time (the early 2000s) and discuss the search for connection with a member of the previous generation challenged by history. The realization of the parent's silencing act by the child is a common and main theme that cannot be dissolved completely due to the loss of the parent, the authentic source. Interestingly, while Péter György's and Márta Mészáros' parent figures died after the political change, György Száraz, the father of the author, György Száraz Miklós, had already died in 1984. In this case, the death of the mother means the realized loss of the authentic source, which is also marked in the dedication of the novel: "This book is my mother's. Who else would it be?" György Száraz Miklós' mother died in 2004, twelve years before the novel was published, and she would have been able to answer any question by orally completing the notes from her diary, which serves as one of the main sources of the book. The three chosen artistic representations have many bases of comparisons (such as the main topic silencing in intergenerational context or the mobilization of diverse sources to retrospectively find out the past) but still use significantly different techniques (due to the diverse genres as well) to represent their main themes. Such plurality also resembles the depicted young post-socialist society, and the parallelly existing standpoints regarding how to handle the recent past. The next section discusses the role of remembering and silencing in the depicted society and the analyzed examples.

REMEMBERING AND SILENCING IN POST-SOCIALIST HUNGARY

Even though memory, in contrast to imagination, is supposed to communicate the truth of the past, there are personal, communal, circumstantial, and other factors that transform or modify memory.[14] As personal memories are not just

---

[14] András Keszei, *Emlékek formájában* (Budapest: L'Harmattan Kiadó, 2015), 10–18.

images or processes of the past, their interpretations can be influenced by sociocultural and historical contexts too.[15] Hence, neither a person's own nor collective memory should be understood as a clear, one-to-one copy of the past.[16] Accordingly, instead of narrative discourse interpretation, an integrated analysis of reconstructing memories is needed with interdisciplinary and comparative research to understand the complex relationship of all the influencing factors possibly modifying personal and collective memories.[17] This is why all the analyzed authors used multiple sources and detailed research in advance to find answers for the act of silencing. Péter György turned to aesthetic and scientific analysis, György Száraz Miklós – based on an interview and the footnotes in his book – conducted research in archives about his father's past.[18] Márta Mészáros also collected information about the children of Soviet soldiers' attacks, many of which she could collect in Austria, where numerous Hungarians ran away during and right after the historic events.[19]

Remembering activates double time periods; it evokes the past,[20] emotionally emphasizing and ideologizing certain aspects and interpretations.[21] Remembering recreates the past also based on the current circumstances.[22] Accordingly, the two-time segments: present and past, are connected, and their separation is ensured. All three case studies can be understood as remembering. While Péter György evoked the past by analyzing certain aspects, institutions, and ideologies of the previous political period, he realized them via contemporary knowledge and mainly from a contemporary point of view. Similarly, the period of the Second World War, when the father's Jewish origin led to serious consequences (forced labor camp), was first

---

[15] Barbara Skarga, "Tożsamość ja i pamięć," *Znak* 5 (1995): 4–18.

[16] Daniel L. Schacter, Scott A. Guerin, and Peggy L. St. Jacques, "Memory Distortion: An Adaptive Perspective," *Trends in Cognitive Sciences* 15, no. 10 (2011): 467–74.

[17] Daniela Szymańska, Elżbieta Grzelak-Kostulska, and Beata Hołowiecka, "Polish Towns and the Changes in Their Areas and Population Densities," *Bulletin of Geography Socio-economic Series* 11, no. 11 (2009): 15–30.

[18] Orsolya Péntek, "Pokolsár: Száraz Miklós György a Felvidékről, Erdélyről, Andalúziáról és Rómáról," *Magyar Napló* 25, no. 11 (2013): 33–44.

[19] Ferenc Dobi, "Csapás a múltból," *Filmtett*, October 11, 2017.

[20] Paul Connerton, *How Societies Remember* (Cambridge: Cambridge University Press, 1989).

[21] Katalin Sinkó, "A politika rítusai: Emlékműállítás, szobordöntés," in *A művészet katonái: Sztálinizmus és kultúra*, eds. Péter György and Hedvig Turai (Budapest: Corvina Kiadó Vállalat, 1992), 67–79.

[22] János Pótó, *Emlékművek, politika, közgondolkodás* (Budapest: MTA Történelemtudományi Intézete, 1989), 79.

silenced (in the previous political period) and re-addressed after the political change of 1989. Hence, the past event was both separated and connected to the contemporary time segment. Interestingly, only this father figure supported the previous political system, despite the fact that the fates of the other two parent figures were also changed for the better during the same period. György Száraz Miklós and Márta Mészáros stated next to each other the presence of their storylines and the depicted past events through diary segments or remembering scenes. In the case of the *My father in pieces*, different chapters and marked dates of the letters express the different time segments. In the film, different actors play the same character at different ages, and the memory scenes of the far past (the youth of the mother figure before escaping from Hungary) have a special warm-brown color tone, like the old photographs. Accordingly, these two examples separate more explicitly the past and present of the storylines, but by putting scenes from the two-time segments interchangeably after each other, their interconnectedness is expressed not just content-wise.

The social practice of remembering many times is directed by the ruling political power.[23] It can be a pre-requisite in the formation and management of collective identity by supporting the envisaged message.[24] The lack of remembering can also serve the same aim, as in the case of the 1956 revolution and freedom fights in Hungary that was not remembered during the previous political period, and accordingly, the critique of the system was not a topic on any official level. Communist regimes, as non-democratic systems, are almost unquestionably characterized by silencing on many levels. The ruling power's influence appears in different ways in the three pieces. Péter György's book speaks about its "indirect" influence; the father figure could achieve professional success by following the required behavior and not speaking out. György Száraz Miklós' work describes the limitation of free speech, that the father figure could express criticism only in a coded way, via his literary pieces. Márta Mészáros' main figure has no connection to the ruling power, but her first love was a member of the former aristocracy, who was completely intimidated by the ruling power, and could not find any other solution than leaving the country.

The top-down silencing effort was present in daily-life matters as well. People were not supposed to speak out freely or tell the truth to their neighbors. No one could talk about the fact that everyone was stealing this or that from the workplace or doing things "illegally." Hence, silencing could become an "anti-remembering" process both in the case of personal and

---

[23] Bennedict Anderson, *Imagined Communities: Reflections on the Origin and the Spread of Nationalism* (London: Verso, 1983).
[24] Péter György, "Az emlékezet szétesése – az olvashatatlan város," *2000* 10 (2006): 5–10.

collective memory. This top-down and internalized silencing could be changed during the political transformation. In the case of Hungary (similar to the trends in other former socialist countries), after the political change, there were vivid public discussions and even an attempt for legal enforcement to discuss the silenced atrocities of the previous political system, and to punish the then participating actors.[25] However, an intention to speak about the memories of the previous political period was not universal, especially on a personal level. Even the "in-between" generation, who were born and raised in the previous area, becoming young adults after the political change in the 1990s, were shocked by the level and realization of this silencing. This was one of the motivations of the authors regarding the represented publications as well. Polish sociologist Piotr Sztompka (1944) gave an explanation for this silencing: "[A]s long as the majority of the population consists of the people whose young, formative years, and therefore crucial socializing experiences, fall under the rule of the communist regime - one can expect the continuing vitality of the bloc culture."[26]

Despite the fact that sharing memory is possible and even promoted after the political change, the still existing silencing practice has opened up numerous contestations and searches for explanations on personal and institutional levels. The analyzed pieces serve as examples of personal-level contestations, while the examples of opening up archives and curating exhibitions about the previous political period are signs for institutional level attempts.[27] German sociologist, born in 1941, Wolf Lepenies warned about any expectations by saying: "[Y]ou can neither buy nor sell [...] a sense for individual justice in a society, which has never [...] experienced legal procedures comparable to those of the civil societies in the West."[28] The unpredictable result or even belatedness of the intention to overcome silencing can be identified in the three works, too, as all three storylines are explained retrospectively, when even remembering could hardly be realized

---

[25] The legal proposal was evaluated as unconstitutional by the Hungarian Constitutional Court on March 5, 1992 (https://net.jogtar.hu/getpdf?docid=992H0011.AB&targetdate= &printTitle=11/1992.+%28III.+5.%29+AB+hat%C3%A1rozat&getdoc=1), but the same intention could be identified even in the Hungarian political life in 2010s. Gábor Halmai, *Memory Politics in Hungary: Political Justice without Rule of Law* (Den Haag: Asser Institute, 2018).

[26] Piotr Sztompka, "Looking Back: The Year 1989 as a Cultural and Civilizational Break," *Communist and Post-Communist Studies* 29, no. 2 (1996): 126.

[27] Ljiljana Radonić, "Post-communist invocation of Europe: memorial museums' narratives and the Europeanization of memory," *National Identities*, 19, no. 2 (2017): 269–88.

[28] Wolf Lepenies, *Folgen einer unerhörten Begebenheit: Die Deutschen nach der Vereinigung* (Berlin: Siedler, 1992), 3.

due to the loss or impaired health state of the "witnesses." The following subchapters comparatively analyze the three chosen pieces regarding the depicted remembering and silencing practices and their artistic representations.

EXPRESSING COMMUNICATIVE- AND CULTURAL REMEMBERING

Jan Assmann, the German thinker on social and cultural memory (1938), differentiated communicative and cultural remembering based on the time frame the covered remembering process. Communicative remembering points to the recent past and includes the shared and commonly experienced elements. Hence, the memory of such an experienced recent past is necessarily partial, biased, subjective, and, therefore, highly variegated. While cultural remembering is connected more to a community, and past becomes symbolic.[29] Both kinds of remembering appear in the case studies. All three cases describe the historical (enclosed) period, the socialist time of Hungary, as well as scenes when the parent and the child figures at present are sharing common experiences. Examples of the latter case are when Péter György explains a heated fight with his dead, a childhood memory in the family circle in the case of György Száraz Miklós' book, and the discussions of common memories (for instance, the main heroin, Mária's husband, the not-biological father of the daughter, Olga) in Márta Mészáros' film.

These shared experiences, highly personal and intimate, are expressed by different techniques in the three analyzed cases. Péter György uses a strikingly subjective tone in these segments in contrast to the academic investigations and analysis of the historical context. György Száraz Miklós was born in the year (1958) when the storyline of the novel ends. Accordingly, he "appears" only in some extra scenes or comments used to complete the depicted narratives of the parents' letters, such as cherished childhood memories. The author exclusively and explicitly chooses these elements. Márta Mészáros often used extreme close-ups, recording the conversations of the mother and daughter, while adapting long shots when the two figures complain silently, adjusting the (recently acknowledged) past.

In the case of a historic rupture, the distance of the cultural and communicative remembering is more psychological than time-related. If it was not allowed or preferred to share the commonly experienced elements, the recent past can also become symbolic. As Péter György did not have information about his father's personal memory for a long time, he could only share cultural remembering processes that he contested with scholarly

---

[29] Jan Assmann, *Az emlékezés kultúrája*, trans. Hidas Zoltán (Budapest: Osiris Kiadó, 1999), 51–55.

research. In an interview, György Száraz Miklós explained that he talked about politics and the 1956 events with his father but never in detail, and he was also urged never to talk about it with anyone else.[30] The topic of Márta Mészáros' film was not even part of the cultural remembering, as the first public art dedicated to the victims of military sexual violence is about to be inaugurated only in the near future.[31] Similarly, the depicted individual life stories do not exclude certain similarities arising from both biographical and historical patterns, such as the effect of 1956 events on personal lives in the case of György Száraz Miklós' father and the mother figure in Márta Mészáros' film.

The realization of remembering is always specific in time and place and incorporates the remembering communities' characters and contexts. The time segments and locations of the valued past for Márta Mészáros' and György Száraz Miklós' main characters are at a specific and separated (distanced) time and (with borders) place: the youth of the characters in Hungary and Slovakia. While for the father figure in Péter György's text, the chronologically and physically distanced but defining past resembles negative memories, the forced labor camp at the end of the Second World War in Bor, today's Serbia. The character was reminded of this distanced past after the political change when he was identified as a survivor by the newly formed commemorating organizations. The connection could no longer be denied, "[a]nd this was what he least wanted." For example, the defining context in which remembering can take place is the health state of the mother figure in Mészáros Márta's *Aurora Borealis* movie. Her oppressed memories can be verbalized only in her unconscious talk during sickness in the hospital.[32]

David Lowenthal, the American historian and geographer (1923—2018), saw the past as being integral to the individual and communal representations of identity and understood its connotations that provide human existence with meaning, purpose and value.[33] This direct connection of memory and identity was explained by the French historian (1931) Pierre Nora as "almost synonymous, [whose] convergence characterizes a new organization of the historical and social dynamics."[34] When the memory of the recent past is

---

[30] Gabriella Szíjjártó, "Apám, a világítótorony - Száraz Miklós Györggyel beszélgettünk," *Szabadföld*, May 3, 2016.

[31] Andrea Pető, "The New Monument to Victims of Military Sexual Violence in Budapest," *Hungarian Studies Review* 48, no. 2 (2021): 209–15.

[32] Charles B. Stone et al., "Toward a Science of Silence: The Consequences of Leaving a Memory Unsaid," *Perspectives on Psychological Science* 7, no. 1 (2012): 39–53.

[33] David Lowenthal, *The Past is a Foreign Country* (Cambridge: Cambridge University Press, 1985).

[34] Pierre Nora, "Reasons for the Current Upsurge in Memory," *Transit* 22 (2002): 1.

unknown or is questioned, "the senses of identity [become] highly fluid and unstable" as Craig Young and Duncan Light, who, as geographers, research the connections of political representation, tourism and space, formulated regarding the post-socialist world.[35] This is also why the children of the three analyzed examples are so eager to understand their parents, as this information of the past also defines their identities that were shaken by the realization of the silenced past (Whose sons or daughters are they?). The sons of the books and the daughter figure in the film intend to explore the circumstances and facts so they can put themselves into the same situations that resulted in their parents' choice to silence the past. The connection between identity and memory is even more emphasized in Márta Mészáros' film. According to the plot of the film, the previously untold past incorporates the fact that the daughter, Olga, is not the biological child of the mother figure, and hence, finding out the past means realizing her identity as well. The final parallel scene of the film when the mother figure, Mária, peacefully dies after seeing a photo of her abandoned daughter. Olga, the daughter, gazes at the aurora borealis and artistically alludes to the certain acknowledgement of the past and acceptance of identity for both characters. But as the film ends at these scenes, the viewer is not assured. The next sub-chapter focuses on the silencing act and its realization by the different actors.

SILENCING TECHNIQUES OF THE CHARACTERS

As Liem Ramsay, a researcher of community psychology interested in contemporary legacies of significant historical events, phrased, "[s]ilence about historical trauma is common among survivors, often serving as a medium, through which the intergenerational effects of catastrophic experiences are transmitted."[36] Silencing, as a social practice, common in the Central and Eastern European context of, and about the previous political period, is targeted by the three analyzed literary pieces working against such intergenerational effects.

Silencing is realized by the main characters either by completely denying the past (in the case of the father figure in the *Instead of My Father* and almost until the end of the mother figure's life in *Aurora Borealis*) or by consciously analyzing and hiding the past via theater plays and with the firm knowledge of what aspects can or cannot be discussed (like the father figure in the *My*

---

[35] Craig Young and Duncan Light, "Place, national identity and post-socialist transformations: an introduction," *Political Geography* 20 (2001): 947.

[36] Ramsay Liem, "Silencing Historical Trauma: The Politics and Psychology of Memory and Voice Peace and Conflict," *Journal of Peace Psychology* 3, no. 2 (2017): 153–74.

Father is Pieces).[37] The mother figure of the film, Mária, is forced to tell the truth but warns her daughter: "It will be very painful for me. And for you too." The father figure of György Száraz Miklós' novel does not speak explicitly about the past and his critique of the system, but the son's character feels that. The basis of the heated arguments between the son and the father in Péter György's book is the internalized lie of the father figure. The father figure silenced his Jewish origin during the previous political system, so he could concentrate only on the present and his profession: natural sciences.[38] A very descriptive segment, showing a small hesitance in that almost complete denial state, is about the fate of the father's diary from the forced labor camp in Bor that was first given and then taken from the son. As the author states: "[h]iding the text has much more meaning than its actual content what he aimed to silence."[39]

Interestingly, the characters, who act against the continuation of silencing, are never the main characters. In the case of the books, even the titles appoint the parent figure to be the main character: *Instead of My Father* or *My Father in Pieces*. Even though Péter György wrote his text in the first person singular with long analytical segments, he created distance, and his own figure becomes less emphasized. György Száraz Miklós "represented himself" only as a child in the storyline and through some comments. In *Aurora Borealis*, the daughter's supporting role is also ensured with the directing technique: she gets informed about details belatedly compared to the viewers. One possible justification for not putting the active character (who searches the past) in the main role is to express that neither of the analyzed examples is a unique storyline, but most families might have certain secrets. Moreover, it is not the leading figure, the "hero/heroin," who aims to stop the transmission of silencing, but an almost unrealizable person in a supporting role.[40]

Interestingly, in all three analyzed pieces, the other parents are depicted as positive, supporting figures, even though in *My Father In Pieces*, the other parent's active role is in the storyline. Moreover, György Száraz Miklós' novel starts the moment when the two parents-to-be get to know each other and fall in love. Péter György's mother character is depicted in the present during the

---

[37] Eszter Laik, "Atya, fiú," *Irodalmi Jelen*, August 31, 2016.

[38] Matthias Schwartz, Nina Weller, and Heike Winkel, "After Memory: Introduction," in *After Memory World War II in Contemporary Eastern European Literatures*, eds. ibidem. (Berlin: De Gruyter, 2021), 1–21.

[39] Péter György, "Az apám Piros emlékezete," *Élet és Irodalom*, October 31, 2008.

[40] Kerreen Ely-Harper, "Record keeping: family memories on film," in *Female Agency and Documentary Strategies: Subjectivities, Identity and Activism*, eds. Boel Ulfsdotter and Anna Backman Rogers (Edinburgh: Edinburgh University Press, 2018), 84–99.

dispute between the son and the father characters. Meanwhile, Márta's husband and Olga's non-biological father appear only in their represented memories. These other parent figures also cooperate in the silencing. None of these figures speaks about the silenced part of the past, even though the two mother figures wrote diaries about those periods, and the husband in the film also knew the entire silenced youth of Márta.

The comparative analysis of the three examples also points out the possible variety and uncertain results of the intention to get to know the past and stop the silencing technique of the previous generations. Interestingly, even though the past cannot be fully reconstructed, all characters acknowledge the decision of the previous generation. The narrator of Péter György's book understands but does not accept the father figure's choice of silencing. He sees it as a part of the memory about the father that is even on the book cover. It depicts a young man sailing away from the center with huge physical intensity, as the father figure made all the efforts throughout his life to escape the need to face his origin and the lived through past. In an interview, Péter György said that with his book, he intends to speak out instead of his father and his generation, as he realized in those circumstances and with such traumatic experience, the named generation was unable to speak for himself. Accordingly, the depicted process is not 'a pact of silence'[41] for the protection of the next generation, but a pure incapability to do anything otherwise.

György Száraz Miklós' storyline ends without any result. The collected data and primary sources of the letters and diaries cannot wholly complete and identify the past. The connected diaries and other memories remained unfinished, being in pieces which resemble the title *Father in Pieces*. Still, the entire book is five hundred pages, which might allude to the fact that someone's past in 'longue durée' is more important than the silenced segments (e.g., the father figures' imprisoned years). In the case of the movie, no summarizing conclusion is presented either. There is no information on whether the daughter figure accepts or acknowledges the revealed personal past of her mother and herself. The decision is left open for the viewers; hence, the director expresses that the contemporary society has the task and possibility to overcome and dissolve the silencing of the recent past.

While aurora borealis is a meteorological phenomenon resulting from a disrupter, it is also called the messenger of the sun, hence a possible sign of hope. These adapted symbols: the figure sailing away from facing reality; the

---

[41] Aleida Assmann and Ute Frevert, *Geschichtsvergessenheit, Geschichtsversessenheit. Vom Umgang mit deutschen Vergangenheiten nach 1945* (Stuttgart: Deutsche Verlags-Anstalt, 1999), 76–78.

puzzle-like father figure, who can never be fully completed; or the natural phenomenon as a sign of hope, are picturesque essences of the diverse realizations and consequences of silencing. Moreover, these symbols might contribute to the transformation of these personal stories to become part of the collective memory, as Maurice Halbwachs, French philosopher and sociologist, the father of researching collective memory (1877—1945), wrote: "In order for a person or historical event to enter social memory, it has to be transformed into an instruction, a concept, a symbol. It is invested with meaning; it becomes an element in the system of ideas of a society."[42] Whether the analyzed art pieces become part of the collective memory is subject to future investigation and requires a longer time perspective.

CONCLUSION

This chapter discussed specific examples of the interaction between memory and literary studies. The three chosen Hungarian contemporary examples discuss a kind of anti-remembering act regarding certain elements of the recent past. As remembering is a communicative activity and a tool for intergenerational relations, the denial or prevention of such communication can lead to long lasting consequences.[43] Memories play a role in the formation of identity not just as a source of knowledge about the past, but as a defining relation to the present as well.[44] This is pointed out by presenting the question of silencing in parent-child relationship in all three cases. The parent figures are the ones who silence certain aspects of the past, and stay in the center of the analyzed art pieces. Members of the next generation motivate the dissolution of silencing in order to form or protect not just their relationships and their knowledge of the past, but also their own self-images as well. The two publications and one film production were analyzed through memory studies literature, and the investigation focused on remembering on personal and community levels, as well as the realization and dissolving intentions of silencing.

Barry Schwartz, an American psychologist focusing on social theory and action (1946), together with his colleagues, emphasized the "commemorative narrative" feature of collective memory, defined as a story about a significant historical event that has been re-crafted many times in order to convey the

---

[42] Maurice Halbwachs, *Das Gedächtnis und seine sozialen Bedingungen* (Frankfurt: Suhrkamp, 1985), 389–90.

[43] Paul Ricoeur, "Fragility and responsibility," *Philosophy and Social Criticism* 21, no. 5–6 (1995): 15–22.

[44] Barbara Szacka, *Czas przeszły, pamięć, mit* (Warszawa: Wydawnictwo Naukowe Scholar, 2006), 16–18.

envisaged moral lesson.[45] The analyzed examples are also intended to re-craft the recent past, but they use personal, many times untold stories that much rather complement the canonized narrative than strengthen it. Along these lines, it is important to mention that even though collective memory contains less information and fewer details than community members' personal memories, it has a greater impact on transforming both personal memories and the officially narrated memory of the past.[46] That can be why the represented members of the parent generation transformed their personal memories and silenced them to fit the collective memory. Similarly, the authors intend to enrich the officially narrated memory about the depicted time period and historic events by making the chosen personal memories part of the collective through art. The art of memory through, for instance, writing, film, and monument,[47] can stabilize memory throughout generations by transforming personal memory to collective cultural memory,[48] from orality to writing or other modalities of storing information.[49] Moreover, media technologies can therefore be defined as "tools that mediate between personal and collective cultural memory."[50]

Among others, Maria Todorova, a Bulgarian historian born in 1949, emphasized that both collective and personal memories can shed light on elements of the social and cultural life of the previous political period.[51] By focusing on the rupture between personal and collective memories of communism, Kaja Kaźmierska, a Polish sociologist and cultural anthropologist, researches the relationship between biography and memory, called "asymmetry of biographical and collective memory."[52] The analyzed art pieces address both and enrich the knowledge about the past period for the future generation. While the depicted stories are highly personal, they

---

[45] Barry Schwartz, Yael Zerubavel, Bernice M. Barnett, and George Steiner, "The Recovery of Masada: A Study in Collective Memory," *The Sociological Quarterly* 27, no. 2 (1986): 147–64.

[46] Adam D. Brown, Nicole Kouri, and William Hirst, "Memory's Malleability: Its Role in Shaping Collective Memory and Social Identity," *Frontiers in Psychology* 3 (2012): 1–3.

[47] Astrid Erll and Ann Rigney, eds., *Mediation, Remediation, and the Dynamics of Cultural Memory* (Berlin: De Gruyter, 2009).

[48] Bernhard Giesen, *Triumph and Trauma* (Berkeley: University of California Press, 2000).

[49] Jacques LeGoff, *Histoire et Memoire* (Paris: Gallimard, 1986).

[50] José Van Dijck, *Mediated Memories in the Digital Age* (Stanford: Stanford University Press, 2007), 19.

[51] Maria Todorova, *Remembering Communism: Genres of Representation* (New York: Social Science Research Council, 2010), 12.

[52] Kaja Kazmierska, "Biographical and Collective Memory. Mutual Influences in Central and Eastern Europe Context," in *Memory and Change in Europe: Eastern Perspectives*, eds. Joanna Wawrzyniak and Małgorzata Pakier (New York: Berghahn Books, 2015), 96–112.

represent common copying methodologies of individuals in a totalitarian system. By depicting the possible dissolution of silencing the past in an intergenerational setting, the three case studies also address the issue of identity creation in post-communist societies on an individual level.

REFERENCES

Anderson, Benedict. *Imagined Communities: Reflections on the Origin and the Spread of Nationalism.* London: Verso, 1983.

Assmann, Aleida, and Ute Frevert. *Geschichtsvergessenheit, Geschichtsversessenheit: Vom Umgang mit deutschen Vergangenheiten nach 1945.* Stuttgart: Deutsche Verlags-Anstalt, 1999.

Assmann, Jan. *Az emlékezés kultúrája.* Translated by Hidas Zoltán. Budapest: Osiris Kiadó, 1999.

Axelsson, Majgull. *My name is not Miriam.* Stockholm: Brombergs, 2014.

Brown, Adam D., Nicole Kouri, and William Hirst. "Memory's Malleability: Its Role in Shaping Collective Memory and Social Identity." *Frontiers in Psychology* 3 (2012): 1–3.

Brunnbauer, Ulf, and Stefan Troebst, eds. *Zwischen Amnesie und Nostalgie: die Erinnerung an den Kommunismus in Südosteuropa.* Köln, Weimar, Wien: Böhlau, 2007.

Connerton, Paul. *How Societies Remember.* Cambridge: Cambridge University Press, 1989.

Dahrendorf, Ralf. *Reflections on the Revolution in Europe.* London: Chatto and Windus, 1990.

Dobi, Ferenc. "Csapás a múltból," *Filmtett,* October 11, 2017.

Eckstein, Harry. "A Culturalist Theory of Political Change." *American Political Science Review* no. 3 (1988): 789–804.

Ely-Harper, Kerreen. "Record keeping: family memories on film." In *Female Agency and Documentary Strategies: Subjectivities, Identity and Activism,* edited by Boel Ulfsdotter and Anna Backman Rogers, 84–99. Edinburgh: Edinburgh University Press, 2018.

Eörsi, László. "A Corvin közi emléktáblák." *História* 31, no. 9 (2009): 60–62.

Erll, Astrid, and Ann Rigney, eds. *Mediation, Remediation, and the Dynamics of Cultural Memory.* Berlin: De Gruyter, 2009.

Forster, Kurt. "Introduction." In *The Renewal of Pagan Antiquity,* Aby Warburg, 1–75. Los Angeles: Getty Research Institute, 1999.

Giesen, Bernhard. *Triumph and Trauma.* Berkeley: University of California Press, 2000.

György, Péter. "Az emlékezet szétesése – az olvashatatlan város." *2000* 10 (2006): 5–10.

György, Péter. "Az apám Piros emlékezete." *Élet és Irodalom,* October 31, 2008.

Halbwachs, Maurice. *Das Gedächtnis und seine sozialen Bedingungen.* Frankfurt: Suhrkamp, 1985.

Halmai, Gábor. *Memory Politics in Hungary: Political Justice without Rule of Law.* Den Haag: Asser Institute, 2018.

Kazmierska, Kaja. "Biographical and Collective Memory: Mutual Influences in Central and Eastern Europe Context." In *Memory and Change in Europe: Eastern Perspectives*, edited by Joanna Wawrzyniak and Małgorzata Pakier, 96–112. New York: Berghahn Books, 2015.

Keszei, András. *Emlékek formájában*. Budapest: L'Harmattan Kiadó, 2015.

Laik, Eszter. "Atya, fiú." *Irodalmi Jelen*, August 31, 2016.

LeGoff, Jacques. *Histoire et Memoire*. Paris: Gallimard, 1986.

Lepenies, Wolf. *Folgen einer unerhörten Begebenheit: Die Deutschen nach der Vereinigung*. Berlin: Siedler, 1992.

Liem, Ramsay. "Silencing Historical Trauma: The Politics and Psychology of Memory and Voice Peace and Conflict." *Journal of Peace Psychology* 3, no. 2 (2017): 153–74.

Lowenthal, David. *The Past is a Foreign Country*. Cambridge: Cambridge University Press, 1985.

Milward, Alan S. "Bad Memories." *Times Literary Supplement*, April 14, 2000.

Nora, Pierre. "Reasons for the Current Upsurge in Memory." *Transit* 22 (2002): 1.

Péntek, Orsolya. "Pokolsár. Száraz Miklós György a Felvidékről, Erdélyről, Andalúziáról és Rómáról." *Magyar Napló* 25, no.11. (2013): 33–44.

Pető, Andrea. "The New Monument to Victims of Military Sexual Violence in Budapest." *Hungarian Studies Review* 48, no. 2. (2021): 209–15.

Pótó, János. *Emlékművek, politika, közgondolkodás*. Budapest: MTA Történelemtudományi Intézete, 1989.

Radonić, Ljiljana. "Post-communist invocation of Europe: memorial museums' narratives and the Europeanization of memory." *National Identities* 19, no. 2 (2017): 269–88.

Ricoeur, Paul. "Fragility and responsibility." *Philosophy and Social Criticism* 21, no. 5–6 (1995): 15–22.

Schachter, Daniel Lawrence et al., eds. *Memory distortion: How minds, brains, and societies reconstruct the past*. Cambridge, MA: Harvard University Press, 1995.

Schacter, Daniel L., Scott A. Guerin, and Peggy L. St. Jacques. "Memory Distortion: An Adaptive Perspective." *Trends in Cognitive Sciences* 15, no. 10 (2011): 467–74.

Schwartz, Barry, Yael Zerubavel, Bernice M. Barnett, and George Steiner. "The Recovery of Masada: A Study in Collective Memory." *The Sociological Quarterly* 27, no. 2 (1986): 147–64.

Schwartz, Matthias, Nina Weller, and Heike Winkel. "After Memory: Introduction." In *After Memory World War II in Contemporary Eastern European Literatures*, edited by ibidem., 1–21. Berlin: De Gruyter, 2021.

Sinkó, Katalin. "Oh, Amnézia úrnő (ne) jöjj el! (Gondolatok a szobordöntögetésről)." *Magyar Narancs*, May 3, 1990.

Sinkó, Katalin. "A politika rítusai: Emlékműállítás, szobordöntés." In *A művészet katonái: Sztálinizmus és kultúra*, edited by Péter György and Hedvig Turai, 67–79. Budapest: Corvina Kiadó Vállalat, 1992.

Skarga, Barbara. "Tożsamość ja i pamięć." *Znak* 5, (1995): 4–18.

Stone Charles B. et al. "Toward a Science of Silence: The Consequences of Leaving a Memory Unsaid." *Perspectives on Psychological Science* 7, no. 1 (2012): 39–53.

Szacka, Barbara. *Czas przeszły, pamięć, mit.* Warszawa: Wydawnictwo Naukowe Scholar, 2006.

Szíjjártó, Gabriella. "Apám, a világítótorony - Száraz Miklós Györggyel beszélgettünk." *Szabadföld,* May 3, 2016.

Sztompka, Piotr. "Looking Back: The Year 1989 as a Cultural and Civilizational Break." *Communist and Post-Communist Studies* 29, no. 2 (1996): 115–29.

Szymańska, Daniela, Elżbieta Grzelak-Kostulska, and Beata Hołowiecka. "Polish Towns and the Changes in Their Areas and Population Densities." *Bulletin of Geography Socio-economic Series* 11, no. 11 (2009): 15–30.

Todorova, Maria. *Remembering Communism: Genres of Representation.* New York: Social Science Research Council, 2010.

Todorova, Maria, Augusta Dimou, and Stefan Troebst, eds. *Remembering Communism: Private and Public Recollections of Lived Experience in Southeast Europe.* Budapest: Central European University Press, 2014.

Troebst, Stefan, ed. *Postdiktatorische Geschichtskulturen im Süden und Osten Europas: Bestandsaufnahme und Forschungsperspektiven.* Göttingen: Wallstein-Verlag, 2010.

Van Dijck, José. *Mediated Memories in the Digital Age.* Stanford: Stanford University Press, 2007.

Verdery, Katherine. *The Political Lives of Dead Bodies: Reburial and Postsocialist Change.* New York: Columbia University Press, 1999.

Winter, Jay. "The Generation of Memory: Reflections on the 'Memory Boom' in Contemporary Historical Studies." *Bulletin of the German Historical Institute* 27 (2000): 69–92.

Young, Craig, and Duncan Light. "Place, national identity and post-socialist transformations: an introduction." *Political Geography* 20 (2001): 941–55.

Chapter 6

Shaping the Future by Reconstructing the Past. Polish-Jewish Autobiographical Writings beyond the Holocaust (Agata Tuszyńska, Piotr Paziński, Mikołaj Grynberg)

Elisa-Maria Hiemer

Herder Institute for Historical Research on East Central Europe, Germany

Abstract: The article is based on the observation that contemporary research on Jewish literature and culture is usually reduced to aspects of heritage, survivorship and the state of "non-being." This post-catastrophic way of reading ignores that identity-building processes also require forward-looking references to Jewishness and Judaism. With my text sample (Agata Tuszyńska's *A Family History of Fear*, Piotr Paziński's *The Boarding House*, Mikołaj Grynberg's *Tumult*) I aim to explore which narrative strategies recent (fictionalized) Jewish self-descriptions have applied. Their narrators actively shape Jewish spaces in a mainly non-Jewish surroundings and have begun to question binary identity patterns (being either Polish or Jewish). Applying a close reading strategy through a spatial theory lens, I emphasize the generational, national, temporal boundaries that the narrators consciously cross. The need for belonging and a secure location in Poland is challenged by anti-Semitic beliefs, which all three examples oppose.

Keywords: Poland, Autobiography, Post memory, Jewishness, Polish-Jewish Identity

***

Today's Europe makes up only one part of the West; it has lost its historical hegemony. It has shrunk with respect to its previous self since 1989. It is slowly acquiring a new character: a continent united by a common, tormented past and, more importantly, a common future.[1]

The revival of Jewish communities and the sense of Jewishness in Central Europe have been receiving academic attention since the end of the Cold War. What unites manifold contributions from history, literary studies, or social sciences is that European Jewry is seen through the lens of deprivation. Post-catastrophic approaches incorporate the changing meaning and perception of the Holocaust[2] but emphasize: "The authors of the second and third generation conceptualize the legacy of the Shoah as a task and an obligation."[3] The literary scientist Magdalena Marszałek explicitly states that, in the case of Polish literature, "it is also relevant to all other (auto)biographical figurations of Jewishness that the literary encodings of Jewishness appear as inextricably bound to the caesura of genocide."[4]

Twenty-five years have passed since the statement on the Jewish future in Europe by the historian Diana Pinto. However, the Holocaust remains the main point of reference in research regarding the image society ascribes to Jews. I argue that the common usage of terms such as *second* and *third generation*

---

[1] Diana Pinto, "A New Jewish Identity for Post 1989 Europe?" Institute for Jewish Policy Research, accessed October 19, 2021, https://archive.jpr.org.uk/object-eur44. Pinto considers 1989 a turning point for Jewish communities, since it was the first time that they could feel an equal part of Europe and not torn between emigration or assimilation.

[2] I use the term *Holocaust*. However, in direct quotations that use *Shoah*, I retain the original. *Holocaust* is more common; however, its etymology refers to the ancient sacrificial ritual of burning animals, and implies a fateful coincidence. The biblical term *Shoah* refers to the visitation upon the people of Israel of events threatening their existence.

[3] Anna Artwińska and Anja Tippner, "Postkatastrophische Vergegenwärtigungen – eine Positionsbestimmung," in *Nach dem Holocaust: Medien postkatastrophischer Vergegenwärtigungen in Polen und Deutschland*, eds. Anna Artwińska and Anja Tippner (Frankfurt: Peter Lang, 2017), 27.

[4] Magdalena Marszałek, "Von jüdischen Müttern: Geheimnistropen in der polnisch-jüdischen autobiographischen Gegenwartsliteratur," in *Osteuropäisch-jüdische Literaturen im 20. und 21. Jahrhundert: Identität und Poetik = Eastern European Jewish Literature of the 20th and 21st Centuries*, ed. Klavdia Smola (München: Otto Sagner, 2013), 271.

implies an (erroneous) continuity of Holocaust narrations.[5] Hence, research too is responsible for reducing Jewish literature and Jewish life in Central Europe to aspects of cultural heritage, survivorship and the state of "non-being." This post-catastrophic way of reading ignores that identity-building processes also require forward-looking references to Jewishness and Judaism.

This article explores narrative strategies recent (fictionalized) Jewish self-descriptions have applied. I assume that the reconstruction of the past confirms Jewish roots and helps to position the narrator more confidently in a mainly non-Jewish society.[6] Considering the idea of the initial quote by Pinto, I also examine the relationship between local identity discourses and their position in global Jewish communities. Starting with examples of the academic discourse on Jewish life in Poland around the turn of the millennium, I will add voices from debates within the Jewish community that show how Jews perceive political and social discussions that regularly question the place of Jews in Poland. It is this binary character of the debates (post-memory vs. forward-looking perspectives, historical roots of Polish Jewry vs. "victim rivalry") that becomes a main issue for all the selected texts: Agata Tuszyńska's *Family History of Fear* (*Rodzinna historia lęku*, 2005), Piotr Paziński's *The Boarding House* (*Pensjonat*, 2009) and Mikołaj Grynberg's *Tumult* (*Rejwach*, 2018).[7]

The examples will show how the narrators approach this issue of ambiguous identity. From the perspective of literary studies, the associative triad of

---

[5] Natalia Żórawska, *Dziedzictwo (nie)pamięci: Holocaustowe doświadczenia pisarek drugiego pokolenia* (Katowice: Wydawnictwo Uniwersytetu Śląskiego, 2018), Jagoda Budzik, ed., *Work in progress: konfrontacje trzeciego pokolenia po Zagładzie* (Nowy Sącz: Wydawnictwo Pasaże, 2018).

[6] This contribution continues the main ideas of my PhD thesis. Compared to the published version, I consider new insights from current political and cultural discourses as well as a third book in my literature sample. See Elisa-Maria Hiemer, *Autobiographisches Schreiben als ästhetisches Problem: Jüdische Vielfalt in der polnischen und deutschen Gegenwartsliteratur* (Wiesbaden: Harrassowitz, 2019).

[7] Polish-Jewish relations in non-fictional literature have a long tradition. Especially in the 1980s, both Jewish and non-Jewish authors like Hanna Krall, Andrzej Szczypiorski, Paweł Huelle or Piotr Szewc demonstrated that Jewish history was not a separate part but an integral part of Polish historical identity. While the decade after the fall of communism was the time of late testimonies, we can observe an increasing interest in depicting Holocaust and Jewish topics as part of the pop cultural or every day memory in recent literature (e.g., Szczepan Twardoch, Magdalena Tulli, Zyta Rudzka). An overview of the post–1945 history of Polish Holocaust literature is provided by Elisa-Maria Hiemer et al., "Introduction," in *Handbook of Polish, Czech, and Slovak Holocaust Literature: Works and Contexts*, ed. Elisa-Maria Hiemer, Jiří Holý, Agata Firlej, and Hana Nichtburgerová (Berlin: De Gruyter, 2021), 1–17.

Jewish origin – autobiography – Holocaust seems unbroken. In the case of Polish literature, autobiographical approaches and literary testimonies play a particular role in shaping the memory.[8] In addition, Marianne Hirsch's post memory theory strongly influenced the field of humanities as it scrutinized the transgenerational phenomenon of passing on a traumatic experience. Despite this valuable contribution, the focus on trauma is problematic insofar as discussion on the esthetic form of Jewish literature seems to be secondary. Referring to Gaston Bachelard's idea of 'topophilia' (positive places), I pay particular attention to the spatial organization of the texts. Following Wolfgang Hallet and Birgit Neumann's theoretical approach, I consider the texts not only as a movement of the narrator across spaces, but above all, a movement across boundaries that are liable to shift.[9] In particular, the monolithic notion of identity (being either Polish or Jewish) is challenged by recent literature.

The contribution demonstrates that contemporary literature of Jewish origin is no longer centered around the inherited trauma of the Holocaust and how its authors demand their place in the country by actively creating Jewish spaces. On the wider political and social level, I consider this approach indispensable to building a counter-narrative to recent right-wing debates on Polish-Jewish relations.

CHANGING NARRATIVES OF THE PAST, INSIDE AND OUTSIDE THE JEWISH COMMUNITY

Diana Pinto argues that European Jewry was given a realistic opportunity to develop new communities after the end of the Cold War. She uses the term "voluntary Jews"[10] to underline that European Jews had, for the first time, more options than a choice between assimilation or emigration. To realize this, however, she demands a conceptual break from the usual cultural narratives and an acceptance that pre-war structures of European Jewry were irreversible. Pinto's approach has been frequently criticized for its overly

---

[8] Małgorzata Czermińska summarizes the importance of autobiographical/non-fictional devices in Polish literature after 1989 as follows: "non-fiction prose in the 20th century exists in some sense against the novel. It thrives on the 'crisis of the novel', it feeds on the 'death of the novel', it is read instead of the novel." Małgorzata Czermińska, *Autobiograficzny trójkąt: Świadectwo, wyznanie, wyzwanie* (Kraków: Universitas, 2000), 12.

[9] Wolfgang Hallet and Birgit Neumann, "Raum und Bewegung in der Literatur: Zur Einführung," in *Raum und Bewegung in der Literatur: Die Literaturwissenschaften und der Spatial Turn*, ed. Wolfgang Hallet (Bielefeld: transcript, 2009), 17–18.

[10] Pinto, "A new Jewish identity," 1.

optimistic view and lack of historical sensibility.[11] Jonathan Webber writes: "In other words, the Jewish people have undergone an identity crisis – or, more accurately, a succession of identity crises."[12]

It is only since the turn of the millennium that voices in favor of a more individualistic approach to Jewishness have emerged: Nick Lambert deconstructs the notion of a worldwide spiritually and historically rooted Jewishness of which every Jew automatically wants to be part of. In his 2008 book *Jews and Europe in the Twenty-First Century*, he states that the so-called Jewish bonds (e.g., a common origin and history, Israel, the topos of chosenness) are a narrative that has to be reconsidered. He reveals a problematic overlap between memory and history (as a science), which is particularly evident in the historical representations of Israeli and U.S. historians, and he asserts that this approach is Eurocentric as it excludes the different histories of Jewish communities, e.g., in Ethiopia or China:[13]

> Those familiar with Jewish communal discourse today will recognize that the term 'the Jewish people' is often founded upon the emotional and ideological baggage which accompanies those who make reference to it, bound by the protagonists' desire to communicate a personal vision, rather than premised upon encounters with the expense of Jewish human and written data, pertaining to the condition of that people today.[14]

In his opinion, historians tend to construct an identity-shaping narrative of the past meant to serve as a point of reference for Jews worldwide. However, this standpoint is not only Eurocentric but also does not represent the reality of Jewish life in Poland. Current research still focuses on the Holocaust as a determining factor for Jewish identities that is virulent even in foreign literature. Amongst others, the image of Poland as a Jewish cemetery has

---

[11] Michael Brumlik calls her theory "a castle in the air" (quoted from Jörg Lau, "Was heißt hier jüdisch?" *Die Zeit*, January 5, 2000, 99), see also: Hans Joachim Hahn, "'Europa' als neuer 'jüdischer Raum': Diana Pintos Thesen und Vladimir Vertlibs Romane," in V*on der nationalen zur internationalen Literatur: Transkulturelle deutschsprachige Literatur und Kultur im Zeitalter globaler Migration*, ed. Helmut Schmitz (Amsterdam: Rodopi, 2009), 295–310.

[12] Jonathan Webber, "Modern Jewish Identities," in *Making Holocaust Memory*, ed. Gabriel N. Finder, Natalia Aleksiun, Antony Polonsky, and Jan Schwarz (Oxford: Littman, 2008), 75.

[13] Nick Lambert, *Jews and Europe in the Twenty-First Century: Thinking Jewish* (London, Portland: Routledge, 2008), 61.

[14] Lambert, *Jews and Europe*, 47.

become commonplace for describing the state of Jewry in that country and – as I argue – overshadows other issues Jews in Poland are currently dealing with.[15]

"For the Jews of Poland (...) the Second World War ended only in 1989 with the fall of communism"[16]

Academic discourses on Central European Jewry, in particular, serve as a good example of the bonds that Lambert questions, since all efforts to make Jewish life visible are focused on the reconstruction of the past and on heritage-making. Since the 1980s, US journalist Ruth Ellen Gruber has been researching emanations of Jewish cultures in Central Europe. In her publications,[17] she describes relics of the communal and social infrastructures of former Jewish centers. The unnoticed but visible Jewish heritage has degenerated into a kind of memorial that is evident not only in Polish cities, but also in the voids in history and memory left by the extermination, and ultimately, the expulsion of Jews from Poland in 1968.[18] In her book, an inhabitant of Kazimierz, the

---

[15] Izabela Suchojad, *Topografia żydowskiej pamięci: Obraz krakowskiego Kazimierza we współczesnej literaturze polskiej i polsko-żydowskiej* (Kraków: Universitas, 2010). Jagoda Budzik, "Topos Polski jako żydowskiego cmentarza w hebrajskiej literaturze trzeciego pokolenia," *Narracje o Zagładzie*, no. 2 (2016): 88–100. Żórawska, *Dziedzictwo (nie)pamięci*, 2018. Józef Wróbel, "Z prześladowanymi w późnym, nieprzemilczanym promienistym związku: Drugie pokolenie po Holokauście," *Ruch Literacki* 57, no. 3 (2016): 343–59.

[16] Konstanty Gebert and Helena Datner, "Życie żydowskie w Polsce: Osiągnięcia, wyzwania i priorytety od upadku komunizmu," accessed October 11, 2021, http://www.jpr.org.uk/documents/Jewish%20life%20in%20Poland%20 (Polish).pdf, 7.

[17] Ruth Ellen Gruber, *Upon the Doorposts of Thy House: Jewish Life in East-Central Europe, Yesterday and Today* (New York: Wiley cop., 1994) or Ruth Ellen Gruber, *Jewish Heritage Travel: A Guide through Eastern Europe* (New York: Wiley cop., 1992).

[18] Following the Israeli victory over the Arab states in the 1967 Six-Day War, the USSR demanded that the Eastern Bloc states broke off diplomatic relations with Israel. At the same time, a large part of the Polish population welcomed a victory over those Arab States that were supported by the Soviets. (Yet another, unofficial, part was pleased that Israel had defeated the Arab States.) Władysław Gomułka, chairman of the Polish United Workers' Party (*Polska Zjednoczona Partia Robotnicza*, PZPR) and thus head of state, called on all "Israel sympathizers" to leave Poland and denigrated the Jewish population as "a fifth column" seeking to destabilize the internal order. This initiated the most massive persecution of Jewish citizens to have taken place in Poland since 1945, resulting in denunciation lists in companies and mass dismissals of Jewish employees. As a direct consequence of the March events, about thirteen thousand people left the country. Those who remained mostly decided to stay silent about their Jewish roots.

former Jewish district of Cracow, even states that the decay of this part of the city serves nowadays only as a "touristic outpost to Auschwitz."[19]

These early observations negated the possibility of a continuation of Jewish culture and tradition in Poland and represent an antithesis to Diana Pinto's postulations. Gruber's follow-up work, *Virtually Jewish. Reinventing Jewish Culture in Europe* demonstrates, however, a completely new development in approaching Jewish heritage in Central Europe: Around the turn of the millennium, manifold initiatives on enhancing the visibility of Jewish history and on considering it as part of the national history can be observed in the former Eastern Bloc countries (e.g., erection of monuments, restoration of former Jewish residential areas and cemeteries). Recently, (social) media and urban lifestyles have also contributed to these developments (see the growing popularity of Jewish festivals and gastronomy in larger cities) aiming at a wider perception of contemporary Jewishness – one that, according to Monika Adamczyk-Garbowska, a professor for comparative literature and Jewish studies, does not exist.[20] For Gruber, Central European Jewishness remains an artificial concept, and she thereby questions the very idea of a rebirth of Jewry in post-socialist states.

If we look into the Jewish discourse itself, we can observe divergent narratives when it comes to Jewish self-perception of institutionalized Jewry and individual concepts: The Jewish community in Poland[21] seems to be divided regarding the importance of religion. In a 1999 newspaper article, Shoshana Ronen, a Jewish scholar and publicist living in Poland, warned of the radicalization of Polish Jews. According to Ronen, there was an increasing popularity of orthodox Judaism and of the display of outward appearances (for example, kosher food and strict observance of the Sabbath). In the words of the writer Abraham B. Yehoszua, she favored a liberal definition of Jewishness: a person who considers himself or herself a Jew is indeed a Jew. She argued that establishing an open structure in which everyone can decide what being a Jew means to him or herself is preferable to emphasizing the

---

[19] Gruber, *Upon the Doorposts*, 186.

[20] Monika Adamczyk-Garbowska and Magdalena Ruta, "Od kultury żydowskiej do kultury o Żydach," in *Następstwa zagłady Żydów: Polska 1944–2010*, ed. Felix Tych and Monika Adamczyk-Garbowska (Lublin: Wydawnictwo UMCS, 2011), 715–32.

[21] The *Concise Statistical Yearbook of Poland 2021* counts 1,795 Jews. See Główny Urząd Statystyczny, *Mały rocznik statystyczny Rzeczypospolitej Polskiej 2021* (Warszawa: Zakład Wydawnictw Statystycznych, 2021), 120. Other sources estimate the number of Jews to be about 4,500–7,000. See Helena Datner, "Współczesna społeczność żydowska w Polsce a Zagłada," in *Następstwa zagłady Żydów: Polska 1944–2010*, ed. Feliks Tych and Monika Adamczyk-Grubowska (Lublin: Wydawnictwo UMCS, 2011), 666.

specificity and, thus otherness of Judaism. This was also important in terms of the dialogue with the majority society, so as not to run the risk of establishing a counterculture with far less acceptance.[22] A few days later, "Gazeta Wyborcza," one of the most widely-read Polish daily newspapers, published a reply from Konstanty Gebert, a Jewish journalist. He accused Ronen of lacking expertise regarding the Polish situation and suspected that she equated the situation in Poland with the conflict in her home country, Israel, regarding the rejection of Orthodoxy. Gebert emphasized the community-forming importance of faith/religion and considered the secularization of the Jewish faith to be a regrettable development.[23]

Nonetheless, institutionalized and academic discourses on Jewish life do not seem to capture a true image of Jewish life in Poland. Katka Reszke's study of the third-generation narratives of Jews in Poland is a valuable contribution to understanding their lived realities: Many of her respondents describe a liberal attitude towards Jewish identity and a wish to open the Jewish community to those who might not be Jewish halachically. Reszke summarizes that "[i]ronically though, more than half of the young Jews in today's Poland are 'non-halachic Jews'."[24] Helise Lieberman (since 2009, director of the Taube Center for the Renewal of Jewish Life in Poland) emphasizes:

> If, however, someone feels himself to be a Jew only because others want him to be, then his path to self-knowledge becomes very difficult. Can one want to be a Jew at all if only negative aspects are associated with it - in fact, nothing inspires to search, but much tempts to shut oneself in, to hide, to withdraw... That is exactly why we must try, each for herself/himself, to make possible a positive Jewish environment in which people feel at home.[25]

---

[22] Shoshana Ronen, "Jak w Polsce być Żydem?" *Gazeta Wyborcza*, September 8, 1999, 18.

[23] The discussion needs to be contextualized within the 1990s developments in Central Europe, when questions of identity were closely linked to questions about political involvements. See also Marci Shore, *The Taste of Ashes: The Afterlife of Totalitarianism in Eastern Europe* (London: Windmill Books, 2014). The author also interviewed Konstanty Gebert.

[24] According to the Halakha, Jewish descent is to be traced through the maternal line, that is, if only a person's father has Jewish origins, they cannot themselves be Jewish. Katka Reszke, *Return of the Jew: Identity Narratives of the Third Post-Holocaust Generation of Jews in Poland* (Boston: Academic Studies Press, 2013), 121.

[25] Ewa Koźmińska-Frejlak, "Nie można być Żydem samotnie: Z Helise Lieberman rozmawia Ewa Koźmińska-Frejlak," *Midrasz*, no. 10 (2006): 15.

Leaving behind the intra-Jewish discussion and personal identity-related issues, we must recognize a new level of destabilization of the Polish-Jewish dialogue. In the context of the recollection of the Holocaust, in recent years, the victim rivalry between Poles and Jews has been taken up once more. In 2018, an attempted amendment to the Act on the Institute of National Remembrance (*Ustawa Insytutu Pamięci Narodowej*, Ustawa IPN) that penalized public speech when attributing responsibility for the Holocaust to the Polish nation[26], showed how the current Law and Justice party (*Prawo i Sprawiedliwość*, PiS) government seeks to fight for Poland's good name by emphasizing the suffering of Polish people during the Nazi occupation.[27] The goal of this debate, which is led by right-wing extremists and right-wing conservatives, is to establish a new Polish memory practice oriented toward ethnic-confessional patterns. The debate on the amendment and the expression "Polokaust" (brought up first by the author Marek Kochan in response to international criticism[28]) became vivid in the year of the 50th anniversary[29] of the events of March 1968.[30] Michał Bilewicz, a social psychologist and head of the Warsaw Center for Prejudice Research, explains the term as follows:

---

[26] Katarzyna Liszka, "Articles 55a and 55b of the IPN Act and the Dialogue about the Holocaust in Poland," *Archiwum filozofii prawa i filozofii społecznej* 21, no. 3 (2019): 82–84, https://doi.org/10.36280/AFPiFS.2019.3.81.

[27] Katarzyna Andersz, "Żeby Polska była Polską [wywiad z Michałem Bilewiczem]," *Chidusz* 47, no. 2 (2018), https://chidusz.com/zeby-polska-byla-polska-michal-bilewicz-marzec-68/. These kinds of policies seem to replace the preceding discussion about Polish-Jewish relations during the Second World War. Jan Tomasz Gross' book *Neighbors* (*Sąsiedzi*, Sejny: Pogranicze, 2000) describes Polish co-responsibility for the massacre of Jews in Jedwabne, whereas *Fear* (*Strach*, Kraków: Znak, 2008) addresses the topic of postwar antisemitism in Poland. Together with his wife Irena Grudzińska-Gross, he wrote *Golden Harvest* (*Złote Żniwa*, Kraków: Znak, 2011), which focuses on theft of Jewish property and desecration of Jewish graves by Poles. All these publications have challenged the historical consciousness and led to polarized discussions between the political wings.

[28] Kochan considers the idea of a "Polokaust Museum" as an opportunity for Poland to rebuild its reputation. Marek Kochan, "Zbudujmy szybko Muzeum Polokaustu," *Rzeczpospolita*, February 19, 2018, accessed July 25, 2022, https://www.rp.pl/opinie-pol ityczno-spoleczne/art2109721-marek-kochan-zbudujmy-szybko-muzeum-polokaustu.

[29] See also Andrzej Czyżewski, "The Myths of March '68: Negotiating Memory in Contemporary Poland," in *Unsettled 1968: Origins – Myth – Impact*, eds. Aleksandra Konarzewska, Anna Nakai, and Michał Przeperski (Routledge: New York, London, 2020), 163–87.

[30] See footnote 18.

The coining of this term to mean the Holocaust to which Poles are said to have fallen victim, shows the need to recognize the suffering of Poles during the Nazi occupation. A necessity taken to the extreme, because the Poles were not victims of the genocide; they were not – like the Jews – condemned to extermination as a whole nation.[31]

And he continues:

This need is nothing new. The reactions to the use of the term "Polish concentration [sic!] camps,"[32] as it was termed by Barack Obama in 2012, show the need to fight for the good historical name of Poland, which is also nothing new. However, this fight has never been exploited in politics to the extent that it is now. The attempt to attach oneself to the Shoah is a phenomenon that actually began only in the last few months, after the adoption of the amendment to the IPN law.[33]

The discussion about victim congruence is already echoed in some literary texts, for example, in Anna Janko's autobiographical text *Mała Zagłada* (*Little Annihilation*, 2015), which focuses on the massacre of Polish children in Sochy. From the perspective of the daughter of a survivor, she develops the narrative "in such a way that the reader gets the impression that both Poles and Jews suffered common atrocities."[34] Chmielewska considers this a clear minimization or even exclusion of Jewish losses from the common Polish historical narrative: "The Polish witness as a discourse figure strives to take over the symbolic capital of Jewish trauma."[35]

What do these developments mean for authors of Jewish descent? I argue that the chosen books mirror the political and social circumstances in which they were written, but that their authors all find alternative solutions to cope with this unfavorable environment.

---

[31] Andersz, "*Żeby Polska była Polską.*"

[32] Bilewicz confuses Obama's original wording that was "Polish death camps," for which Obama later apologized. See: "President on Barack Obama's letter", accessed July 22, 2022, https://www.president.pl/president-komorowski/news/president-on-barack-oba mas-letter,38594.

[33] Andersz, "*Żeby Polska była Polską.*"

[34] Katarzyna Chmielewska, "Der polnische Zeuge: Traumabildung, Symmentrien und feindliche Übernahme des (jüdischen) Traumas," in *Nach dem Holocaust: Medien postkatastrophischer Vergegenwärtigungen in Polen und Deutschland*, ed. Anna Artwińska and Anja Tippner (Frankfurt: Peter Lang, 2017), 142.

[35] Chmielewska, "Der polnische Zeuge," 144.

TROUBLING SNAPSHOTS VS. SELF-CONFIDENT BOUNDARIES: RECENT POLISH LITERATURE OF JEWISH ORIGIN

In the case of the selected authors, conclusions on the state of Jewish life can be drawn on the basis of special constructions of Jewish places.[36] The temporospatial aspect is important insofar as the character of the Jewish community is non-territorial and is always opposed to the territorial character of the country. Spatial arrangements embody power structures; oppositions such as near/far, and central/peripheral can be indications of the cultural organization of spaces.

"I Belong to both." Agata Tuszyńska's Family History of Fear (2005).

At the age of 19, Agata Tuszyńska (1957) learned of her mother's Jewish origins.[37] At the age of 48, she published *Family History of Fear*, in which, with the help of witnesses and archive material, she traces her family's history back to the nineteenth century. The narrator chooses mostly female fates and describes them in such a way that the "schizophrenic dichotomy"[38] of Jewish life in Poland becomes visible, i.e., the feeling of not fitting in, of not feeling aligned with either a Polish or a Jewish identity, as the example of the Jewish Street (*ulica Żydowska*) in Łęczyca shows. At this address, in an anonymous building, resides the history teacher and amateur historian Mirek, who will become an important companion and source of information to Agata Tuszyńska. When moving there, he "was ashamed of his address on Żydowska Street"[39]. Over time, however, his bias gives way to an awareness of the place's historical significance, so he begins to ostentatiously note his street on envelopes and forms. He provides the narrator with a variety of files from the city archives and points out individuals who are connected to the family history. The narration emphasizes private and especially positive spaces that previously existed. Their re-*construction* reassures the narrator that she is

---

[36] See Erica Lehrer and Michael Meng, eds., *Jewish space in contemporary Poland* (Bloomington, Indiana: University Press, 2015).

[37] Agata Tuszyńska writes theatre plays and poems but is mainly known for her biographies and reportages, e.g., about the Polish-Jewish singer Wiera Gran (*Oskarżona Wiera Gran*, Kraków: Wydawnictwo Literackie, 2011).

[38] Agata Tuszyńska, *Rodzinna historia lęku* (Kraków: Wydawnictwo literackie, 2005), 407. (My own translation if not specified otherwise. The English edition differs extensively from the original; in particular, quotes referring to anti-Jewish sentiments or Socialist everyday life are not part of the translated version. In addition, the last chapter, *Addresses/Adresy*, where the narrator summarizes her journey and its impact on her definition of Jewishness, is drastically shortened).

[39] Agata Tuszyńska, *Family History of Fear: A Memoir* (New York: Anchorbooks, 2017), 137.

doing something important and right, whereas conflicting spaces are limited to the *descriptive* level. Meanwhile, positive memory spaces are actively shaped by the narrator and are an act of self-agency. According to Bachelard, space in literature is often an expression of the most elementary and ordering principles of being. He pays particular attention to the concept of 'topophilia', by which spaces are praised and defended with the power of memory.[40] Thereby, the street lives up to its name again: "He wrote. I telephoned, and I rushed up as soon as I could to Żydowska Street to sit by the tile stove [...] to be able to speak of her as if she had just stepped outside the room for a moment."[41] However, the narrator enjoys the revival of the Jewish past only in the company of Mirek. Without him, she not only feels out of place and disoriented, but also accuses herself of unlawfully violating the order of the present that soaked up past traces: "In the afternoon sun, I was only an intruder there, trying to violate the present by my very presence. What I was looking for had been buried by the half century after the war."[42]

Her writing is not restricted to Polish spaces but also refers to global aspects, which can be seen in an important chapter about Tuszyńska's relatives living abroad: The events of March 1968 cause a feeling of loss and betrayal in Tuszyńska's family. Emotionally and politically, however, the Polish Jews are committed to Poland's socialist future: "Leave? Why should he [the grandfather, E.-M. H.] leave? He had a homeland, after all."[43] The maternal side of the family, the great-aunt and the great-uncle leave the country, traveling first to Denmark and finally settling in the US. Not only the geographical distance, but also the cultural and socioeconomic changes the emigrants go through distance the family members from each other ("America took her from me completely."[44]) The narrator's journey to the US helps her to overcome this negative perception and – again – this positive place of Jewish diaspora is presented in a performative way.

> I slowly began to come out of hiding. But the question of whether I was a Jew, I could not answer in the affirmative for a long time. [...] I was listening to klezmer music on the Lower East Side, which was full of traces of Jewish emigrants. I was catching up on residues. But a

---

[40] Gaston Bachelard, *La poétique de l'espace* (Paris: Les Presses universitaires de France, 1961), 17.

[41] Tuszyńska, *Family History of Fear*, 139.

[42] Tuszyńska, *Rodzinna historia lęku*, 182. (This sentence is missing in the English edition completely).

[43] Ibid., 213.

[44] Tuszyńska, *Family History of Fear*, 368.

confession did not cross my lips. It wasn't about them, it was about me. In time, I stopped denying. Jewish? Polish?[45]

The quote allows for two interpretations. On the one hand, commercialized cultural heritage is effective for gaining access to Jewish culture, although the pure consumption of it as described in the quotation, might appear naïve. On the other hand, the approach of focusing first simply on consumable cultural goods is an important part of the processes of self-questioning and self-recognizing, which are, according to Katka Reszke, typical for the generation of 'sudden Jews'.

As for the outside world in Poland, the narrator's perception of its cultural, political, and historical dominance as a threat has been inherited from her mother: "At all costs, she wanted to spare me the fear and humiliation that had befallen her. She wanted to protect me from the Polish world, which – in her opinion – could be a threat."[46] The daughter's behavior mirrors this experience unconsciously: Agata acts in the background, evaluates archival material at home, and does not want to draw attention to herself, yet it is only through her that it is possible to revive the Jewish space in the Polish town. The strongest gestures are the attachment of the *mezuzah*[47] to her front door and the transfer of the *mazewot*[48] to the cellar of her home in Warsaw. In short, her inherited fear of non-belonging turns into an acknowledgment of her Jewish descent. The Jewish remnants, found mainly on the periphery today, are transferred to the capital. This act signifies that Warsaw will continue to be a place of Jews. On the last page, the narrator claims self-confidently: "I belong to both. And let it remain that way."[49] The importance of the parental home as a *topophilia* becomes obvious as she finally expresses the wish to invite all of her relatives to gather in one room: "Into my childhood room where you never came. Where you were missing. In this empty space, in this silence. There where I missed you so much although I didn't know of your existence, I am here and wait."[50]

---

[45] Tuszyńska, *Rodzinna historia lęku*, 407–8.

[46] Ibid., 32.

[47] Small capsule to be attached to the door frame of a Jewish house. On the parchment are written parts of the prayer Shma Yisrael.

[48] Jewish grave stones.

[49] Tuszyńska, *Family History of Fear*, 401.

[50] Ibid., 401.

"A completely different world": Piotr Paziński's Boarding House (2009)

The Boarding House is Piotr Paziński's (1973) debut novel[51] and describes a young man's short stay in a vacation home. The trip signifies returning to the place of his childhood, where the former vacationers, having reached retirement age, now seem to have settled for good. After initial skepticism about the unexpected visit, the elderly begin to recount their lives, focusing on spiritual and political topics, not omitting those of March 1968. The Holocaust is treated only marginally and from the narrator's point of view, in paratactic foreshortenings: "Between the pines they made them dig a ditch, a few meters long, corpse-wide. A dozen or so salvos, there was no need for more."[52] The dominance of a childlike point of view and the mixing of chronological and ontological levels give the narrative an oneiric character. Regarding the way to the boarding house, it reads, "to disappear into a hidden tunnel hollowed out in the sky and then begin running again on the other side, in a completely different and unknown world."[53] The narrator's motivation to reassure himself of his childhood visions is muted when he becomes aware of the irretrievability of the Jewish community. "Instead, a bitter taste of passing. And too many reminders of old age? Too many meds, coughs, and memories of those who are no longer here."[54] Additionally, the omission of the parents' generation throughout the whole story verbalizes the cultural and emotional rupture that has taken place. Instead of looking for possible means to overcome this gap, the book has a surprising ending: On his journey back, both the deceased Jews the older residents told stories about and the still living pensioners appear to the visitor in a clearing. The usually introverted and taciturn narrator cries out, "I am coming to you!"[55] and rushes back to the Jews, who are in the process of intoning the prayer for the dead. Later that night, however, he arrives at the train station, so the previous action turns out to be an imagined scenario. But will the restoration of the broken generational chain remain wishful thinking?

The author himself is rather skeptical of the rebirth of Jewish life in his country: "one must state it clearly: there will be no more Jews in Poland. They

---

[51] The author was the editor in chief of the Jewish culture monthly *Midrasz*, which was closed down in 2019. He published *Ptasie Ulice* (Birdy streets) in 2013, the plot of which is situated in the former Jewish district of Warsaw and which continues the search for Jewish remnants using characters from *The Boarding House*.

[52] Piotr Paziński, *The Boarding House* (Dublin: Dalkey Archive, 2018), 47–48.

[53] Paziński, *The Boarding House*, 1.

[54] Ibid., 64.

[55] Ibid., 117.

will still exist for some time, but there will be fewer and fewer of them."[56] Additional feuilletonistic remarks and sales-promoting references place the novel within the survivor narrative and therefore, seemingly provide an interpretive frame. Paziński is said to be the "first literary voice of the third generation in Poland after the Holocaust"[57] and his Czech translator states, "the narrator of The Boarding House describes ghosts, those who no longer exist - the last Polish Jews, among whom he should also be."[58]

Yet, in this boarding house, the narrator depicts an understanding of being Jewish in Poland that is increasingly a question of choice and, in addition to the personal dimension, touches upon the socio-political constructions. Taking a look at the spatial constructions of the auto-fictional novel, it is worth considering Gaston Bachelard's statements on the house – the topos to which the whole plot of *The Boarding House* is reduced: "For the house is our corner of the world. It is – it has often been said – our first universe."[59] The spatial constructions in the case of *The Boarding House* can be described as "fixations of happiness"[60] as the flashbacks to his childhood prove:

> But Mr. Abram wouldn't scare away so easily, he continued his story, and our garden, empty thus so far, would grow green, shooting up with colorful flower petals and serrated leaves of ferns; it was filling up with the juicy scent of grass and the thickening bitterness of juniper. And things I couldn't see before were appearing around us as if they were becoming visible only thanks to Mr. Abram's stories.[61]

In the course of the novel, contrasting spatial semantics become evident in the juxtaposition of the past and the present place. The reconstructed image of a peace-loving past is contrasted with the metaphor of the ark. "A tiny, dingy tabernacle in the desert, a place of rest during the journey. Our ark. Here, they were – we were – at home. And we will always be here."[62] The ambiguous character of the metaphor corresponds to the varying emotional load the narrator has to cope with: "the principle of Noah's Ark, because it is not the apocalypse, but also because it casts a pessimistic glance at the future,

---

[56] Piotr Paziński, "Przyszłość społeczności żydowskiej w krajach postkomunistycznej Europy i rola żydowskiej prasy," *Midrasz*, no. 12 (2005): 40.

[57] Justyna Sobolewska, "Taniec z cieniami," *Polityka*, no. 31 (2009): 40.

[58] Piotr Paziński, *Letní byt*, trans. Lucie Zakopalová (Praha: Havran, 2012), 117.

[59] Gaston Bachelard, *Poetik des Raumes* (Frankfurt am Main: Ullstein, 1975), 36.

[60] Bachelard, *Poetik des Raumes*, 37–38.

[61] Paziński, *The Boarding House*, 80.

[62] Ibid., 109.

stands in the middle between paradise and hell, between apocalypse and the principle of hope" as the literary scientist Joanna Jabłkowska emphasizes.[63]

Furthermore, the current state of the house and its localization are telling: Not only is the boarding house located on an almost forgotten railroad line, but the surrounding sanatoriums also seem to have lost their attractiveness and clientele over the years. Hence the house becomes a place whose future is uncertain but to be defended against being forgotten.

The Jewish residents of the guesthouse belong neither ontologically nor spatially to Polish society. At the same time, the Jewish community aims to preserve its microcosm. The boarding house thus holds the quality of a heterotopia, an identity bound to collective places of remembrance, whose access is not equally possible for everyone. I consider this to be a conscious act of demarcation. Yet, simultaneously, the narrator creates an image of a group-specific, consensual memory space that fluctuates between daydreaming and disillusionment. Overall, the Jews' place in Poland is claimed and defended by a group-specific solidarity. Constructive acts are, for example, the discussion of the pre-war period, or the holding on to the paraphernalia of those who have emigrated to Israel. As much as life in the boarding house seems to be outside time and not to belong to the reality of Polish life, the narrator tries hard to construct the boarding house as an emotional surrogate for living a Jewish life. Despite rejection from some of the elderly ("What are you still doing here? Stop snooping, go back to your place."[64]), the narrator seeks to close the emotional gap with the residents: "It's sad to be among old people, isn't it?' He didn't wait for my answer. [...] A few days, a few moments, and I stayed for my whole life. Indeed, it couldn't be any other way."[65]

The "German" Jew in Poland: Mikołaj Grynberg's Tumult (2018)

Mikołaj Grynberg's (1966) collection of short stories entitled *Tumult* deals with the issue of a Jew being exposed to public opinion.[66] The original title, *Rejwach*, derives from Yiddish, and its meaning (chaos, mess) stands emblematically for the narrator's experience of his own Jewishness: Hard to put into words, even harder to defy against an environment that questions the place of Jews in the country, the book is a collection of snapshots of Polish-

---

[63] Joanna Jabłkowska, *Literatur ohne Hoffnung: Die Krise der Utopie in der deutschen Gegenwartsliteratur* (Wiesbaden: Deutscher Universitätsverlag, 1993), 94.

[64] Paziński, *The Boarding House*, 106.

[65] Ibid., 112.

[66] Since 2012 Grynberg has published several works (often applying collage techniques) on Jewish life in contemporary Poland, e.g., *Oskarżam Auschwitz, Opowieści rodzinne* (Wolowiec: Wydawnictwo Czarne, 2021).

Jewish encounters in socialist and contemporary Poland. The autobiographical hints are omnipresent and often refer to the narrator's childhood. Unlike Paziński, *Tumult* emphasizes a painful past that the narrator's younger self experiences as a feeling of powerlessness, culminating in reluctant acceptance: Due to his last name, the narrator was labeled "the German" on a holiday camp for teenagers. "During my short life, I was already the Jew who killed Jesus, so I thought that it might be better to be a defeated German."[67]

Grynberg's narrator does not question his place in Poland, but at the same time, he never actively defends it as Tuszyńska's and Paziński's narrators do. He takes an observational position, detaching himself from the discussion,[68] as seen in the last sentence of *At Hitler's* (*U Hitlera*), when the narrator addresses himself in the second person: "this little boy with glasses who was frantically afraid of Hitler, was you."[69] This technique not only serves to make the stories less autobiographical and more inclusive or universal, but also bears witness to the author's ongoing struggle to reconcile the Polish and Jewish parts of his identity.

In *Arkadia*, the narrator describes Jewish tourists looking for traces of the Jewish ghetto. Guiding them to places of interest, he keeps a safe distance and smiles nicely "so they can feel safe. I am wondering what their parents and grandparents told them about us, the Poles."[70] Sometimes tourists draw attention to his friendliness that they – apparently – did not take for granted, as they state: "ju are a gud Pol"[71]. Spatiotemporal issues are addressed subtly: *Arkadia* is the popular Warsaw shopping mall that plays a main role in the grotesque novel *Night of the living Jews* (*Noc żywych Żydów*, 2012) by Igor Ostachowicz, in which Jewish zombies wander around the mall and literally try to find their place among the Poles who are going shopping. The location is next to the Jewish cemetery on Okopowa Street, to which Grynberg's narrator accompanies the foreign tourists. Therefore, the story is both about the omnipresence of Jewish traces of the past and an interference to a previous literary example. Meanwhile, the reasons why the narrator does not reveal his Jewish background may be varied: Firstly, a strong affirmation of his Jewishness at this point would have detached the narrator from the home

---

[67] Mikołaj Grynberg, *Rejwach* (Warszawa: Nisza, 2018), 44.
[68] Elisa-Maria Hiemer, "Tumult (Rejwach)," in *Handbook of Polish, Czech, and Slovak Holocaust Fiction: Works and Contexts*, ed. Elisa-Maria Hiemer, Jiří Holý, Agata Firlej, and Hana Nichtburgerová (Berlin: De Gruyter, 2021), https://doi.org/10.1515/978311 0671056-106, 432.
[69] Grynberg, *Rejwach*, 77.
[70] Ibid., 11.
[71] Ibid., 12.

country, which seems an equally important part of the way that he views his own identity. Secondly, since the foreigners' opinions of Poles seem negative, he – as a Jew – would automatically have to defend his choice to reside in his home country.

In some stories, the autobiographical aspect becomes even more obvious, as we can observe parallels with the author's own professional life: *The Common Good* (*Wspólne dobro*) is about a discussion with the audience after a public lecture. Like a stream of consciousness, the whole text is composed of short statements made by the audience as they express disapproval of the author's view on Polish-Jewish history.

> 'You have to know the limits, for God's sake! Do you want to convince the nation that Jews were Poles?' 'To whom do you owe your life? To the Poles after all. We put the lives of our families at risk to save you, you may recall it, Sir. And you just go on about the Poles being worse than the Germans. If you want to go on living here, you'll have to reconcile with the truth.' 'Well, who accepted you, when nobody else wanted you? Casimir the Great – Praise him for that.'[72]

Instead of arguing or framing the disturbing assertions, the narrator remains silent and absent. *Tumult* is thus a literary testimony to the current Polish opinion on Jews. At best, the people appear ignorant and oblivious to history. At worst, they choose to mock and attack the narrator. Despite this provocation, the narrator does not protest loudly, preferring to fight such verbal attacks with calmness and the power of his snapshots, which force the Poles into self-reflection.

BETWEEN IDYLLIZATION AND DISILLUSIONMENT. JEWISH LIFE IN POLAND IN THE TWENTY-FIRST CENTURY

In the examples I have examined, I have proposed an alternative way of reading the texts and have shown that Jewishness is no longer understood solely as a deprivation: In their works, the authors either consciously create spaces with positive connotations, which are indispensable to the formation of a self-confident Jewish identity or – as *Tumult* shows – give us a critical diagnosis of Polish society and Polish-Jewish relations. Given the impossibility of monolithic identities, it is surprising that all the works repeatedly refer to the dichotomy of Polish vs. Jewish. All the narrators clearly see their place in Poland, but while Tuszyńska attempts to overcome these boundaries, Paziński

---

[72] Ibid., 87–89. The latter statement refers to the fact that King Casimir allowed Jewish people to settle in Poland in the fourteenth century.

and Grynberg pursue a demarcation of the Jewish community. However, I would not consider this procedure to perpetuate binary identity structures, since it is done to strengthen the personal path to Jewishness (Paziński) or means of self-protection (Grynberg). Thus, the works do not clearly state what it means to be Jewish – nor do the Jewish respondents in Reszke's study. Every definition is the result of personal experience. Jewishness has to be understood as an individual identity feature that defies categorization.

All the books show how Jews are physically located on the periphery, which emphasizes their marginalized position in society.[73] In Paziński's book, the Jewish boarding house is located far away from the railway and is accessible only to members of its community. However, Tuszyńska tries to overcome this marginalization by, for example, placing a mezuzah at her house in Warsaw. Paziński's narrator chooses to cultivate this marginal position instead: He contrasts the harmonious image of childhood in the boarding house with the metaphor of the ark. The main feature of the boarding house is its protective value. Far away from the majority society, conflicts can be avoided if one can claim a place of one's own. Grynberg's manifold examples of anti-Jewish sentiments and antisemitism are "moving and frightening"[74] as the Polish Nobel Prize winner, Olga Tokarczuk, comments on the book. But the book's subtext reads: There have always been Jews in Poland, and there always will be. His example is thus an affirmation of the place that Jews have in the country.

The attempt to overcome the generational rupture caused by the de facto absence of Jewishness in Poland after 1968 unites all three books. However, this is also achieved by accentuating positive examples of family history and, in two cases (Tuszyńska, Paziński), by a nostalgic appropriation of the past. The often-contradictory actor-narrator relationship (i.e., the relationship between the narrative voice and the acting character, which is congruent here) refers to the conflictual process of positioning oneself as Jewish: *Family History of Fear* and *The Boarding House* pursue a strategy of idealization, while *Tumult* aims to present a realistic picture of contemporary Polish attitudes towards Jews. For this reason, the collage becomes a common strategy: By quoting "the other", the book aims at a panoramic view of Polish opinions.

None of the chosen works omit the Holocaust, but it is not the main concern anymore: They intend not only to draw attention to historical or contemporary conflicts, but also to shape a Jewish future in the country by acts of self-agency: This "renegotiation of the boundaries between periphery and

---

[73] Martin Kindermann, *Zuhause im Text: Raumkonstitution und Erinnerungskonstruktion im zeitgenössischen anglo-jüdischen Roman* (Berlin: Neofelis, 2014), 267.
[74] See back cover of the Polish original.

center"[75] that Tuszyńska pursues with her excursions into the surrounding countryside is symptomatic of the return of the Jewish life into the center of Polish memory. In this way, Tuszyńska is also conducting a social discourse against silence. In the case of *Boarding House*, one can speak of an imaginative counter-discourse to the Polish majority society. The need to belong is enormous (the narrative presence and power of the elderly speak for this). According to Neumann's classification of auto-narratives, Tuszyńska and Paziński's works are close to what she classifies as a communal memory novel: It is mainly about the reassurance of belonging to a collective identity and the stabilization of group-specific characteristics.[76] In both cases, the positive and negative references to the past consolidate a common Jewish memory and are part of a contemporary narrativization. In contrast, *Tumult* has the characteristics of a socio-biographic memory narrative that puts conflicts at the center of focus. The individual is pushed to the background, and the analysis of society's interactions with him prevails. Grynberg's text directly addresses the issue of victim rivalry, as described in the second chapter. Almost all the short stories show that Jews in Poland are confronted with the issue of victim rivalry, although the Jewish destinies differ widely from Polish opinions. *Tumult* is a literary response to the political "fight for Poland's good name", described earlier.

REFERENCES

Adamczyk-Garbowska Monika, and Magdalena Ruta. "Od kultury żydowskiej do kultury o Żydach." In *Następstwa zagłady Żydów: Polska 1944–2010*, edited by Felix Tych and Monika Adamczyk-Garbowska, 715–32. Lublin: Wydawnictwo UMCS, 2011.

Andersz, Katarzyna. "Żeby Polska była Polską [wywiad z Michałem Bilewiczem]." *Chidusz* 47, no. 2 (2018). https://chidusz.com/zeby-polska-byla-polska-michal-bilewicz-marzec-68/. (Accessed: January 15, 2020).

Archiwum Sejm Rzeczypospolitej Polskiej: *Interpelacja nr 5524 do ministra spraw zagranicznych w sprawie przeciwdziałania propagowaniu, jak również utrwalaniu na forum międzynarodowym fałszywych i szkodliwych dla polskiej racji stanu terminów: "polskie obozy koncentracyjne", "polskie obozy zagłady", "polskie obozy śmierci*, 01.06.2012, https://www.sejm.gov.pl/sejm7.nsf/InterpelacjaTresc.xsp?key=59F48D27, (Accessed: July 18, 2022).

Artwińska, Anna, and Anja Tippner. "Postkatastrophische Vergegenwärtigungen – eine Positionsbestimmung." In *Nach dem Holocaust: Medien postkatastrophischer Vergegenwärtigungen in Polen und Deutschland*, edited by Anna Artwińska and Anja Tippner, 15–35. Frankfurt: Peter Lang, 2017.

---

[75] Birgit Neumann, *Erinnerung, Identität, Nation: Gattungstypologie und Funktionen kanadischer "Fictions of Memory"* (Berlin, New York: De Gruyter, 2005), 237.
[76] Neumann, *Erinnerung, Identität, Narration*, 237.

Bachelard, Gaston. *Poetik des Raumes.* Frankfurt am Main: Ullstein, 1975.

Bachelard, Gaston. *La poétique de l'espace.* Paris: Les Presses universitaires de France, 1961.

Budzik, Jagoda. "Topos Polski jako żydowskiego cmentarza w hebrajskiej literaturze trzeciego pokolenia." *Narracje o Zagładzie,* no. 2 (2016): 88–100.

Budzik, Jagoda. *Work in progress: konfrontacje trzeciego pokolenia po Zagładzie.* Nowy Sącz: Wydawnictwo Pasaże, 2018.

Chmielewska, Katarzyna. "Der polnische Zeuge: Traumabildung, Symmentrien und feindliche Übernahme des (jüdischen) Traumas." In *Nach dem Holocaust: Medien postkatastrophischer Vergegenwärtigungen in Polen und Deutschland,* edited by Anna Artwińska and Anja Tippner, 131–47. Frankfurt: Peter Lang, 2017.

Czermińska, Małgorzata. *Autobiograficzny trójkąt: Świadectwo, wyznanie, wyzwanie.* Kraków: Universitas, 2000.

Czyżewski, Andrzej. "The Myths of March '68: Negotiating Memory in Contemporary Poland." In *Unsettled 1968: Origins – Myth – Impact,* edited by Aleksandra Konarzewska, Anna Nakai and Michał Przeperski, 163–87. New York, London: Routledge, 2020.

Datner, Helena. "Współczesna społeczność żydowska w Polsce a Zagłada." In *Następstwa zagłady Żydów: Polska 1944–2010,* edited by Feliks Tych and Monika Adamczyk-Grubowska, 661–85. Lublin: Wydawnictwo UMCS, 2012.

Gebert, Konstanty, and Helena Datner. *Życie żydowskie w Polsce: Osiągnięcia, wyzwania i priorytety od upadku komunizmu.* 2011. http://www.jpr.org.uk/documents/Jewish%20life%20in%20Poland%20(Polish).pdf, (Accessed: October 11, 2021).

Główny Urząd Statystyczny. *Mały rocznik statystyczny Rzeczypospolitej Polskiej 2021.* Warszawa: Zakład Wydawnictw Statystycznych, 2021. https://stat.gov.pl/obszary-tematyczne/roczniki-statystyczne/roczniki-statystyczne/maly-rocznik-statystyczny-polski-2021,1,23.html. (Accessed: October 22, 2021).

Gross, Jan Tomasz. *Sąsiedzi.* Sejny: Pogranicze, 2000.

Gross, Jan Tomasz. *Strach.* Kraków: Znak, 2008.

Gross, Jan Tomasz. *Złote Żniwa.* Kraków: Znak, 2011.

Gruber, Ruth Ellen. *Jewish Heritage Travel: A Guide through Eastern Europe.* New York: Wiley cop., 1992.

Gruber, Ruth Ellen. *Upon the Doorposts of Thy House: Jewish Life in East-Central Europe, Yesterday and Today.* New York: Wiley cop., 1994.

Grynberg, Mikołaj. *Oskarżam Auschwitz, Opowieści rodzinne.* Wołowiec: Wydawnictwo Czarne, 2014.

Grynberg, Mikołaj. *Rejwach.* Warszawa: Nisza, 2018.

Hahn, Hans Joachim. "'Europa' als neuer 'jüdischer Raum': Diana Pintos Thesen und Vladimir Vertlibs Romane." In *Von der nationalen zur internationalen Literatur: Transkulturelle deutschsprachige Literatur und Kultur im Zeitalter globaler Migration,* edited by Helmut Schmitz, 295–310. Amsterdam: Rodopi, 2009.

Hallet, Wolfgang, and Birgit Neumann. "Raum und Bewegung in der Literatur: Zur Einführung." In *Raum und Bewegung in der Literatur: Die Literaturwissenschaften und der Spatial Turn*, edited by Wolfgang Hallet, 11–32. Bielefeld: transcript, 2009.

Hiemer, Elisa-Maria. *Autobiographisches Schreiben als ästhetisches Problem: Jüdische Vielfalt in der polnischen und deutschen Gegenwartsliteratur.* Wiesbaden: Harrassowitz, 2019.

Hiemer, Elisa-Maria. "Tumult (Rejwach)." In *Handbook of Polish, Czech, and Slovak Holocaust Fiction: Works and Contexts*, edited by Elisa-Maria Hiemer, Jiří Holý, Agata Firlej, and Hana Nichtburgerová, 430–33. Berlin: De Gruyter, 2021. https://doi.org/10.1515/9783110671056-106 (Accessed: October 19, 2021).

Hiemer, Elisa-Maria, Jiří Holý, Agata Firlej, and Hana Nichtburgerová. "Introduction." In *Handbook of Polish, Czech, and Slovak Holocaust Literature: Works and Contexts*, edited by Elisa-Maria Hiemer, Jiří Holý, Agata Firlej, and Hana Nichtburgerová, 1–17. Berlin: De Gruyter, 2021. https://doi.org/10. 1515/9783110671056-106 (Accessed: May 20, 2022).

Jabłkowska, Joanna. *Literatur ohne Hoffnung: Die Krise der Utopie in der deutschen Gegenwartsliteratur.* Wiesbaden: Deutscher Universitätsverlag, 1993.

Kindermann, Martin. *Zuhause im Text: Raumkonstitution und Erinnerungs-konstruktion im zeitgenössischen anglo-jüdischen Roman.* Berlin: Neofelis, 2014.

Kochan, Marek. "Zbudujmy szybko Muzeum Polokaustu." *Rzeczpospolita*, February 19, 2018. https://www.rp.pl/opinie-polityczno-spoleczne/art21097 21-marek-kochan-zbudujmy-szybko-muzeum-polokaustu (Accessed July 25, 2022).

Koźmińska-Frejlak, Ewa. "Nie można być Żydem samotnie: Z Helise Lieberman rozmawia Ewa Koźmińska-Frejlak." *Midrasz*, no. 10 (2006): 13–16.

Lambert, Nick. *Jews and Europe in the Twenty-First Century: Thinking Jewish.* London, Portland: Routledge, 2008.

Lau, Jörg. "Was heißt hier jüdisch?" *Die Zeit*, January 5, 2000: 99.

Lehrer, Erica, and Michael Meng. *Jewish space in contemporary Poland.* Bloomington, Indiana: University Press, 2015.

Liszka, Katarzyna. "Articles 55a and 55b of the IPN Act and the Dialogue about the Holocaust in Poland. "*Archiwum filozofii prawa i filozofii społecznej* 21, no. 3 (2019): 82–84. https://doi.org/10.36280/AFPiFS.2019.3.81 (Accessed July 21, 2022).

Marszałek, Magdalena. "Von jüdischen Müttern: Geheimnistropen in der polnisch-jüdischen autobiographischen Gegenwartsliteratur." In *Osteuropäisch-jüdische Literaturen im 20. und 21. Jahrhundert. Identität und Poetik = Eastern European Jewish Literature of the 20th and 21st Centuries*, edited by Klavdia Smola, 271–80. München: Otto Sagner, 2013.

Neumann, Birgit. *Erinnerung, Identität, Nation: Gattungstypologie und Funktionen kanadischer "Fictions of Memory."* Berlin, New York: De Gruyter, 2005.

Paziński, Piotr. "Przyszłość społeczności żydowskiej w krajach postkomunistycznej Europy i rola żydowskiej prasy." *Midrasz*, no. 12 (2005): 40.

Paziński, Piotr. *Pensjonat.* Warszawa: Nisza, 2009.

Paziński, Piotr, *Letní byt*. Translated by Lucie Zakopalová. Praha: Havran, 2012.

Paziński, Piotr. *Ptasie ulice*. Warszawa: Nisza, 2013.

Paziński, Piotr. *The Boarding House*. Dublin: Dalkey Archive, 2018.

Pinto, Diana. "A new Jewish identity for post 1989 Europe." Institute for Jewish Policy Research. February 6, 1996. https://archive.jpr.org.uk/object-eur44 (Accessed: October 19, 2021).

"President on Barack Obama's letter", June 1, 2012. https://www.president.pl/president-komorowski/news/president-on-barack-obamas-letter,38594 (Accessed July 22, 2022).

Reszke, Katka. *Return of the Jew: Identity Narratives of the Third Post-Holocaust Generation of Jews in Poland*. Boston: Academic Studies Press, 2013.

Ronen, Shoshana. "Jak w Polsce być Żydem?" *Gazeta Wyborcza*, September 8, 1999, 18.

Roth, Markus, and Sascha Feuchert. "Einleitung." In *Holocaust Zeugnis Literatur: 20 Werke wieder gelesen*, edited by Markus Roth and Sascha Feuchert, 7–29. Göttingen: Wallstein Verlag, 2018.

Shore, Marci. *The taste of ashes: the afterlife of totalitarianism in Eastern Europe*. London: Windmill Books, 2014.

Sobolewska, Justyna. "Taniec z cieniami." *Polityka*, no. 31 (2009): 40.

Suchojad, Izabela. *Topografia żydowskiej pamięci: Obraz krakowskiego Kazimierza we współczesnej litera-turze polskiej i polsko-żydowskiej*. Kraków: Universitas, 2010.

Tuszyńska, Agata. *Rodzinna historia lęku*. Warszawa: Wydawnictwo literackie, 2005.

Tuszyńska, Agata. *Oskarżona Wiera Gran*. Kraków: Wydawnictwo Literackie, 2011.

Tuszyńska, Agata. *Family History of Fear: A Memoir*. New York: Anchor Books, 2017.

Webber, Jonathan. "Modern Jewish Identities." In *Making Holocaust Memory*, edited by Gabriel N. Finder, Natalia Aleksiun, Antony Polonsky, and Jan Schwarz, 74–85. Oxford: Littman, 2008.

Wróbel, Józef. "Z prześladowanymi w późnym, nieprzemilczanym promienistym związku. Drugie pokolenie po Holokauście." *Ruch Literacki* 57, no. 3 (2016): 343–59.

Żórawska, Natalia. *Dziedzictwo (nie)pamięci: Holocaustowe doświadczenia pisarek drugiego pokolenia*. Katowice: Wydawnictwo UŚ, 2018.

PART III.
PRESERVING IDENTITY

Chapter 7

The Literary Representability of the Shoah in the Novel *Gec i Majer* from David Albahari: Language between Documentation and Imagination

Philine Bickhardt

University of Zurich, Switzerland

Abstract: This paper examines the role of the relationship between documentation and imagination as a mode of thematizing the inexpressibility ("unsayable") of the Shoah in the novel *Gec i Majer* (1998) by the Serbo-Canadian author of Jewish origin David Albahari (*1948). As one of the first novels about the extermination of Jews in South-Eastern Europe written in 1990s, it focuses on *Staro Sajmište*, the former central concentration camp in the Western Balkans' largest city, Belgrade. Incorporating theoretical theses about the witnesses (Hannah Arendt, Theodor Adorno, Georgio Agamben) and comparing them with the first-person narrator of the novel, this study demonstrates that difficulties of remembering are shown with the help of numerous stylistic elements and breaks in narrative structures. Thereby, the "gaps" in memory and the lack of knowledge about everyday life in the camp determine the literary representation of the Holocaust

Keywords: Jewish history, Holocaust literature, Serbo-Canadian author, unsayable, concentration camp

***

In the field of Shoah[1] literature from South-Eastern Europe of the 1990s, the short novel *Gec i Majer* (1998) has a unique characteristic in two respects: It is David Albahari's only novel about the extermination of the Yugoslavian Jews in Serbia and the only novel ever about the concentration camp *Staro Sajmište*.[2] As is typical for many novels by the Serbo-Canadian writer of Jewish origin David Albahari (*1948), an autodiegetic first-person narrator tells in *Gec i Majer*, who teaches Serbo-Croatian in Belgrade in the 1990s and at the same time opens up a second level of action by researching and analyzing sources in archives, the search for the fate of his Jewish ancestors, i.e., the 'daily routines' of the Belgrade Jews in the concentration camp *Staro Sajmište*.

When it comes to witnessing and remembering in general, the survivors of the Shoah and the posterity (descendants) are faced with the task of *saying the unsayable*[3] ("unsagbar")[4] – as Theodor W. Adorno and Hannah Arendt call it in relation to the Shoah, although with different connotations. This term and the well-known dictum from Adorno, paradigmatic for the discourse of the inexpressibility, comes from one of the first post-war texts of Adorno *Cultural Criticism and Society* (*Kulturkritik und Gesellschaft*, 1951): "Writing a poem after Auschwitz is barbaric."[5] Also, the philosopher Giorgio Agamben[6] speaks about the "unsayable," both related to the testimony and the limitations of language. His thesis in *What remains of Auschwitz. The archive and the*

---

[1] The word "Holocaust" (in Greek: *holókaustos*, meaning: completely burned) is attempted to be dispensed with in this work, as it is increasingly criticized due to its original meaning as a "fire victim." Instead of this term, the word "Shoah" (Hebrew: catastrophe) is used in this work. Peter Schäfer, *Kurze Geschichte des Antisemitismus* (München: C.H. Beck, 2020), 251–52.

[2] Elena Messner, "David Albaharis Belgradroman *Gec i Majer [Götz und Meyer]*," *Yearbook for European Jewish Literature Studies* 2, 1 (2015): 293–311, https://www.degruyter.com/document/doi/10.1515/yejls-2015-0018/html.

[3] Theodor W. Adorno, "Cultural Critcism and Society," in Theodor W. Adorno, *Prisms*, trans. Samuel and Shierry Weber, ed. Thomas McCarty (n.d.: n.d., 1997), 34, https://moodle.ufsc.br/pluginfile.php/1407246/mod_resource/content/1/Theodor%20W.%20Adorno%20Prisms%20%28Studies%20in%20Contemporary%20German%20Social%20Thought%29.pdf.

The official English translation of Adornos "unsagbar" (ibid., 46) is "unutterable" (ibid., 17). I am using in this work "unsayable" because it is closer to the original. Moreover, Agamben also uses the term of "unsayable": "But why unsayable? Why confer on extermination the prestige of the mystical?," Giorgio Agamben, *What remains of Auschwitz. The archive and the witness* (New York: Zone Books, 1999), 32.

[4] Theodor W. Adorno, *Gesellschaftstheorie und Kulturkritik* (Frankfurt am Main: Suhrkamp Verlag, 1975), 46.

[5] Adorno, "Cultural Criticism and Society," 34.

[6] Agamben, *What remains of Auschwitz*.

witness (*Quel che resta di Auschwitz*, 1999) on the paradox of witnessing, the surviving witnesses bear testimony. There is no testimony anywhere because the actual witnesses did not survive. His thesis is still crucial for the discourse and serves in this work as an approach. There have been very productive insights on the question of Shoah representation in *Gec i Majer*: Masha Volynsky[7], which uses the term "lacuna" (or gap) from Agmaben to analyze the "language within the battle between History and Memory;" Elena Messner[8] focuses on the literary representation of the Shoah in the novel. Stijn Vervaet[9] makes – while analyzing *Baits* and *Gec i Majer* – an emphasis on intergenerational transmission of trauma, using the "Postmemory"-theory of Marianne Hirsch for analyzing the first-person narrator as a member of the second-generation. I follow these approaches insofar as I see the difficulties of witnessing for the first generation, the family trauma for the second generation and generally the representation of Shoah implemented in the imaginations of the first-person narrator. Contrary to the mentioned approaches, I want to focus primarily on the possibilities and limitations of language. Rather than analyzing conditions and ways of remembering represented in the text, I am interested in the first-person narrators' imaginations – in contrast to the documentary function of the text. At the same time, the first-person narrator is the main character (autodiegetic) and the mastermind of the events and fantasies described. I see the above-described character of the inexpressibility (German: *unsagbar*) of Shoah literature processed in the first-person narrator's attempt to fill the gaps in history and witness with imaginations. Through the play of documentation and imagination, *Gec i Majer* gives the gap between the facticity of history and the (im)possibility of speaking and writing about it a literary form.

IMAGINATION AS A 'GAPFILLER': SPLITS

According to statistics from "Der Spiegel" from March 2011,[10] Yugoslavia recorded the highest percentage of the Jewish population murdered in the Holocaust in European countries between 1933 and 1945, with 95%, far ahead

---

[7] Masha Volnynsky, "Language within the Battle between History and Memory in David Albahari's Götz and Meyer," *Serbian Studies: Journal of the North American Society for Serbian Studies* 23, no. 1 (2009): 157–66, https://muse.jhu.edu/journal/405.

[8] Messner, "David Albaharis Belgradroman *Gec i Majer [Götz und Meyer].*"

[9] Stijn Vervaet, *Holocaust, War and Transnational Memory: Testimony from Yugoslav and Post-Yugoslav Literature* (n.d.: Routledge, 2019).

[10] "Anteil der im Holocaust ermordeten jüdischen Bevölkerung in europäischen Ländern in den Jahren 1933 bis 1945," Spiegel, March 2011, https://de.statista.com/statistik/daten/studie/182345/umfrage/anteil-der-im-holocaust-ermordeten-juedische n-bevoelkerung/#professional.

of Poland with 80% and the Soviet Union (excluding the Baltic States) with 70%. Concretely speaking for the Belgrade Jews, Jewish men of Belgrade were executed in the autumn and winter of 1941. After this, the organization "Death" (German: "Tot"), under the direction of the Gestapo, installed the concentration camp "Judenlager Zemun," nowadays known as *Staro Sajmište*, on the former Belgrade fair (Serbian: *beogradski sajam*) on the left bank of the Sava. In the first phase of the camp's existence, from December 8, 1941, to May 10, 1942, sixty-four hundred Jews (mostly mothers and children) and around six hundred Roma were imprisoned. After Hitler-Germany decided on the "Final Solution to the Jewish Question" (German: Endlösung der Judenfrage) at the Wannsee Conference on January 20, 1942, it was resolved to liquidate all Jews who remained in Serbia. The approximately fifty-five hundred Jewish women and children who had survived to that day[11] were systematically killed in spring 1942 within six weeks by SS officers Wilhelm Götz and Erwin Meyer in trucks of the Saurer brand due to carbon monoxide from the exhaust pipe in the interior of the car.[12] These trucks, known as "soul killers" (Serbian: *dušegupka*), were used in the former Yugoslav regions and the territories of Poland and the Soviet Union. These two SS officers are the eponymous characters for the novel *Gec i Majer* by David Albahari.

The discourse of inexpressibility difficulties of remembering is shown through numerous stylistic elements and breaks in the narrative structures. The mutually overlapping levels of time and action compete; countless repetitions do not impair the reading flow, even if they sometimes cause fatigue. On the one hand, the first-person narrator tries to get closer to the perpetrators from 1941/42 through research and imagination and puts the readers in the everyday life of the camp. On the other hand, he worked as a Serbo-Croatian teacher at school in the 1990s – with the class, he tried out various 'visualization strategies' of the past. The relationship of the first-person narrator to the eponymous perpetrator figures, "Gec" and "Majer," is contradictory. A re-enactment game (imitating the gassing of the school class in the school bus) that concludes the novel seems gruesome and absurd. The implied suicide of the main protagonist at the end of the novel suggests the danger of going insane about the past and allows ambiguity.

---

[11] Rena Rädle and Milovan Pisarri, *Mesta stradanja i antifašističke borbe u Beogradu 1941–1944. Priručnik za čitanje grada* (Beograd: Forum za primenjenu istoriji, 2013), 185.

[12] Jovan Bajford, *Staro Sajmište: Mesto sećanja, zaborava i sporenja* (Beograd: Beogradski centar za ljudska prava, 2011), 11.

The novel claims to be "David Albahari's most pronounced historiographical metafiction"[13] in its opening sentences. Phantasy and imagination make it possible to reconstruct the fate of the relatives of the first-person narrator:

Götz and Meyer. Having never seen them, I can only imagine them.[14]

The eponymous perpetrator characters *Gec i Majer* are undoubtedly not just a product of his imagination because the narrator speaks of their acquaintance through dealing with documents from archives and museums in the "now time," the 1990s ("That is how Götz and Meyer came in my life.")[15] Apart from the information on their length of stay, the narrator knows nothing about the perpetrators, let alone their personality traits. At this point, the "imagination"[16] gets to work, which compensates for the lack of the "immediate impressions"[17] that history[18] cannot provide. The first-person narrator repeatedly raises the problem that this does not always work when he delves into conjectures, assumptions, and speculations. Contradicting statements and uncertainties open up fields of interpretation that lead to confusion (e.g., "Quite by chance, though maybe not, Untersturmführer Andorfer, before he dedicated himself professionally to the SS, worked as a business manager of a hotel."[19]). These are integrated into the text and are understood as metafictional references as the commenting, self-questioning narrator's voice.

A clever move is the "apparently logical argumentation [by] converting assumptions into facts"[20]: "Maybe he smokes. He probably smokes. Everyone

---

[13] Eva Kowollik, *Geschichte und Narration: Fiktionalisierungsstrategien bei Radoslav Petković, David Albahari und Dragan Velikić* (Berlin: LIT Verlag, 2013), 129.

[14] David Albahari, *Götz and Meyer*, trans. Ellen Elias-Bursać (Florida: Harcourt, 2004), 1.

[15] Albahari, *Götz and Meyer*, 15. In the documentary film of "My father was a murderer," the two SS officers Wilhelm Goetz and Erwin Meyer are named, who arrive in Belgrade in the "Saurer" gassing car in the first half of March 1941, "'Mein Vater war ein Mörder': Tochter des Gestapo-Chefs von Belgrad über Verbrechen ihres Vaters", Rosa Luxemburg Stiftung, accessed November 10, 2021, https://www.rosalux.de/news/id/5376/mein-vater-war-ein-moerder.

[16] Kowollik, *Geschichte und Narration*, 139.

[17] Ibid., 139.

[18] Quotes on history in Albahari, *Götz and Meyer*, 34: "History was, after all, impersonal, at least as a discipline, it couldn't exist at the level of the individual, because then it would be impossible to grasp." Ibid., 35: "History has no time for feelings, even less for trauma and pain, and least of all for dull helplessness [in the serbian original it is "speechlessness"], for the inability to grasp what is happening."

[19] Ibid., 19.

[20] Kowollik, *Geschichte und Narration*, 139.

smoked back then. As far as that is concerned, the world hasn't changed."[21] In other places, however, the narrator gives his assumptions as facts:

> I never saw Götz or Meyer, so I can only imagine them, but somehow I feel certain that Götz, or Meyer, had a poodle, a small fluffy thing called Lily.[22]

The unreliable but archival first-person narrator is particularly focused on the perpetrators[23], as the introductory text passage and the multiple names of the perpetrators show. Despite the narrator, who claims to be unreliable, the text fulfills a "factographic-documentary function" by "documenting what happened [...] as a precisely created archive that is infinitely networked with itself."[24]

"[The narrator] finds himself in a vacuum constituted by a lack of individual memories and collective repression."[25] With the help of imagination, including dreams and hallucinations, what one does not know is thought up.[26] Eva Kowollik speaks of "gaps" which, lexically and semantically,[27] are reminiscent of an unbridgeable gap between the past and the present attempt at reconstruction, according to Giorgio Agamben: "Testimony, however, contains a lacuna. The survivors agree about this."[28] "Yet here the value of testimony lies essentially in what it lacks; at its center, it contains something that cannot be borne witness to"[29] because they did not have to suffer death themselves. "[T]hey bear witness to a missing testimony."[30] The survivors of the Shoah perceived "their [mostly coincidental] survival as a mistake."[31] It is also described as a *"split of the self"*[32] into "the dead self" as a contradiction to the "living self."[33] This original split of the victim between the "dead me" and

---

[21] Albahari, *Götz and Meyer*, 11.

[22] Ibid., 38.

[23] Cf. Kowollik, *Geschichte und Narration*, 134.

[24] Messner, "David Albaharis Belgradroman *Gec i Majer [Götz und Meyer]*," 297–98.

[25] Kowollik, *Geschichte und Narration*, 136.

[26] Cf. Messner, "David Albaharis Belgradroman *Gec i Majer [Götz und Meyer]*," 300. Kowollik, *Geschichte und Narration*, 138.

[27] In the official german translation of Agamben is used the word "Lücke," which also uses Eva Kowollik. In the official english translation is used "lacuna," which is semantically tantamount to gap. I use "gap" because it stresses the distance and disconnection between two things (for example like a gulf between mountains).

[28] Agamben, *What remains of Auschwitz*, 33.

[29] Ibid., 34.

[30] Ibid., 34.

[31] Kowollik, *Geschichte und Narration*, 143.

[32] Ibid., 141.

[33] Ibid., 143.

the "living me" is evident[34] in the relationship between the readership and the first-person narrator in *Gec i Majer*, who, contrary to surviving victims, was not himself in the camp and who is literarily reshaped as a fictional character. The first-person narrator tries to provide 'proxy testimony' to the cruel crimes committed against his ancestors (because both the author and the first-person narrator are identified as Jewish). The stylistic means and the form (repetition, storytelling from the perpetrator's perspective, cold reporting and leaving out feelings on the victims' side) translate the problem into literary terms. The 'pretended' information is marked as such through the (sometimes obvious) imaginations, such as assumptions, ascriptions, and speculations; as made-up imaginations, which are no longer accessible due to the *separation* of the posterity from the original experience, i.e., the first-person narrator in the 1990s and today's readers.

In addition, one can speak of the narrator's "ego split" due to the simultaneous "identification" with the Jewish, deceased ancestors and the perpetrators, Gec and Majer. It is noticeable that the first-person narrator empathizes with the victims through imaginations (e.g., in day and night dreams). However, this only happens in a descriptive retelling. In the first-person narrator speech, the perpetrator figures are created directly from fiction. In contrast, only those things, which are provable, are mentioned about the descendants. The first-person narrator tries in vain to control all the facts and 'voices' of the victims and perpetrators. The indicated suicide of the first-person narrator at the end of the novel can be interpreted as a way out of the psychological unbearable-ness bordering on delusion and as the failure of the confrontation with the murder of the descendants:

> My life *split* in an orderly and painless fashion into three parallel lives. [...] My second life was one of constant transformations: in that life, staring at the family tree, which; like some sort of masterpiece, I had framed and hung on the wall, I would become, by turns, one of my vanished cousins: sometimes a woman, sometimes a little girl or boy, or perhaps an old man resting his hand on a prayer book, a merchant's assistant among this bolts of cloth, a baker or a pharmacist. The third life had two heads: I was at once both Götz and Meyer, the angel of death and the driver, a soldier and a simple man, the pretend savior and the real executioner. In such confusion, it is not difficult to imagine that there were moments when I did not know who I was. I would pour myself a glass of water, drink it as Götz, or Meyer, but my throat would still feel parched like little Estera's when the door

---

34 Ibid., 143.

slammed at the back of the Saurer. In the evening, I'd get into bed as my father's brother, and I'd be assaulted by dreams of a village in the Austrian Alps. There were countless such examples, which does not mean, I hope no one will think this, that I was a nutcase.[35]

The two storylines create a further *split* in the narrative structures of the novel: the 50-year-old first-person narrator is a Serbo-Croatian teacher; a teacher of a language that will no longer exist in this form after the fall of Yugoslavia. The extermination in the concentration camps in the 1940s and the wars of disintegration still to come in the 1990s reflect two identities, the Jewish and the Yugoslav. Against the background of the questioned Yugoslav identity, the search was on for other impulses to create identification. The first-person narrator defines and explores his Jewish origins as a 'new' affiliation. In this sense, the first-person narrator embodies a Yugoslav society looking for identity under the auspices of disintegration:

The Yugoslav identity, which had been questioned by politicians since the 1960s, has now been displaced and replaced by an ethno-national identity under the pressure of political polarization, even among the majority of the population. For many, this has been a painful process. Particularly affected were the "Yugoslavs," who lost their object of identification and came under enormous pressure to make decisions, as well all those population groups who, in addition to a national or religious affiliation, had also a pronounced Yugoslav identity, including the approximately 9,000 Jews [...].[36]

IRONY AND REPETITION: THE PERPETRATORS "GEC" AND "MAJER"

The narrator suspects that the two perpetrators were possibly married, smoked a cigarette here and there,[37] perhaps had an ailing daughter at home and must have given the children sweets in the camp.[38] All these assumptions give an idea of a picture, but do not give any concrete coordinates of the figures; they are "de-personalized templates."[39] "Facelessness and essencelessness"[40] make

---

[35] Albahari, *Götz and Meyer*, 45–46.

[36] Sundhausen quoted from Kowollik, *Geschichte und Narration*, 137.

[37] Albahari, *Götz and Meyer*, 11: "While the other fellow was in the camp, he was sitting to administrative work or sitting in the truck with his foot on the accelevator, waiting. Maybe he smoked."

[38] Ibid., 10: "The children, for instance, trusted Götz, or was it Meyer, when he strode briskly Into the Camp, warmed by the spring sun, picked them up and gave them candy."

[39] Messner, "David Albaharis Belgradroman *Gec i Majer [Götz und Meyer]*," 298.

[40] Ibid., 298.

them interchangeable, duplicable and multipliable, arbitrary; as faceless phantoms, they can still be terrifying since they are not fully exposed. Besides the 'additional poetry' of human and everyday habits, the first-person narrator adopts the perpetrator's perspective in several moments: "[O]utside history remains the impact of the fact that in all those documents the words *Jew* and *Gypsy* were written 'jew' and 'gypsy,' in lowercase. Inferior people cannot command superior letters."[41] This ironic imitation of a statement that could seriously have come from a staunch SS officer implies the opposite statement to the explicit: people are neither inferior nor should be shaken by the general writing convention of names for people and peoples. In contrast to moral value quotes, irony evokes a distance and aversion desired by the first-person narrator.

The first-person narrator does not ascribe the details to either one or the other but emphasizes that one of them (which one he does not know) has them. It is not two concrete perpetrator characters that are presented, but one type is created; it looks like a profile of a criminal who is wanted by the police. Linguistically, this is implemented in numerous repetitions (a total of 274)[42] and various name combinations, the latter mostly being "Götz and Meyer" and "Götz, or Meyer"; rarer forms are: "Götz, or was it Meyer,"[43] "Götz, although it might have been Meyer,"[44] "Götz, or maybe Meyer,"[45] "Götz was better at, though it may have been Meyer."[46]

When it comes to repetition as an aesthetic principle, there is no "indistinguishability," but on the contrary: every duplication contains an "otherness." A change in space and time alone gives rise to a difference to the first mentioned, so that in each repetition, not only what is repeated is said, but also the "difference" between the two things. The repetition happens in the deviation ("Even the contrary presupposes the already once.").[47] In the case of Götz and Meyer and the many name combinations with each new variant of the naming, their profile or character is enriched. Here the repetition becomes variation: the eventualities, i.e., possible activities and thoughts of these two characters (and original real persons), have a successive effect on the text as the narrative progresses; however, there is also a weariness of this writing style, because with each new mention, nothing more

---

[41] Albahari, *Götz and Meyer*, 36.
[42] Spread over the whole novel, I counted 274 mentions of Götz and Meyer.
[43] Albahari, *Götz and Meyer*, 25.
[44] Ibid., 32.
[45] Ibid., 47.
[46] Ibid., 64.
[47] Cf. Peter Pütz, *Wiederholung als ästhetisches Prinzip* (Bielefeld: Aisthesis Verlag, 2004), 8.

seems to be said, but only suggested; "Continuity and polarity"[48] are dependent on each other, because each mentioning of the figures again proclaims the factuality of their existence, but at the same time the assumptions presented as information in the naming make them unsettling. The repetitions that testify to the existence of the perpetrators (the names Götz and Meyer) are contrary to the arbitrariness caused by speculation, suggestion and assumption ("Meyer, unless it was Götz").[49] The game of factuality and arbitrariness creates fatigue, uncertainty and irritation and literally *gets on your nerves.*

In addition, Peter Pütz sees the representation of "general" and "particular" as a possibility of articulating repetition in the "large" and "small," which is generally known in Aristotle's *Poetic* in the difference between poetry (fiction) and historians (fact writers): "He leaves the special to the historian, who communicates what really happened in its uniqueness; however, he reserves the general for the poet, who does not represent the singular, but the general, what is possible according to the 'rules of probability or necessity.'"[50] These two principles are indirectly represented at Albahari in the form of the interplay of documentation and imagination. In the primary text itself, the skepticism towards the historiography is addressed several times: it is "impersonal," it cannot be understood on the level of the "individual [...]"[51] and has no answer to the "dull helplessness [in the Serbian original it is "speechlessness"], for the inability to grasp what is happening."[52] The speechlessness described here refers to the discourse of "unsayable" (see above Adorno and Agamben). While the elaborately researched historical facts describe the 'special' or the certain concrete case and the first-person narrator has a skepticism towards the histography, the use of phantasy and imagination ("poetry" from Aristoteles) is the "glue" that fills the gap.

In the case of *Gec i Majer*, the numerous repetitions not only contain the implementation of a representation on a secondary, literary level, but also the prohibition of representation ("unsagbar") is suggested, which refers to the discourse of the Shoah that cannot be represented, as the "pathos formula of every catastrophe"[53] per se. It eludes to the conventional aesthetic of representation – by simultaneously conveying truthful statements

---

[48] Ibid., 21.

[49] Albahari, *Götz and Meyer*, 23.

[50] Cf. Pütz, *Wiederholung als ästhetisches Prinzip*, 10.

[51] Albahari, *Götz and Meyer*, 34.

[52] Ibid., 35.

[53] Sigrid Weigel, "Zeugnis und Zeugenschaft, Klage und Anklage," in *Zeugnis und Zeugenschaft*, ed. Rüdiger Zill (Berlin: Akademie Verlag, 1999), 114.

(documentation) and invented, implied eventualities (imagination) and by constantly addressing this problem in the narrator's voice. In *Gec i Majer,* the used documentary notation suggests a certain "pact" with a robustness of the information mentioned and is sometimes also redeemed (e.g., with regards to data, information on processes, trucks of the "Saurer" brand, food rations etc.), although this pact is subverted again and again by fiction.

The re-presentation, in general, aims to bring back what happened originally, i.e., a described and linguistically implemented "re-petition" by Marszałek and Mersch, "to bring to mind and 'truthfully' replicate" the "not-present, whether it is something that has passed in time or something that is spatially absent."[54] Therefore, it assumes that reality can be objectified and that it is faithfully reproduced, although there is no doubt that the perception of reality (even before it is represented) is preceded by visions, ideas, systems – in short: perceptual dispositives – and can only be conveyed through a medium.[55] In contrast to this "old" concept of realism, which was based on the fact that the real can be represented, newer approaches assume a "literary realism as a spelling (écriture), a stylistic process [...] that only uses the real staged as an *effect.*"[56] The goal was no longer a naive portrayal, but rather the insight "that 'reality' arises from the effect."[57] It is about art that does not want to depict, but rather makes an experience real in the aesthetic experience (film, theater, literature). For performative art (e.g., Milo Rau in the theater), the following applies: The documentary – in the sense of documents such as archive material, photos, film recordings, reports, etc. – is used in such a way that in the act of playing or implementing the portrayed and subject of the masterpiece "transferred into an experience"[58] on the on the recipient's side. In Milo Raus' words, it is "a realism [...] that replaces the 'representation of the real [...] with the reality of representation.'"[59] The reality of a representation of the Shoah is limited, which can be experienced very convincingly in the limitations of language – implemented in the play between imagination and documentation – in *Gec i Majer.*

---

[54] Magdalena Marszałek and Dieter Mersch, *Seien wir realistisch: Neue Realismen und Dokumentarismen in Philosophie und Kunst* (Zürich, Berlin: Diaphanes, 2016), 10–11.

[55] Ibid., 10.

[56] Barthes quoted from Marszałek and Mersch, *Seien wir realistisch,* 16.

[57] Ibid., 18.

[58] Ibid., 20.

[59] Ibid.

In relation to Albahari, it is not about a document in the sense of a 'true' contemporary witness report, but rather the "simulated"[60] testimony described by Weigel, i.e., a document in the service of an artistically generated experience that is not just thematizing the difference between fact and fiction (the mixture of which is typical of postmodernism and Albahari). Because: the many fantasies of the first-person narrator in *Gec i Majer* allude to the distinction between fact and fake (as a lie). The lost knowledge or the inaccessible should not be thought up by means of fiction, in the sense of a lie (literature knows no lies anyway), but David Albahari offers possible scenarios (character, activities, etc.) to the readers – always marked in literary terms as a possibility through formulations such as "I have no proof whatsoever that this was what he dreamed, but I find the thought appealing [...];"[61] "I don't know," "It is entirely possible," "Whatever the case."[62]

PARALLELIZATION BETWEEN VICTIMS AND PERPETRATORS: IMITATION AND IMAGINATION OF THE FIRST-PERSON NARRATOR

The perpetrator profile in the novel is marked by possible suggested opposites: married, loving, caring father and husband vs. SS officer on duty to exterminate a people. The arbitrary attribution of made-up habits and behavior of the SS officers by the first-person narrator gives the perpetrators human traits. It is grotesque insofar as this 'humanization' upgrades the 'lower' immoral offenders. For example, the description of the perpetrator as a caring family father: one of the perpetrators hopes that his daughter will eat enough fruits to counteract the recurring sore throat. "You get a sore throat today, tomorrow it's pneumonia, and the day after, it's anybody's guess. A person must remain vigilant; therein lies the art of living. One day you relax your standards, and the next day you are in a camp, so it goes."[63] Firstly, this discussion about the impending danger of death through physical suffering is parallelized and equated to the perpetrator's society, represented through the SS officer's daughter and the victims. The perpetrators are shown as stupid people with no historical and ethical understanding of their own doing, as if every cold could result in camp detention. Secondly, the narrator characterizes the perpetrators as supposedly "human" incapable of social and family

---

[60] Weigel, "Zeugnis und Zeugenschaft, Klage und Anklage," 116: Since a testimony is based on a person's "gesture of truly bearing" an experience, there can only be real or spurious testimony: "In this respect, there can be no fictitious testimony, but only a simulated one."

[61] Albahari, *Götz and Meyer*, 3.

[62] Ibid., 3–4.

[63] Albahari, *Götz and Meyer*, 32.

responsibility and compassion. The disproportion of the concern for the daughter (because of a cold) and responsibility for daily mass executions is a mind play of the first narrator for causing outrage about these obedient, submissive and naive perpetrators. The 'humanization' of the perpetrators through parallelization, created by imaginative investment, effects the break in perception of the perpetrators as being absolutely "evil". Instead of depicting the perpetrators as absolute evil and proven anti-Semites (Goldhagen 1996), *Gec i Majer* reminds us about Christopher Browning's "ordinary men."[64] But, the 'humanization' of the perpetrators does not lead to a full identification with them, because the aversion-generating irony, tiring repetitions and variations of the perpetrator names break a possible identification again and again. Presenting the perpetrators as "normal" doesn't trivialize their actions, but rather suggests a connecting line between the victims and the perpetrator in the sense that there are many stages in the 'long line' between the 'bad' perpetrators and the 'good' victims. This is reminiscent of the thesis formulated by Primo Levi of the concentration camp as a "zone in which the 'long chain of conjunction between victims and executioners' comes loose."[65] Agamben describes the gray zone from Primo Levi as a "zone of irresponsibility [...]."[66] The real horror of the camp – in the opinion of Hannah Arendt – is that moral categories and standards known to mankind – for instance the difference between victim and perpetrator – are not applicable anymore after the concentration camps because even the victims were often turned into perpetrators and it is nearly impossible (but of course needed) to distinguish victims and perpetrators.[67] In Albaharis' book, there are described Serbian prisoners who had to fetch the corpses from the gassing car, dig mass graves and put them in. The crimes of the totalitarian regime expanded upon the victims. This is why Hannah Arendt called concentration camps "total."[68] Nobody could evade it – and the inconceivability is still a challenge for posterity today.

Moreover, the first-person narrator imagines a card game between the Jewish camp administration and SS officers. He lets the victims' representatives

---

[64] Christopher R. Browning, *Ordinary Men. Reserve Police Battalion 101 and the Final Solution in Poland,* (New York: HarperCollins, 1992).

[65] Primo Levi quoted by Agamben, *What remains of Auschwitz*, 21.

[66] Ibid., 21.

[67] This double standard of the victimized perpetrator is also implemented in the different naming of the Serbian prisoners: Sometimes they just called "Serbian prisoners" (Albahari, *Götz and Meyer*, 26), sometimes marked as perpetrators like the interchangeable Götz and Meyer: "the five Serbian prisoners, or was it seven" (Ibid., 25).

[68] Hannah Arendt, *Elemente und Ursprünge totaler Herrschaft: Antisemitismus, Imperialismus, totale Herrschaft* (München, Berlin, Zürich: Piper, 2017), 930.

'compete' in a game, as if they were equals, against the SS officers.[69] This reminds me of a real football match of SS officers with 'Sonderkommando' members in Auschwitz, described by Primo Levi, which served Giorgio Agamben as an explanation:

> This match might strike someone as a brief pause of humanity in the middle of an infinite horror. I, like the witnesses, instead view this match, this moment of normalcy, as the true horror of the camp. For we can perhaps think that the massacres are over even if here and there they are repeated, not so far away from us. But that match is never over; it continues as if uninterrupted. It is the perfect and eternal cipher of the 'gray zone', which knows no time and is in every place.[70]

Furthermore, the 'candy game' between the perpetrators and the children in the camp 1941 is repeated in a "play" with chocolate candies between the first narrator and his ancestor and survivor in the 1990s. In one scene, this relative recites the names of the ancestors who were killed during the Shoah for a reward of sweets from the narrator as a representative of the second generation.

> [...] I did not manage to establish what it was they played: tablonet or, perhaps, rummy, or some other game meant to pass the time. My cousin, for instance, played solitaire. [...] When I put that first chocolate on the table, he reached out, squeezed it, brought it to his nose, then stuffed it in his mouth and mumbled, 'Klara'. A thin droplet of chocolate drool slipped down his chin. After the second chocolate, he said, 'Flora'. [...] I took out another chocolate, asking him for men's names. [...] I went to my cousin's room three or four more times, always with a big bag of chocolate in my pocket, and I managed to squeeze out a few more first and last names. [...] Then, as I wiped the bites of chocolate and bubbles of drool from his face, I decided I'd end the masquerade [...].[71]

The first-person narrator questioned his extended relatives and witnesses in search of those who remained and to reconstruct the family history. Playing with the candy of the first-person narrator with the descendant drives the first-person narrator's thirst for knowledge and obsessive attitude towards the witness to extremes. It also reminds us of the responsibility that comes with those who grapple with witnesses and their suffering:

---

[69] Albahari, *Götz and Meyer*, 26.

[70] Agamben, *What remains of Auschwitz*, 26.

[71] David Albahari, *Götz and Meyer*, 27–28.

I enticed him with chocolates, which he was not allowed to eat because he had diabetes, and so it was that, for a moment, I pulled aside the curtain of his memory loss. At that point I didn't know that Götz, or was it Meyer, had also used chocolates as a form of deceit, though in his case the candy served to close the curtain of memory loss rather than open it, which, I have to say, is a big difference. A curtain is a curtain, no doubt, but life does not proceed in nouns, life proceeds in verbs.[72]

Astonishingly, his descendant (first narrator), lured the survivor with candies, because he knew the relative had diabetes. Not long after his several visits, the relative died. What does that say about the ethical means and methods of remembering and the first-person narrator himself? The imaginary power and obsession with family trauma and history from the first-person narrator, occasionally drift into negligence and corruption of his fellow human beings, sometimes making him appear unappealing. Instead of the relative's intrinsic motivation, there is now the promised reward as an extrinsic motivation (also known as the repression effect); the chocolate candy.

By "bribing" the diabetic survivor, the repeatability of the game enters in a paradoxical, revolting manner into the immediate context of the first-person narrator and the crumbling Yugoslavia of the 1990s. For Georgio Agamben and Primo Levi, the play (see the example of the football match above) and its repeatability outside of the camp points out the all-encompassing presence from Auschwitz and the still given possibility of repeating nowadays. In this sense, the narrator's imaginations of the perpetrator's thoughts and games with children or other Jewish people in the camp (a) and the candy-play between the survivor and victim's decedent (narrator) in the 1990s (b) resemble the football match from Primo Levi as a metaphor of the suffering of the Jewish. The repetition of the match, especially through the Jewish first-person narrator in opposition to a perpetrator figure, indirectly tackles the question of testimony and the justification of writing about it. In the perfidy of the candy game, a moral dilemma of remembering emerges on the border between permitted questioning and improper moral blackmail.

The opening thesis can be confirmed and specified: the imagination begins where speaking and writing about the mass murder seems impossible despite the certainty about the factuality of the history. Imagination 'fills' the gap left by the witness and the document. David Albahari is not concerned with a forced harmony between documentation (facts, proofed historical evidence) and imagination (placeholder for the lost "truth"), but an interplay that creates semantic breaks on the textual level and is mediated by different

---

[72] Ibid., 25.

stylistic elements (irony, repetition, parallelization etc.). Proximity and distance, understanding and non-understanding, alternate and allow readers to 'experience' the Shoah, more precisely the concentration camp, as a "sayable" and "unsayable" unicum simultaneously.

REFERENCES

Adorno, Theodor W. *Gesellschaftstheorie und Kulturkritik.* Frankfurt am Main: Suhrkamp Verlag, 1975.

Adorno, Theodor W. "Cultural Criticism and Society." In Theodor W. Adorno, *Prisms.* Translated by Samuel and Shierry Weber, edited by Thomas McCarty. n.d.: n.d., 1997, https://moodle.ufsc.br/pluginfile.php/1407246/mod_resour ce/content/1/Theodor%20W.%20Adorno%20Prisms%20%28Studies%20in% 20Contemporary%20German%20Social%20Thought%29.pdf.

Agamben, Giorgio. *What remains of Auschwitz: The archive and the witness.* New York: Zone Books, 1999.

Arendt, Hannah. *Elemente und Ursprünge totaler Herrschaft: Antisemitismus, Imperialismus, totale Herrschaft.* München, Berlin, Zürich: Piper, 2017.

Albahari, David. *Götz and Meyer.* Translated by Ellen Elias-Bursać. Florida: Harcourt, 2004.

Bajford, Jovan. *Staro Sajmište: Mesto sećanja, zaborava i sporenja.* Beograd: Beogradski centar za ljudska prava, 2011.

Browning, Christopher R. *Ordinary Men Reserve Police Battalion 101 and the Final Solution in Poland.* New York: HarperCollins, 1992.

Geulen, Eva. *Giorgio Agamben zur Einführung.* Hamburg: Junius, 2016.

Kowollik, Eva. *Geschichte und Narration: Fiktionalisierungsstrategien bei Radoslav Petković, David Albahari und Dragan Velikić.* Berlin: LIT Verlag, 2013.

Köppen, Manuel and Klaus R. Scherpe. "Zur Einführung: Der Streit um die Darstellbarkeit des Holocaust." In *Der Streit um die Darstellbarkeit des Holocausts in Film – Literatur – Kunst,* edited by Manuel Köppen and Klaus R. Scherpe, 71–73. Köln, Weimar, Wien: Böhlau Verlag, 1997.

Marszałek, Magdalena and Dieter Mersch. *Seien wir realistisch: Neue Realismen und Dokumentarismen in Philosophie und Kunst.* Zürich, Berlin: Diaphanes, 2016.

Messner, Elena. "David Albaharis Belgradroman *Gec i Majer [Götz und Meyer].*" *Yearbook for European Jewish Literature Studies* 2, no. 1 (2015): 293–311, https://www.degruyter.com/document/doi/10.1515/yejls-2015-0018/html.

Rädle, Rena. "'Mein Vater war ein Mörder': Tochter des Gestapo-Chefs von Belgrad über Verbrechen ihres Vaters." Rosa Luxemburg Stiftung, November 17, 2011. https://www.rosalux.de/news/id/5376/mein-vater-war-ein-moerder.

Rädle, Rena and Milovan Pisarri. *Mesta stradanja i antifašističke borbe u Beogradu 1941–1944: Priručnik za čitanje grada.* Beograd: Forum za primenjenu istoriji, 2013.

Schäfer, Peter. *Kurze Geschichte des Antisemitismus.* München: C.H. Beck, 2020.

Vervaet, Stijn. *Holocaust, War and Transnational Memory: Testimony from Yugoslav and Post-Yugoslav Literature.* n.d.: Routledge, 2019.

Volnynsky, Masha. "Language within the Battle between History and Memory in David Albahari's Götz and Meyer." *Serbian Studies: Journal of the North American Society for Serbian Studies* 23, no. 1 (2009): 157–66, https://muse.jhu.edu/journal/405.

Weigel, Sigrid. "Zeugnis und Zeugenschaft, Klage und Anklage." In *Zeugnis und Zeugenschaft*, edited by Rüdiger Zill, 111–35. Berlin: Akademie Verlag, 1999.

Chapter 8

Studying Estonian Gulag Literature: Approaches and Obstacles

Kseniia Tereshchenko
Independent Researcher and Translator

Antonina Puchkovskaia
King's College London, UK

Abstract: Gulag literature is a hybrid genre that does not fall into the category of fiction or nonfiction, as it is often not clear whether events described by the author are documented precisely or with the elements of fiction. Nevertheless, it is mostly books of this kind that represent the history of Gulag in contemporary culture. Such representation, on the one hand, and the dilemma of the (broken) referential pact, on the other, additionally complicate literary research. When it comes to Estonian Gulag literature specifically, one has to also take into account aspects related to the country's cultural and political issues. The goal of our paper is to analyze Estonian Gulag literature and highlight its distinctive features, as well as to shortly report the results of the digital humanities project "Notes from the Camp" (2021), which consisted of illustrations, summaries, and commentary on Estonian Gulag literature was turned into a digital form by means of storytelling and web design.

Keywords: gulag literature, literary studies, digital storytelling, digital humanities

***

INTRODUCTION

With the so-called Digital Age, new methodological approaches to cultural and literary studies appear, but old questions remain. In terms of Gulag literature, they have to do with the nature of this genre, as it allows authors to apply literary and stylistic tools to describe historical events. Subsequently, both readers and researchers struggle to separate the latter from the former and either treat such books as trustworthy sources or detect historically inaccurate facts and conclude that this undermines the value of such writings. We believe such an approach does not do justice to Gulag literature, a primary genre representing the cultural memory of Soviet repressions. Unfortunately, few attempts have been made to study this topic, and they mostly have to do with the Gulag prose of Russia, while that of Eastern Europe remains even less studied. Therefore, we chose Estonian Gulag literature as a research object to shed light on its literary features and historical context and discuss the controversy surrounding Gulag history and culture and its place in the modern world and academia in general.

GULAG STUDIES IN THE DIGITAL AGE

Gulag (an acronym for *Glavnoe upravlenie lagerei*, "chief administration of the camps," a governmental agency in the USSR existing from 1918–1960) has become a general term for the Soviet repressive system. The typical image of Gulag camps includes exceptionally severe conditions in which the prisoners had to exist, including harsh forced labor[1] and lack of food and hygiene.[2] However, the negative approach to Gulag and related repressions is not shared by everyone: almost half of the population of the Russian Federation considers them necessary[3], while almost half of the respondents aged 18–24 have not heard of them.[4] Thus, even though Joseph Stalin's repressions and Gulag are wide-known phenomena, profound research is still needed.[5] Moreover, the already obtained data may be available to scholars but remains not as widely known as the cultural image of these events.

An example of the commonly discussed characteristic of the Gulag is that, supposedly, many of its prisoners were political prisoners who committed no actual crimes but were convicted for not supporting the Soviet regime or were subject to false accusations.[6] Among non-historians, such points of view are formed by cultural texts (autobiographies, memoirs, poetry) rather than historical sources, as they are more available to the public. Thus, the cultural

---

[1] Robert W. Thurston, *Life and Terror in Stalin's Russia 1934–1941* (London, New Haven: Yale University Press, 1996), 102–104.

[2] Jonathan Brent, *Inside the Stalin archives: discovering the new Russia* (New York: Atlas and Company, 2008), 1–18.

[3] "Stalinskie repressii: prestuplenie ili nakazanie?," VCIOM, June 5, 2017, https://wciom.ru /analytical-reviews/analiticheskii-obzor/stalinskie-repressii-prestuplenie-ili-nakazanie-.

[4] "Repressii XX veka: pamyat o blizkih," VCIOM, October 5, 2018, https://wciom.ru/an alytical-reviews/analiticheskii-obzor/repressii-khkh-veka-pamyat-o-blizkikh.

[5] Edwin Bacon, *The Gulag at war: Stalin's forced labour system in the light of the archives* (London: MacMillan, 1994), 7.

[6] John Keep, "Recent Writing on Stalin's Gulag: An Overview," *Crime, Histoire & Sociétés* 1, no. 2 (1997): 91–112.

significance of Gulag literature is evident. It has to do with cultural memory rather than historical accounts, as the books of this genre are subjective and represent a specific aspect of Soviet repressions. One of the factors contributing to it is the authorship of existing sources.

There are many memoirs, publications, correspondence, and other sources of information about the prisoners' experience in the Gulag. They provide great insight into the life of Gulag victims and their perception of what has happened. However, they should be attended to with a certain level of skepticism. They do not provide a clear image because most of the authors of such writing were political prisoners. Therefore, it might seem that most Gulag prisoners were also accused of anti-Soviet beliefs, but this is a distortion caused by the fact that "actual" criminals did not write about their experience. Moreover, some prisoners died in the camps and did not leave their accounts of the events. Therefore, even though many sources are available, they may not be representative of the entire phenomenon.[7]

We believe that the problem with studying Gulag literature lies in the essence of this genre. Thus, the most popular book on Gulag – Aleksandr Solzhenitsyn's *Gulag Archipelago*, is defined, genre-wise, as a "historical research/fiction book,"[8] which does not specify the line between fiction and history.

Even though works of this genre are not purely historical or autobiographical, they still are one of the main media through which Gulag is reflected in modern culture.[9] These writings postulate a particular version of historical events, and discussions around this topic do not tone down to this day, complicating research and making it hard for the researcher to stay objective. Considering that the cultural images of phenomena are based on facts, and the human perception and experience or cultural artifacts associated with a different event or era, some might not represent the reality of a situation:

> Literature is culture's memory, not as a simple recording device but as a body of commemorative actions [...] Writing is both an act of memory

---

[7] Bacon, *The Gulag at war*, 11–12.

[8] "художественно-историческое произведение" in Russian. See Aleksandr Solzhenitsyn, *Arkhipelag Gulag* (Moskva: Litres, 2021).

[9] 52% of the respondents of a survey conducted in 2017 have stated that the main source of their knowledge about Stalin's repressions is «документальная литература» – a term in Russian for a genre close to autobiographical fiction we discuss in this paper. See "Stalinskie repressii."

and a new interpretation, by which every new text is etched into memory space.[10]

An example of such a widely known but questionable artifact when it comes to its historical accuracy is a series of illustrations created in the 1980s by the policeman, prison warden, and collector of prison art and folklore Danzig Baldaev (1925—2005). The series is supposed to represent life in the Gulag and include ferocious imagery. These drawings are often used to illustrate the Soviet repressive system, although Baldaev has never been to Gulag and based his work on folklore stories, which may or may not be true.[11]

We see similar problems in other genres, such as military literature,[12] particularly in books about the Great Patriotic War in Russia, which are based on actual events and propagate a certain attitude towards them. This genre concerns cultural memory, not fact-checking, as it does not objectively represent historical events. However, unlike Gulag literature, this representation follows the widely accepted agenda and causes fewer disputes.

For instance, examples of propaganda in Soviet military literature can be found in several books about the Brusilov offensive, such as *Brusilov Offensive* (*Брусиловский прорыв*, 1943) by Sergei Sergeev-Tsensky (1875—1958). The Brusilov offensive is an event from the history of the First World War that became a symbol of heroism of the Russian army in its fight against German forces, especially at the beginning of the Great Patriotic War, when Soviet propaganda needed to refer to past victories against Germany to motivate people in the new war.[13]

Gulag literature, one of the essential means through which the cultural image of Soviet repressions is formed, is hard to investigate for several reasons. The

---

[10] Renate Lachmann, "Mnemonic and Intertextual Aspects of Literature," *Cultural memory studies: an international and interdisciplinary handbook*, ed. Astrid Erll and Ansgar Nünning (Berlin, New York: Walter de Gruyter, 2008), 301.

[11] See, for example, "*Avtorstvo 'tjuremnyh risunkov' polkovnika Danciga Baldaeva postavili pod somnenie*," *ARD: portal delovoj informacii*, April 2, 2015, https://asiarussia.ru/news/6734/.

[12] Elena Mihajlik, "Ne otrazhaetsja i ne otbrasyvaet teni: 'zakrytoe' obshhestvo i lagernaja literatura," *Novoe literaturnoe obozrenie*, no. 100 (2009): chap. 1. Accessed November 24, 2021. https://magazines.gorky.media/nlo/2009/6/ne-otrazhaetsya-i-ne-otbrasyvaet-teni-zakrytoe-obshhestvo-i-lagernaya-literatura.html.

[13] Olesya Starodubova, "Khudozhestvennaya literatura kak sredstvo propagandy: formirovanie obraza brusilovskogo proryva v sovetskoi khudozhestvennoi literature 1940-kh godov." Accessed November 21, 2021, https://cyberleninka.ru/article/n/hudo zhestvennaya-literatura-kak-sredstvo-propagandy-formirovanie-obraza-brusilovskogo-proryva-v-sovetskoy-hudozhestvennoy-literature.

first difficulty lies in the genre's essence: real-life events get mixed with an author's exaggerations, edits, or additions; to make the text more readable or exciting for their readers, writers change the storyline and develop new characters. As a result, it is frequently not clear how to tell the truth from fiction, but this also can provide the text with an additional value:

> Studies have shown that fiction (as in the historical novel) is a great help when it comes to narrativizing events since narrators who are free to design their own stories can more easily evoke vivid characters and give closure to events (Rigney, *Imperfect Histories* 13–58). Those who "stick to the facts" may paradoxically end up with a more historical and authentic story, but also a less memorable one, than the producers of fiction. The latter enjoy poetic license when narrativizing their materials and often have creative, specifically literary skills that help give an added aesthetic value to their work. This aesthetic dimension means that they can attract and hold the attention of groups without a prior interest in the topic, but with a readiness to enjoy a good story and suspend their disbelief (Landsberg 25–48).[14]

For example, in Raimond Kaugver's (Estonian author, 1926—1992) books on Gulag, the protagonists are different in each novel, and although all of them are the author's alter ego, they are different, which allows readers to see the situation (common for all of them – imprisonment in Gulag) from different points of view. If Kaugver were strictly autobiographical, we would only see one viewpoint.

In *Letters from the Camp*,[15] the author uses his name. This book is written from a first-person perspective. Although not many bibliographical facts of the protagonist are mentioned, those correspond to Kaugver's biography, as he was imprisoned in the Vorkutlag camp and worked in the medical department there.

At the same time, the protagonists in the three other books about Gulag by Kaugver all have different stories. However, what primarily unites them is the experience of being a prisoner in the Gulag and how they reflect on it. According to Keskküla, this author created his books quickly and, without

---

[14] Ann Rigney, "The Dynamics of Remembrance: Texts Between Monumentality and Morphing," *Cultural memory studies: an international and interdisciplinary handbook*, ed. Astrid Erll and Ansgar Nünning (Berlin, New York: Walter de Gruyter, 2008), 347.

[15] Raimond Kaugver, *Kirjad laagrist* (Tallinn: Eesti Raamat, 1989).

making many edits, passed them further to the publisher[16], which might indirectly imply that, for the most part, he used his own experience rather than those of an imaginary character. Therefore, while the biographical facts of the characters and the author differ, their inner worlds are in focus. They are similar, if not the same.

When one approaches such books from the historical point of view, they are first and foremost interested in the biographical aspect. Unfortunately, as one of the consequences of such an approach, Gulag literature is often considered historical literature whose only goal is to document real-life events. As a result, everything the author added, edited, or cut out, is treated as an error. This is a mistake they should have avoided if they wanted their writings to be treated seriously. We reconsider such an approach for the study of autobiographical literature:

> If other genres or sub-genres or forms can be read as life-writing – such as novels, poems, short stories, travel writings, topographical books, historiography – they can all be used as routes into cultural memory. Nevertheless, if we are to use such literary texts as evidence for cultural memory studies, we cannot use them naively as historical 'documents' or 'sources' of first-hand testimony. Indeed, we must approach them as literary critics, aware that what we are dealing with are, precisely, texts.[17]

One of the most common claims against Aleksandr Solzhenitsyn, the key author of Gulag literature, is the excessive number of Gulag prisoners. In his magnum opus, *Gulag Archipelago* (*Архипелаг ГУЛАГ*, 1973), he states that the approximate number of victims is 66,5 million.[18] Many consider this as several Gulag prisoners, whereas other sources name the total number of around 7,6 million prisoners,[19] only a tiny portion of which was, in fact, political, as their number is often exaggerated.[20] However, the author was misinterpreted. The named number is not only about Gulag prisoners but also includes all victims of the communist regime, including those lost to hunger,

---

[16] Kalev Kesküla, "Elukutselt menukirjanik," *Eesti Ekspress*, December 11, 2001, https://ekspress.delfi.ee/kuum/elukutselt-menukirjanik?id=69021969.

[17] Max Saunders, "Life-Writing, Cultural Memory, and Literary Studies," in *Cultural memory studies: an international and interdisciplinary handbook*, ed. Astrid Erll and Ansgar Nünning (Berlin, New York: Walter de Gruyter, 2008), 322.

[18] Solzhenitsyn, *Arkhipelag Gulag*.

[19] Evgeny Krinko and Sergey Kropachev, "Masshtaby stalinskih repressii v otsenkah sovetskih i sovremennyh rossiiskih issledovatelei," *Bylye gody. Rossiiskii istoricheskii zhurnal*, no. 4, (2012), 26.

[20] Vasily Popov, "Gosudarstvennyi terror v sovetskoi Rossii," in *1923-1953 gg.: istochniki i ih interpretatsiya, Otechestvennye arhivy* no. 2 (1992): 20–32.

civil war, collectivization, and so on.[21] Moreover, the inaccuracies were inevitable, as the author had no access to archives and other trustworthy sources, which does not undermine the general integrity of the book. It is just an example of the disputes that go on to this day.

At the same time, the value of these books as works of art is compromised, too. Both modern and Soviet readers and researchers have treated them primarily as a historical source, while its literary aspect remains ignored. Regardless of the historical context, such works are cultural texts with peculiar stylistic features and ideas that must be acknowledged. However, little research was conducted in this field, including Estonian Gulag literature, as discussed in the next section.

The study of artistic features of Gulag literature is crucial as it helps study the historical events through the prism of the contemporaries' point of view. Like books about the Second World War, Gulag literature, by its existence, puts historical events on the map – they become a part of the culture of our worldview that only cultural artifacts have processed. They are tools that help perceive such events. Historical textbooks serve other purposes and do not imply the emotional processing of historical events. It makes Gulag literature an irreplaceable medium for cultural memory.[22] Research of this genre is possible through a unique approach that would consider both historical and cultural aspects of the texts. In this manner, it would be possible to gain more knowledge regarding literature, in particular, and human perception of history overall.

ESTONIAN CASE

Andrea Gullotta, Alexander Safronov, Mikhail Mikheev, Lyudmila Starikova, and other researchers studied Gulag literature.[23] However, their works mainly

---

[21] Krinko and Kropachev, "Masshtaby stalinskih repressii v otsenkah sovetskih i sovremennyh rossiiskih issledovatelei," 26.

[22] Astrid Erll, "Cultural Memory Studies: An Introduction," in *Cultural memory studies: an international and interdisciplinary handbook*, ed. Astrid Erll and Ansgar Nünning (Berlin, New York: Walter de Gruyter, 2008), 322.

[23] Andrea Gullotta, "Trauma and Self in the Soviet Context: Remarks on Gulag Writings," *Avtobiografiia: Journal on Life Writing and the Representation of the Self in Russian Culture*, no. 1 (2012): 73–87; Alexander Safronov, *Zhanrovoe svoeobrazie russkoj khudozhestvennoj dokumentalistiki (ocherk, memuary, 'lagernaya' proza): uchebno- metodicheskoe posobie* (Riazan': Federal'noe Gosudarstvennoe Bjudzhetnoe Obrazovatel'noe Ukhrezhdenie Vysshego Professional'nogo Obrazovanija "Rjazanskij Gosudarstvennyj Universitet Imeni S.A. Esenina," 2015); Mikhail Mikheev, "O 'novoi' proze Varlama Shalamova," *Voprosy literatury*, no. 4, (2011): 183–214; Lyudmila Starikova, "Lagernaya proza" v kontekste russkoi literatury XX veka: ponyatie, granitsy, spetsifika," *Vestnik Kemerovskogo gosudarstvennogo universiteta*, no. 2 (2015): 169–74.

focus on books (novels, memoirs, poetry, etc.) written in Russian. In contrast, our research framework states that this genre goes beyond one national literature and should include the appropriate works by authors from Eastern Europe who wrote in their native languages.

Gullotta considers Gulag prose a part of another, more prominent genre – literature of Soviet repression that he defines as a group of texts that are created by people who in some way experienced Soviet repression, are directed towards real undetermined readers, have either an aesthetic or a moral function (can be combined), and sometimes bear stylistic features that appeared due to the Soviet repression.[24] In Gullotta's view, Gulag memoirs, Gulag poetry, and Soviet repression fiction are subgenres of Soviet repression literature.[25] However, it is worth noting that such an approach does not imply that Gulag literature is part of a particular national literature – it is only a genre with specific features. This notion is vital for us, as going beyond more well-known literature helps analyze this genre more efficiently.

Among the common features of Gulag prose identified by Lyudmila Starikova, based on the works of various researchers, are the discussion of life in a camp supplemented by existential and metaphysical questions; documentality and direct relation to history, but with poetic and artistic features; author's reflection based on their own experience; separation of a camp from the rest of the world, etc.[26]

As we can see, there are different approaches to determining Gulag literature. However, the core of this concept is the same and lies in autobiographical elements, common problematics, and the hybridization of fiction and documentality. Estonian Gulag literature, in general, corresponds to the characteristics mentioned above but is much less studied. However, there are investigations conducted by Eneken Laanes[27] and Anneli Kõvamees[28] that provide an overview of Estonian Gulag literature. When it comes to the definition of the discussed genre, Kõvamees uses a quotation from Matt Oja's work:

---

[24] Gullotta "Trauma and Self in the Soviet Context: Remarks on Gulag Writings," 74.
[25] Ibid., 75.
[26] Starikova, "Lagernaya proza," 173.
[27] Eneken Laanes, "TRAUMA KEELDE TÕLGITUD (Kultuurideülesed mäluvormid eesti laagri- ja küüditamismälestustes," *Keel ja Kirjandus* no. 4 (2017), 241–57.
[28] Anneli Kõvamees, "Taboos and Rules: Insights into Prison Camp Novels by Estonian Writers," INTERLITTERARIA 2,1 no. 2 (2016): 318–32.

Literary text that includes a description of a camp or discussion of this phenomenon is an example of camp prose, regardless of where, when, or by whom it was written (Oja 1989: 272).[29]

As we can see, the lack of need to attach Gulag literature to specific national literature is also highlighted here. Laanes, on the other hand, discusses the task of the first Estonian works on the Soviet forced-labor camps and repressions and concludes that it is to

> document the experience contained in the social memory of the repressed. Its details were largely unknown to the public in Soviet times.[30]

Kõvamees also supports this notion by stating:

> While the survivors of the Nazi camps have had the chance to talk about their experience – there is a large number of books, documentaries, and feature films, the survivors of the Soviet camps have been forced into silence for a long time.[31]

Laanes further writes that

> to solve this task, the form of a traditional autobiographical short story and fiction were used most often,[32]

which, once again, highlights the fact that authors of Gulag literature typically chose to reflect on their experience not in the form of memoirs but that of (autobiographical) fiction, which allowed the author to have more chances of being published in the times of censorship, when such autobiographical but partially fictional literature was one of few available ways to document the social memory of repressed people. Therefore, the goals that authors of Gulag

---

[29] Ibid., 320.

[30] Laanes, "TRAUMA KEELDE TÕLGITUD," 247.

[31] Original quotation: "Kui natsilaagrite üleelanutel on olnud võimalus oma kogemustest rääkida, ilmunud on väga palju sellekohast kirjandust ning tehtud dokumentaal- ja mängufilme, siis need, keda karistati Nõukogude vangilaagritesse saatmisega, on pikka aega pidanud vaikima." Kõvamees, "Taboos and Rules," 319.

[32] Original quotation: "Selle eesmärgi täitmiseks kasutati pigem traditsioonilisi autobiograafilise jutustuse vorme ja ilukirjanduslikke žanre," Laanes, "TRAUMA KEELDE TÕLGITUD," 247.

literature attempt to reach are clear – it is to document the experience of Gulag survivors in an artistic, not strictly historical, way.

Among Estonian authors who worked on books of Gulag literature are Jaan Kross (1920—2007), Arved Viirlaid (1922—2015), Agu Kask (1906—1977), Aili Helm (1921—2009), Albert Uustulnd (1925—1997), and Raimond Kaugver.[33] We focus on the works of Kaugver, one of the most prominent representatives of Estonian Gulag prose. We conducted a literary analysis of his works, and its results helped us form the concept for our digital humanities project, which can be found in the next section.

NOTES FROM THE CAMP PROJECT

There have been attempts to approach the topic of Gulag history using digital tools. Mostly this has to do with, broadly speaking, digital humanities projects – websites containing information presented in various ways that aim to make Gulag-related knowledge accessible to everyone. Some of them, such as online databases *Immortal Gulag* (*Бессмертный барак*)[34] and *The open list* (*Открытый список*)[35] created by social activists, aim to collect information both about the victims of Gulag and their executors and share stories of those who were repressed. Other projects are using the approach of geographic information systems (GIS): for example, *This is right here* (*Это прямо здесь*)[36] by Memorial Foundation that visualizes the network of Gulag-related locations in Moscow on an interactive map, as well an international *Gulag Online*[37] project created by the Gulag.cz (http://gulag.cz/ru) community[38] with a website containing a map of Gulag camps. Another common format of a project on the Gulag is digital exhibitions. Examples of such an approach can be found in the resources of the GULAG History Museum,[39] a sizable state institution that deals with Gulag history. Another integral approach is storytelling, represented by projects like *Gulag Retrospective*,[40] created by a

---

[33] *Halleluja* (1990) and *Vürst* (1994) by Jaan Kross; *Kes tappis Eerik Hormi?* (1974), *Surnud ei loe* (1975), *Märgitud* (1980), and *Vaim ja ahelad* (1961) by Arved Viirlaid; *Varjud udus* (1956) by Agu Kask; *Vägivallamaa* (1982) and *Režiim – see kõlab uhkelt* (1984) by Aili Helm; *Acheroni kaldal* (1991) by Albert Uustulnd.
[34] "Bessmertnyi Barak," accessed November 21, 2021, https://bessmertnybarak.ru/.
[35] "Otrkrytyi spisok," accessed November 20, 2021, https://ru.openlist.wiki/.
[36] "Eto pryamo zdes'," accessed November 20, 2021, https://topos.memo.ru/.
[37] "Gulag online," Gulag Online virtual museum, accessed November 20, 2021, https://gulag.online/.
[38] "Gulag.cz," Organizace Gulag.cz, accessed November 20, 2021, gulag.cz.
[39] "GULAG History Museum," accessed November 20, 2021, https://gmig.ru/.
[40] "Gulag Retrospective," accessed May 24, 2021, https://gulag.dh-center.ru/.

student of the Art & Science program at ITMO University. What makes it unique is the section where biographies of Gulag prisoners are re-written from the first-person view, giving them additional meaning, and bringing out new aspects of information.

Existing projects primarily focus on the digital representation of available data rather than its analysis. However, due to the lack of digital humanities projects that would cover the history of the Gulag and cultural artifacts related to it and the lack of research on Estonian Gulag literature in general, we decided to start a project of our own in the form of a website[41] with a visualization of the results of our literary studies research.

In our case, by cultural artifacts, we mean books belonging to the genre of Gulag literature. This choice is determined by offering a peculiar, elaborate narrative at the intersection of personal experiences and fiction. Other than the discussion of Gulag, a topic represented by several other projects already, our project also touches upon the problem of Estonian prisoners in particular.

We believe that illustration, narrative design, and interactivity can be utilized productively in the research of literature. These means allow us to make our research results accessible to a vaster audience than academic papers. Such instruments help with books that have yet to be translated into major languages like English. Therefore, the format of a digital project that we propose can spark an interest in books that are not available to the global community but deserve its attention for previously discussed reasons.

Before coming up with the initial concept for the project, a manual literary study of books was conducted. This step was necessary since this topic was not well-researched, and we had little external material to base our work on; we had to perform the analysis ourselves.

It aims to provide literary analysis of Estonian Gulag literature in an accessible and visually appealing way using digital storytelling. Novels and short stories by Kaugver chosen as the material for the project are not translated into English and Russian. Therefore, they remain unknown to readers outside of Estonia. We provide summaries of them and illustrations and literary commentary to help users gain better insight into this author's work and the way the life of a Gulag prisoner is described there.

Kaugver was an Estonian writer and author of over twenty novels, four dedicated to his experience in a prison camp (Vorkutlag) in Vorkuta, Siberia. He spent five years (1945—1950) there, being accused of being the

---

41 "Notes From the Camp," accessed September 20, 2021, https://notesfromcamp.dhcenter.com/.

motherland traitor for his service in Finnish Infantry Regiment 200 (also known as "*Soomepoisid*" – the Finnish Boys). He started to work on his books about Gulag during his imprisonment, but they were published years later. Soon after his return to Estonia, he began to work as a professional writer and became a best-selling author. He lived in Tallinn, died in 1992, and was buried at Metsakalmistu Cemetery.[42] Kaugver was chosen since he is the only Estonian writer who has written a whole series of works that belong to the genre of Gulag literature.[43] He was also an accomplished professional writer who was not primarily famous for his writings on Gulag but also acclaimed for his work in general.[44]

Upon analyzing Kaugver's Gulag prose, we managed to distinguish certain features that characterize his writings, and some of them have further determined the project's design and concept. Those are:

1) Autobiographism is crucial, but elements of fiction are also present. It means that although the books are based on personal experiences, in some respects do not correspond with actual events.

   Although crucial events of the protagonist's life often correspond to the author's, the details differ greatly. In "Forty Candles," some pivotal events that can be found in both the protagonist's and author's biographies are: joining the Finnish Infantry Regiment 200 and being imprisoned in Vorkutlag. One of the differences is the fact the Kaugver, upon leaving the army, returned to Estonia and was not accused straight away and worked as a teacher for a while until questioned by the commission,[45] whereas the protagonist had little to no "eventless" periods in his adult life, which adds to the integrity of the book, leaving no "blanks."

2) The simplicity of language. The author avoids lengthy descriptions, colorful adjectives, etc. Instead, the text is quite dry, simple, and brief.

---

[42] Sven Vabar, "Raimond Kaugver," Estonian Writers' Online Dictionary, accessed November 21, 2021, https://sisu.ut.ee/ewod/k/kaugver.

[43] *Nelikümmend küünalt* (1966), *Kirjad laagrist* (1989), *Postuumselt rehabiliteeritud* (1990), *Põhjavalgus* (2010) by Raimond Kaugver.

[44] Raimond Kaugver, *Kirjad Sigridile: Sõjatandrilt ja Vangilaagrist 1944–1949* (Tallinn: Underi ja Tuglase Kirjandusk, 2020).

[45] Raimond Kaugver, *Elulookirjeldus*, TLA (Tallinna Linaarhiiv), f R-52, n 2, s 4.

For example, he writes in *Letters from the Camp* (*Kirjad Laagrist*, 1989; fragment translated by us from Estonian):

I knew that more than 8,000 prisoners were in the camp and asked how a hospital with twenty beds could be enough for them.

Vincent Pavlovich – that was my colleague's name – shrugged and pointed somewhere in the direction of the forest.

'Most of the ill ones find their cure there,' he said coldly. 'We only admit the ones who might be useful later.'

At first, I did not understand what he meant and thought that there was another bigger hospital somewhere in the forest. I was very naive.[46]

3) Fragmented composition. The chapters are short and often end with a tragic, expressive notice. It prevents readers from having a smooth reading experience: they are forced to make stops between chapters.

Two of the books that our research was primarily based on – *Letters from the Camp* and *Forty Candles* (*Nelikümmend Küünalt*, 1966) – have a similar structure, as they both contain short chapters that do not consequently follow each other's story but end rather abruptly and begin with a description of a new unrelated episode, which leaves no space for tracing the protagonist's or the author's relation towards the described events. The difference lies in the fact that *Letters from the Camp* is more of a compilation of short stories about different people (although the storytelling protagonist and the set are the same, which makes the text more integral), but *Forty Candles* is a novel focused on one protagonist.

4) Retrospection. The described events are those of the past. The protagonist – the alter ego of the author – reminisces about his life. He does not describe events as they unravel.

---

[46] Original quotation: "Teadsin, et laagris viibib üle kaheksa tuhande mehe, ja küsisin imestusega, kuidas neile jätkub sellest napilt paarikümne nariga laatsaretist. Vintsent Pavlovitš – see oli minu kolleegi nimi – kehitas õlgu ja viipas kuhugi metsa suunas. "Enamus haigeid leiab oma ravi seal," ütles ta jahedalt. "Meil peetakse siin ainult niisuguseid, kellest veel asja saab." Ma ei taibanud kohe tagamõtet ja järeldasin tema sõnadest, et kuskil lähedal peab asetsema mõni suurem ja täielikum hospidal. Ah naiivsust!" from Raimond Kaugver, *Kirjad laagrist*, 63–64.

For example, *Forty Candles* is an inner monolog of a 40-year-old man who reflects upon each year of his life, starting with his birth. In addition, it may be worth noting that the author was 40 when this book was published, which implies or at least adds to the autobiographical nature of the text.

5) The books are not wholly dedicated to life in a camp. The writer also describes events before and after the imprisonment but are still related to it, being either "causes" of conviction or subsequent problems the protagonist faced after being freed.

For instance, in *Forty Candles*, about 50 of 244 pages, are dedicated to the eight years the protagonist spent in Gulag, while *Posthumously Rehabilitated* (*Postuumselt Rehabiliteeritud*, 1990) is almost entirely focused on after Gulag, traumas, and adaptation to the new life.

6) Some of the texts were modified due to censorship or other reasons. It adds to the fictitious nature of the genre itself, making it even harder to decide what is based on reality, what was the author's intention, and what he was forced to change.

In Kalev Kesküla's article *A popular writer by profession* (*Elukutselt menukirjanik*), the author says that Kaugver attempts to make the protagonist as cynical and selfish as possible because a former prisoner was not supposed to be a positive character in the Soviet times. At the same time, given that the distance between the author and the protagonist is relatively narrow, this criticism towards oneself is, at times, noticeably insincere.[47]

7) The character's emotions are barely described. It adds to the simplicity of language, making the text even drier, transmitting the moving part to the reader.

Mikhail Mikheev, a researcher who wrote a paper on Varlam Shalamov's (1907—1982) Gulag literature, distinguished a literary feature applicable to Kaugver's prose as well: anti-catharsis, a way to describe a scene of violence when the reader "observes" it. Since the author's or the protagonist's emotions are not discussed, the reader finds no closure and cannot experience a catharsis that brings purgation of emotions. On

---

[47] Kalev Kesküla, "Elukutselt menukirjanik."

the contrary, it evokes more anxiety as the traumatic event remains unprocessed.[48]

These conclusions helped us figure out the preliminary concept and design of the project. For example, the simplicity of language and the author's briefness is mirrored in the length and style of the texts we intend to use on the project's website. The same goes for the fragmented composition. It led us to the idea of using collage artwork for illustrations rather than only pictures. Thus, we apply collage and photomontage and do not create illustrations from scratch like how traditional images would be displayed. Still, we use pre-existent pictures and photographs (some even taken in Gulag or at the exact locations). We also mix factual sources with artistic features, as authors of Gulag literature do.

Textual annotations suit the fragmented composition of studied books, as they appear one by one instead of via smooth transmission. Thus, even without paying attention to the content, our sole format can transmit our approach to the studied objects to a certain extent.

By creating illustrations, we supplement our research object with our perception of it and allow users to interact with it:

> We thus insist on considering visualizations as aesthetic objects with the ability to move those who encounter them and to intervene in their perceptions. The aesthetic object is often thought of as an object which arrests our attention, interrupts perceptual automatisms (Shklovsky, 1916), and slows us down, inviting contemplation and critical and playful engagement. The aesthetic object, through its very form, can defamiliarize the things we most often take for granted.[49]

This is beneficial for the popular science aspect of our project. The combination of illustrative materials explicitly created to highlight these aspects of the studied books and actual literary studies research makes our design more accessible and adds to the used approach. The artistic element adds an extra point of view that is lacking when it comes to the interpretation

---

[48] Mikheev, "O 'novoi' proze Varlama Shalamova."
[49] Uta Hinrichs, Stefania Forlini, and Bridget Moynihan, "In defence of sandcastles: research thinking through visualization in dh," *Digital Scholarship in the Humanities* 34 (2017): 6.

of scientific articles. The use of different methods helps visualize complex concepts and helps users understand our ideas better.[50]

The interface of the project's website includes two major types of content: illustrations and text annotations, connected by interactive design elements. Interactive elements allow the user to form their way through the story.

As mentioned above, illustrations were created using the method of collage because this format fits studied books. An artist designed the collages based on our instructions. Images used as artwork fragments are photographs and other types of graphic material.

Text annotations are brief descriptions of specific objects seen in illustrations. They allow us to provide details regarding both events of the books and literary analysis. One of the objectives of our project is to make literary analysis more accessible for readers, as it is often, if not always, required for a deeper understanding of this or that author.

CONCLUSIONS

The complex relationship between historical and cultural memory, the political controversy surrounding the Gulag, and the ambiguity of the genre of Gulag literature – are the reasons, we believe, lead to the lack of research on these topics. If we want to explore said genre in a historical and cultural context, we need to look for new complex approaches that mix the methods of different fields of study.

The ambiguity of the Gulag as a historical event is represented in cultural artifacts. It demands further research using new approaches and critical attitudes, as existing papers and projects do not cover the topic's complexity. To avoid repetitive information and subjectivity, we have conducted our research by considering different approaches to analyzing famous and obscure materials. Furthermore, a lot should be done.

Existing digital platforms for discussion and research are essential and help raise awareness but do not cover it in all its complexity. Further interdisciplinary research is needed to gain a better understanding of the problem.

Our main contribution, the *Notes From the Camp* project, aims to cover an often-overlooked slice of Gulag literature – that of Eastern Europe (Estonia, in particular), and focuses on the cultural aspect of Gulag rather than the

---

[50] Similar ideas are discussed in, for instance, Gordana Novakovic, "The Garden of Hybrid Delights: Looking at the Intersection of Art, Science and Technology," in *Art Practice in a Digital Culture*, eds. Hazel Gardiner and Charlie Gere (London: Routledge, 2016).

historical one. In such a manner, we add to the information already available online in digital projects focused on Gulag history and hope that such an addition will help us see the complete picture more clearly.

Although we do not consider our research exhaustive regarding Estonian Gulag literature, we hope it might pave the way and serve as an example of applying non-quantitative methods (e.g., digital storytelling) in digital humanities and literary studies of overlooked and niche fields. In recent years, several books related to Estonian Gulag literature, such as *Case 5513: Heiti Talvik's Two Moments of Spring* (*Toimik 5513: Heiti Talviku kaks kevadist hetke*, 2021) by Arvi Tapver, and *Kolyma – Terrible Land* (*Kolõma – kole maa, 2021)* by Venda Sõelsepp, have been published, which bodes well for the future research in this area.

Notes: 1) Due to the war and its aftermath, some of the reference links mentioned in the article may already be invalid. 2) Subsequently, we moved our "Notes From the Camp" project to the following web site: https://www.figma.com/proto/MZqxhIJIFMxCm2zoz WXrCW/notes-from-the-camp-project?node-id=69-33&scaling=min-zoom&page-id=0: 1&starting-point-node-id=69:33 (Accessed April 25, 2023).

REFERENCES

Bacon, Edwin. *The Gulag at war: Stalin's forced labour system in the light of the archives.* London: MacMillan, 1994.

Bessmertnyi Barak. "Bessmertnyi Barak." Accessed November 21, 2021. https://bessmertnybarak.ru/.

Brent, Jonathan. *Inside the Stalin archives: discovering the new Russia.* New York: Atlas and Company, 2008.

Erll, Astrid. "Cultural Memory Studies: An Introduction." In *Cultural memory studies: An International and Interdisciplinary Handbook*, edited by Astrid Erll and Ansgar Nünning. 1–18. Berlin, New York: Walter de Gruyter, 2008.

Gulag Dh-Center. "Gulag Retrospective." Accessed May 24, 2021. https://gulag.dh-center.ru/.

Gulag Dh-Center. "Notes From the Camp." Accessed September 20, 2021. https://notesfromcamp.dhcenter.com/.

Gulag History Museum. "GULAG History Museum." Accessed November 20, 2021. https://gmig.ru/.

Gulag Online virtual museum. "Gulag online." Accessed November 20, 2021. https://gulag.online/.

Gullotta, Andrea. "Trauma and Self in the Soviet Context: Remarks on Gulag Writings." *Avtobiografiia: Journal on Life Writing and the Representation of the Self in Russian Culture*, no.1 (2012): 73–87.

Hinrichs, Uta, Stefania Forlini, and Bridget Moynihan. "In defense of sandcastles: research thinking through visualization in dh." *Digital Scholarship in the Humanities* 34 (2017): 80–99.

Kaugver, Raimond. *Elulookirjeldus*, TLA (Tallinna Linaarhiiv), f R-52, n 2, s 4.

Kaugver, Raimond. *Kirjad laagrist.* Tallinn: Eesti Raamat, 1989.

Kaugver, Raimond. *Kirjad Sigridile: Sõjatandrilt ja Vangilaagrist 1944–1949.* Tallinn: Underi ja Tuglase Kirjandusk, 2020.

Keep, John. "Recent Writing on Stalin's Gulag: An Overview." *Crime, Histoire & Sociétés* 1, no. 2 (1997): 91–112.

Kesküla, Kalev. "Elukutselt menukirjanik." *Eesti Ekspress,* December 11, 2001. https://ekspress.delfi.ee/kuum/elukutselt-menukirjanik?id=69021969.

Kõvamees, Anneli. "Taboos and Rules: Insights into Prison Camp Novels by Estonian Writers." INTERLITTERARIA 21, no. 2 (2016): 318–32.

Krinko, Evgeny, and Sergey Kropachev. "Masshtaby stalinskih repressii v otsenkah sovetskih i sovremennyh rossiiskih issledovatelei." *Bylye gody. Rossiiskii istoricheskii zhurnal,* no. 4 (2012): 86–99.

Laanes, Eneken. "TRAUMA KEELDE TÕLGITUD (Kultuurideülesed mäluvormid eesti laagri- ja küüditamismälestustes." *Keel ja Kirjandus* no. 4 (2017): 241–57.

Lachmann, Renate. "Mnemonic and Intertextual Aspects of Literature." In *Cultural memory studies: an international and interdisciplinary handbook,* edited by Astrid Erll and Ansgar Nünning, 301–10. Berlin, New York: Walter de Gruyter, 2008.

Mihajlik, Elena. "Ne otrazhaetsja i ne otbrasyvaet teni: 'zakrytoe' obshhestvo i lagernaja literature." *Novoe literaturnoe obozrenie* no. 100 (2009): chapter 1. Accessed November 24, 2021. https://magazines.gorky.media/nlo/2009/6/n e-otrazhaetsya-i-ne-otbrasyvaet-teni-zakrytoe-obshhestvo-i-lagernaya-liter atura.html.

Mikheev, Mikhail. "O 'novoi' proze Varlama Shalamova." *Voprosy literatury* no. 4 (2011): 183–214.

Novakovic, Gordana. "The Garden of Hybrid Delights: Looking at the Intersection of Art, Science and Technology." In *Art Practice in a Digital Culture,* edited by Hazel Gardiner and Charlie Gere, 117–39. London: Routledge, 2016.

Organizace Gulag.cz. "Gulag.cz." Accessed November 20, 2021. gulag.cz.

Otrkrytyi spisok. "Otrkrytyi spisok." Accessed November 20, 2021. https://ru. openlist.wiki/.

Popov, Vasily. "Gosudarstvennyi terror v sovetskoi Rossii." *1923-1953 gg.: istochniki i ih interpretatsiya, Otechestvennye arhivy* no. 2 (1992): 20–32.

Rigney, Ann. "The Dynamics of Remembrance: Texts Between Monumentality and Morphing." In *Cultural memory studies: an international and interdisciplinary handbook,* edited by Astrid Erll and Ansgar Nünning, 345–56. Berlin, New York: Walter de Gruyter, 2008.

Safronov, Alexander. *Zhanrovoe svoeobrazie russkoj khudozhestvennoj doku-mentalistiki (ocherk, memuary, 'lagernaya' proza): uchebno- metodicheskoe posobie.* Riazan': Federal'noe Gosudarstvennoe Bjudzhetnoe Obrazovatel'noe Ukhrezhdenie Vysshego Professional'nogo Obrazovanija "Rjazanskij Gosudarstvennyj Universitet Imeni S.A. Esenina," 2015.

Saunders, Max. "Life-Writing, Cultural Memory, and Literary Studies." In *Cultural memory studies: an international and interdisciplinary handbook,* edited by Astrid Erll and Ansgar Nünning. Berlin, New York: Walter de Gruyter, 2008.

Solzhenitsyn, Aleksandr. *Arkhipelag Gulag.* Moskva: Litres, 2021.

Starikova, Lyudmila. "Lagernaya proza v kontekste russkoi literatury XX veka: ponyatie, granitsy, spetsifika." *Vestnik Kemerovskogo gosudarstvennogo universiteta* no. 2 (2015): 169–74.

Starodubova, Olesya. "Khudozhestvennaya literature kak sredstvo propagandy: formirovanie obraza brusilovskogo proryva v sovetskoi khudozhestvennoi literature 1940-kh godov." Accessed November 21, 2021. https://cyberlenin ka.ru/article/n/hudozhestvennaya-literatura-kak-sredstvo-propagandy-for mirovanie-obraza-brusilovskogo-proryva-v-sovetskoy-hudozhestvennoy-lit erature.

Thurston, Robert W. *Life and Terror in Stalin's Russia, 1934–1941.* London, New Haven: Yale University Press, 1996.

Topos Memo. "Eto pryamo zdes'." Accessed November 20, 2021. https://topos. memo.ru/.

Vabar, Sven. "Raimond Kaugver." Estonian Writers' Online Dictionary. Accessed November 21, 2021. https://sisu.ut.ee/ewod/k/kaugver.

VCIOM, "Repressii XX veka: pamyat o blizkih." October 5, 2018. https://wcio m.ru/analytical-reviews/analiticheskii-obzor/repressii-khkh-veka-pamyat-o-blizkikh.

VCIOM, "Stalinskie repressii: prestuplenie ili nakazanie?" June 5, 2017. https: //wciom.ru/analytical-reviews/analiticheskii-obzor/stalinskie-repressii-pre stuplenie-ili-nakazanie-.

Chapter 9

In Search of Upper Silesian Women. Counter-histories in Contemporary Silesian Literature

Monika Glosowitz

University of Silesia, Poland

Asbtract: The paper examines the role of literary images of women's reproductive labor as a carrier of cultural memory in the process of social transformation of Upper Silesia. The first part stands as a reconstruction of the history of women's labor in a historical, social, and economic context, presenting the historical moments of wars and social transitions, when women had to take upon themselves the role of family providers, while at the same time, what is obvious but not always articulated, continuing their reproductive role. The second part analyses selected literary texts, which amounts to the reconstruction of the voices of Upper Silesian women. I present different narrative strategies for shaping the memories of women's roles in society and shaping the definitions of women's emancipation. This study demonstrates that literature works as one of the most important tools used to regain one's own place in the collective memory.

Keywords: Upper Silesia, women's emancipation, reproductive labor, coal region, mining culture, Silesian literature

***

INTRODUCTION

The objective of this article is to analyze selected literary texts, which amounts to the reconstruction of both the issues depicted, and the voices of Upper Silesian women. First and foremost, I will focus on narratives depicting the daily lives of mining families, treating them as a carrier of cultural memory in order to reconstruct the process of social transformations. I will analyze whose perspectives of narration are in them, who the owners of the voices telling the stories are, and whether the stories do, in fact, contain women's experiences.

For the sake of this article, it seems appropriate to emphasize that today's definition of the term "Upper Silesia" encompasses exclusively the territory of an erstwhile Free State of Prussia's Upper Silesia province (German *Provinz Oberschlesien*) while leaving outside its borders the former Austrian Silesia (Cieszyn Silesia and Opava Silesia). My analysis and the sources I rely on relate almost exclusively to the pre-First World War German territories, a considerable portion of which was incorporated into the territory of the new Polish state after the end of the First World War. This choice is significant not only because of – as researchers say – cultural differences between Upper Silesia and Cieszyn Silesia, but foremost because of the difference in the numbers of coal mines, especially those active today. At the current time, no coal mines are working in Cieszyn Silesia. Rather, the region and its people currently stand at the threshold of the revolution triggered by the need to adjust to the resolutions of The European Green Deal, which is intended to transform the EU into a modern, resource-efficient, and competitive economy. This allows for critical reflection on the powers at play in twenty-first-century modernization. If we venture to assume a broader perspective in this regard, we will see the future ramifications of the "ambitious decarbonization" on a global scale. To this end, it is hard not to agree with some researchers, who promote a thesis of the imminent arrival of the "new green colonialism," amounting to a model of progress based on demands issued by the Global North that are to be implemented by the workforce concentrated in the Global South.[1] Another axis of capital flow should be added here – that being is the one that stretches between Eastern and Western Europe.

Last but not least, I wish to redirect attention away from the division made alongside gender roles and corresponding categories of "tradition" and "progress" toward a definition of work that serves to highlight the hitherto unidentifiable concept of what constitutes "women's work."

THE HISTORY OF WOMEN IN UPPER SILESIA

The region of Upper Silesia is bordered by the Polish voivodships (provinces) of Greater Poland in the north, Lower Silesia in the west, and Lesser Poland in the east, with the Czech border, where the smaller Czech Silesia is located, constituting the southern border. Among the most important cities in the region are places like Katowice, Opole, Ruda Śląska, Bytom, Rybnik, Racibórz, and Zabrze. The region's history has been marked by conflicts and animosities

---

[1] Harpreet Kaur Paul and Dalai Gebrial, ed., *Climate Justice in a Global Green New Deal. Perspectives on a Global Green New Deal* (London: Rosa-Luxemburg-Stiftung, 2021), 7–13.

involving Poles, Czechs, Prussians, and Austrians going as far back as First Silesian War, which began in 1740. The process of industrialization in the region relates mostly to the rapid development of mining.

The extraction of coal from deposits in Polish territories has been carried out for at least 500 years. [...] However, for decades or even centuries the use of this mineral resource was quite restricted: hard coal was utilized to heat iron in smithies, in saltworks, and in lime kilns, as well as in other industrial plants, yet it took place solely in the vicinity of where the deposits were near the surface and were easy to access. Mass exploitation began when the coal started to be used in steam engines and in such processes as smelting crude iron and metallic zinc. This transpired in Upper Silesia, when in the year 1788, the first steam-powered pump was activated in a silver-lead ore mine in the vicinity of Tarnowskie Góry.[2]

As a rule, at the turn of the nineteenth and twentieth centuries, women in Prussia would not cease to perform their work duties after giving birth to their first child. They usually resumed their daily chores, and sometimes those related to employment, the day after giving birth.[3] Back then, they were mostly employed as seamstresses, but at times they also worked in heavy industry. By 1895, most employed in heavy industry worked in private mines. By way of illustration, let us look at the statistics from three mines in Zabrze. In the Queen Louise (*Königin Luise*) mine, nine thousand men were employed, in comparison to a mere thirty-four women. However, the Concordia coal mine employed 1,384 males and 133 women, while at the Hedwigswunch mine, the ratio was eight men per woman. The women were, among other things, employed as manual coal sorters and other surface workers, where job responsibilities were less physically demanding. Beyond this, by the turn of the nineteenth and twentieth centuries, as many as 20% of work crews in Upper Silesian zinc mines were composed of women, and at iron and steel mills – circa 25%, while at iron ore mines, the number was 40%.[4] Those numbers do not exist in the local cultural memory. There is a movement

---

[2] Jerzy Jaros, "Z dziejów górnictwa węglowego," in *Górniczy stan: W wierzeniach, obrzędach, humorze i pieśniach,* ed. Dorota Simonides (Katowice: Śląski Instytut Naukowy, 1988), 9.

[3] Beata Piecha-van Schagen, "Rodzina i żona: Feministyczna ewolucja," in *Narracje górnicze z terenu Zabrza: Kopalnia Kopalnia to je do mie wszystko,* ed. Bernard Linek (Muzeum Górnictwa Węglowego w Zabrzu: Zabrze, 2016), 372.

[4] See Elżbieta Górnikowska-Zwolak, *Szkic do portretu Ślązaczki: Refleksja feministyczna* (Wydawnictwo Śląsk: Katowice, 2000), 99.

for telling "Silesian herstories," associated with an organization called Szlak Śląskich Kobiet (the Path of Silesian Women). Different projects labeled with this "brand" present stories of Silesian women, most of those whose lives were "significant" for the history of the region. The fact that women worked underground has been profoundly forgotten.

The situation changed with the outbreak of the First World War due to the almost universal conscription of men. It was then that women not only had to take upon themselves the responsibility of providing for their families (by undertaking gainful employment), but also had to incur additional burdens derived from the ideas of *Heimatfront* ('the homeland front') and *Frauenfront* (the women's front).[5] Women also played an active part in the German Revolution of 1918–1919 and the establishment of workers' councils, which also emerged in large numbers in (Upper) Silesia. As Matthäus Wehowski puts it:

> It strikes one, how great a role women played in both the elections of representatives and the organization of councils. For instance, describing the Gleiwitz [Gliwice] council, the editor-in-chief of *Der Oberschlesische Wanderer*, Peter Weber, underscores 'the immense significance of the women's movement' in the creation of new councils'. Police spies also reported on the active contribution of women, who many a time constituted the majority of participants in the organizational activities, and largely decided about their personal composition.[6]

The First World War thwarted the economic development of coal mining regions, and its end resulted in the redrawing of state borders, allotting the eastern part of Upper Silesia to Poland while leaving the region's western part

---

[5] "It meant contributing to warfare by becoming socially (and emotionally) involved in it. Among other things, women partook in commissions dealing with the distribution of rationed food. Most of all, however, the realities of the post-war world 'without men' propelled and compelled them to emancipate themselves. Many of them had to undertake hard physical work, since the strategic importance of the mining and smelting industries triggered the hiring of adolescent males and women, in which capacity there was a fourfold increase during the final year of the war as compared to 1913." Piecha-van Schagen, "Rodzina i żona," 373.

[6] Matthäus Wehowski, "Demokratyzacja i konflikt narodowościowy. Rady żołnierskie i robotnicze. W okresie przełomu na Górnym Śląsku, listopad 1918 – styczeń 1919," in *Rok 1918 na Górnym Śląsku: Przełom społeczno-polityczy i jego konsekwencje*, ed. Sebastian Rosenbaum (Instytut Pamięci Narodowej – Komisja Ścigania Zbrodni przeciwko Narodowi Polskiemu & Muzeum w Gliwicach: Gliwice, 2020), 90.

with Germany.[7] In 1923, 73.3% of hard coal production in Poland was derived from Upper Silesia, which matched the region's percentage contribution to the country-wide output of crude iron, steel, zinc, and lead. So, Upper Silesia was virtually decisive in terms of the country's economic potential. Yet, there is no precise data available regarding the class structure of the early 1920s. The workers' estate was estimated to constitute over 70% of the entire Silesian population.[8] The 1920s and 1930s, however, were a period of economic difficulties pertaining to the search for new potential markets for Polish coal. Since Germany slapped Poland with punitive transit tariffs, exporting the coal abroad involved increased costs of rail transport. The said situation was then further exacerbated by the policies of foreign capital owners, who at the time owned the majority of coal mines in Poland. They sought to increase output while keeping production costs low. In the Polish part of Upper Silesia prior to the war, working wives were considered "a cause of disgrace."[9] In 1931, merely 24% of adult women were actively employed in the region. On March 29, 1926, the Silesian parliament enacted the so-called Celibacy Act, the Law on Termination of Teaching Service Contract [i.e., dismissal] of Women Teachers Arising from Marriage. The law remained in force until April 9, 1938, and triggered mass layoffs among female teachers.[10]

During the Second World War, Silesia became a part of Germany once again. By sending forced laborers and prisoners of war to work in the mines, the Germans succeeded in increasing output. This was accompanied by the decapitalization of many mines and their resultant technical decrepitude. In 1945 the Upper Silesian basin fell entirely to Poland, yet due to the overexploitation of mines, the seized industrial sites were in poor condition. The situation stabilized in the 1950s, particularly with the advent of improved working conditions in the latter part of the decade, which had been brought about by reducing the size of work crews. The end of the Second World War also brought about significant social change – women were once again encumbered with providing for their families. Female workers were employed

---

[7] Ibid., 17–18.

[8] Mirosława Błaszczak-Wacławik, "Miejsce i rola regionalnej kultury w procesach życia społecznego Górnego Śląska do roku 1945," in *Górny Śląsk. Szczególny przypadek kulturowy*, eds. Mirosława Błaszczak-Wacławik, Wojciech Błasiak, and Tomasz Nawrocki (Kielce: Wydawnictwo Naukowe Jan Szumacher, 1990), 12–13.

[9] Agata Komosa, "Żony górników nie powinny pracować? Szef Solidarności oderwał się od rzeczywistości," NaTemat, accessed september 20, 2021, https://natemat.pl/13009 1,kopalni-nie-mozna-zamykac-bo-zony-gornikow-nie-powinny-pracowac-to-jeden-z-argumentow-piotra-dudy.

[10] See Jerzy Piotrowski, "Zawód a struktura rodziny," in *Rodzina a zawód* (Biuletyn ŚIN nr 39), ed. Wanda Mrozek (Katowice: Śląski Instytut Naukowy, 1963), 18–32.

to dismantle industrial machines, appliances, and entire factories, that were earmarked for expropriation by the Soviets. Women also undertook regular physical work (e.g., hard coal excavation) during that period.[11] During the 1950s, the government initiated a top-down activation of women's labor, but it hardly translated into a new model of gender-role distribution in mining families. "Therefore, for instance, when in mining families 15% of wives on average were employed, in textile workers' families the number of working wives was over 70%."[12] In 1958 after the very notable and widely discussed accident at the Marcel Mine, in which Halina Karbownik lost her arm, an official ban was enacted concerning the permanent employment of women for underground work in mines. In the 1960s and 1970s, childless women most commonly did work, but they left the workforce after bearing children.[13] Increased mechanization led to a spike in work efficiency such that at the end of the 1970s, the extraction of hard coal doubled over two decades.[14] Also, in the 1970s, there was an observable tendency related to the motivation to undertake professional work; the need to fulfill one's professional aspirations. However, this would not have been possible without the impact brought about by the increase in labor rights and entitlements for working women and more pronounced benefits, in particular, regarding maternity.[15] There were many social privileges for miners working in the uneasy post-war labor reality. These were implemented in order to mitigate the effects of heavy and dangerous underground work, and they were applied preferentially to different social groups (from the "G stores" that were accessible exclusively to miners to new social security retirement plans).[16] As part of the centralized social policies of the Polish People's Republic, the privileges associated with working as a miner preclude one from referring to any common status of miners or generalizing about the situation of miners in Europe at the time.

Another crucial yet tragic moment for mining in Upper Silesia came with the radical transformation of the region ushered in by the events of 1989, which resulted in the liquidation, bankruptcy, and privatization of numerous workplaces. The overall number of jobs shrank by three hundred thousand,

---

[11] Piecha-van Schagen, "Rodzina i żona," 374–75.

[12] See Piotrowski, "Zawód a struktura rodziny," 30.

[13] Piecha-van Schagen, "Rodzina i żona," 375.

[14] Ibid., 20–25.

[15] See Lucyna Frąckiewicz, "Możliwości i konsekwencje aktywizacji kobiet w województwie katowickim," in *Górnośląskie Studia Socjologiczne*, vol. 11., ed. Wanda. Mrozek (Katowice: ŚIN, 1975). See Górnikowska-Zwolak, *Szkic do portretu Ślązaczki*, 119.

[16] See more Arkadiusz Przybyłka, "Przywileje socjalne związane z pracą w górnictwie w okresie PRL-u," *Studia Ekonomiczne: Zeszyty Naukowe Uniwersytetu Ekonomicznego w Katowicach*, no. 353 (2018).

while families in the region had to incur not only economic impoverishment, but also being stripped of their hitherto high social standing (in terms of prestige).[17] The 1990s, in general, dealt a huge blow to mining families in Upper Silesia, both in terms of their economic standing and social degradation. Not only was this the case for numerous miners who had been made redundant, but also for those whose salaries had been substantially decreased, while their retirement and severance packages were slashed in half, compared to previously collected wages (!). Therefore, women faced the prospect of undertaking wage-paying work, while the principal deterrent to their doing so was their low level of education and the scarcity of job offers available to them.[18] One of many voices advocating for the acknowledgement of a greater women's role during this restructuring process is that of Silesian sociologist Marek Szczepański. However, in his focus on the role of women at the time, he dubs them "closeted maids," indicating that "their labor more often than not remains unacknowledged in terms of prestige, and value for society and economy." He also cites their "being unacquainted with the necessary restructuring," which makes "the majority of females representing this peculiar social and professional category – inordinately numerous in the [former – MG] Katowice voivodeship – oppose the process in question, associating it mainly with the liquidation of industrial plants, looming unemployment, and poverty."[19]

Let's look at the history of women's labor in a historical, social, and economic context. We clearly see the most important occasions when women were mobilized to work outside their homes. Those were the historical moments of wars and social transitions when women had to take upon themselves the role of family providers, while, at the same time, what is obvious but not always articulated, continuing their reproductive role. Dealing with the crucial question of how all those events affected the collective memory of/about women in Silesia, I have to make a fundamental hypothesis. In concurrence with Raymond Williams, an influential Marxist literary critic, I want to see culture as "a particular way of life which expresses certain meanings and values not only in art and learning but also in institutions and ordinary behaviour."[20] However, as a woman with working-

---

[17] Marek Stanisław Szczepański, "Rodzina w procesie restrukturyzacji: instytucja zapoznana? Przypadek województwa katowickiego," in *Kobiety wobec przemian okresu transformacji*, eds. Krystyna Faliszek, Elisabeth McLean Petras, and Kazimiera Wódz (Katowice: Wydawnictwo Śląsk, 1997), 189–191.

[18] Szczepański, "Rodzina w procesie restrukturyzacji,"191.

[19] Ibid., 193.

[20] Raymond Williams, *The Long Revolution* (New York: Columbia University Press, 1961), 41.

class family roots, I'm afraid I have to disagree that the scientific and artistic depiction of Silesian working-class women is the narrative that they would choose for themselves. And we can see that clearly, by comparing the artistic and scientific formulations with oral history archives. The former is built on hypotheses formulated by non-working wives caring for their hard-working miner husbands who allowed them "the luxury of not working at all."[21] It has become a kind of "specific *myth* of the Silesian woman,"[22] which, in fact, as I will argue below, is not a myth, but rather a judgment legitimized by narrative forms, methodological tools, and research background coming from Western liberal feminist theories.

METHODOLOGICAL ISSUES AND CHALLENGES

As German archivist Christina Vanja wrote: "The historiography of mining has largely ignored mining women, as well as the wives of the miners." [23] Rossana Barragán Romano and Leda Papastefanaki, Bolivian and Greek historians, conclude: "The role of women as mineworkers and as household workers has been erased."[24] Eileen Mountjoy and other Greek and American female scholars ask: "But has anyone remembered the women who packed the miners' dinner pails, washed their blackened clothing, and waited in anguish outside the mines when disaster struck?"[25] Only a few studies that would investigate the everyday life of Silesian women up until the present has seen the light of day.

The attentive observer will note that there is a growing interest in the history of Upper Silesia. This wave of interest in Upper Silesia is conspicuous in contemporary Polish culture and can be largely credited to publications such

---

[21] "Women in Silesian Industry," In Your Pocket portal, accessed November 22, 2021, https://www.inyourpocket.com/katowice/silesian-women-of-industry_74973f.

[22] Barbara Markowska, "Silesian Women's Situated Identity and the Question of Subjectivity: The Power of the Past and Promise of the Future," in *Gender and Energy Transition Case Studies from the Upper Silesia Coal-mining Region*, eds. Katarzyna Iwińska and Xymena Bukowska (Cham: Springer, 2022).

[23] Christina Vanja, "Mining Women in Early Modern European Society," in *The Workplace before the Factory: Artisans and Proletarians, 1500-1800*, eds. Thomas M. Safley and Leonard N. Rosenband (Ithaca, NY, London: Cornell University Press, 1993), 100–17.

[24] Rossana Barragán Romano and Leda Papastefanaki, "Women and Gender in the Mines: Challenging Masculinity Through History: An Introduction," *International Review of Social History.* 65, no. 2 (August 2020): 191.

[25] Eileen Mountjoy, "A Woman's Day: Work and Anxiety," Indiana University of Pennsylvania, accessed October 12, 2021, https://www.iup.edu/library/departments/archives/coal/people-lives-stories/a-womans-day-work-and-worry.html.

as Stefan Szymutko's *Nagrobek ciotki Cili* in 2001,[26] Zbigniew Kadłubek's *Listy z Rzymu* in 2008,[27] and later on, Aleksander Nawarecki's *Lajerman*[28] and *Wobec tradycji*. Mariusz Jochemczyk's *Śląskie szkice oikologiczne*[29] is also drawing academic attention after winning the 2021 Nike Literary Prize awarded to Zbigniew Rokita for *Kajś*.[30] However, at the same time, the postulate to "shatter Silesian stereotypes" has little in common with advocating for writing her stories, that is, the practice that commemorates the outstanding females who merit recognition.

This is why voices demand that the "unsung revolution of Polish women" be told.[31] The ultimate goal of the latter version of history and memory is to recode the manner in which one conceives historical narratives and cultural memory. It is not just about rearranging the visibility field "more justly" by rendering the hitherto underrepresented more visible. It is more about approaching critically one's own apparatus in a way proposed by a feminist materialist philosopher Donna Haraway:

> History is a story Western culture buffs tell each other; science is a contestable text and a power field; the content is the form. [...] I am arguing for politics and epistemologies of location, positioning, and situating, where partiality and not universality is the condition of being heard to make rational knowledge claims. These are claims on people's lives. I am arguing for the view from a body, always a complex, contradictory, structuring, and structured body, versus the view from above, from nowhere, from simplicity[32].

The place from which a researcher speaks is, in fact, not only key in the case of anthropologists, who commence their field work by observing other human beings, but also for other humanities scholars, including those for whom texts are the main research material. In the text giving an account of the events and

---

[26] Stefan Szymutko, *Nagrobek ciotki Cili* (Katowice: Wydawnicto Uniwersytetu Śląskiego, 2001).

[27] Zbigniew Kadłubek, *Listy z Rzymu* (Katowice: Wydawnictwo św. Jacka, 2008).

[28] Aleksander Nawarecki, *Lajerman* (Gdańsk: słowo obraz/terytoria, 2010).

[29] Mariusz Jochemczyk, *Wobec tradycji: Śląskie szkice oikologiczne* (Katowice: Wydawnictwo Uniwersytetu Śląskiego, 2015).

[30] Zbigniew Rokita, *Kajś* (Wołowiec: Wydawnictwo Czarne, 2020).

[31] Cf. mostly discussions appearing in social media and referring to such authors as Dariusz Zalega and his book entitled *Śląsk zbuntowany* (Wołowiec: Wydawnictwo Czarne, 2019) which is also the title of a Facebook page.

[32] Donna Haraway, "Situated Knowledges: The Science Question in Feminism and the Privilege of Partial Perspective," *Feminist Studies* 14, no. 3 (Autumn 1988): 577, 589.

circumstances leading up to her being portrayed in the play *Talabot*, performed for the first time by the Odin Teatret in 1988, a Danish anthropologist, Kirsten Hastrup describes how she felt "on the other side," that is, performing the role that she had been casting others in up to that point while she carried out her fieldwork. She ends with the conclusion: "The ethnographer's presence, however violent, is in some way the only alternative to silence about the other worlds because her sharing of this world is a source of authority about its objective reality; no reality can ever be exhaustively apprehended in its own categories."[33]

This statement, however, turns out to be problematic while discussing the portraits of Silesian women (more aptly described as members of working-class mining families). Both female and male researchers, along with popular columnists, subscribed to the thesis about Silesian women's alleged conservatism, i.e., a patriarchal worldview imposed on Silesians by state authorities and the Catholic Church, which were then internalized by these women and adopted as the core of their identity. 'Social change,' in turn, was defined as relinquishing the basic values of "the older generation" – most of all the family and religion – and, what loudly reverberates in all the quoted sociological studies, the undertaking of professional employment.

Let us consider the following excerpts from scholarly works and articles:

Even though the social role of the man has always differed from that of the woman, Upper Silesia has always seemed to have been conducive to such a state of affairs.[34]

Is 'the Silesian family' indeed a homogeneous entity resistant to each and every civilizational change?[35]

Men at work 'prove themselves worthy' as workers and brave persons. Women, even though many of them work professionally, in accordance with the local tradition need to 'prove themselves worthy' as adroit organizers of the family's home life and budget.[36]

---

[33] Ibid., 341.

[34] Magdalena Piłat-Borcuch, "Konflikt ról społecznych – przypadek kobiet na Górnym Śląsku," *Górnośląskie Studia Socjologiczne* 4, no. 8 (2013): 133.

[35] Komosa, "Żony górników nie powinny pracować?."

[36] Irena Bukowska-Floreńska, *Rodzina na Górnym Śląsku* (Katowice: Wydawnictwo Uniwersytetu Śląskiego, 2007), 290.

... a clear tendency occurs amongst women who have not been in employment, namely, about half of them show the propensity to undertake a professional career. The said tendency signifies more of a 'myth of work' than genuine professional endeavour and rather than speaking to an economic need, points to emancipatory attitudes of miners' wives of a younger generation.[37]

In the course of two generations, or sometimes even one, women in Silesia have affected a grand shift in their social position. Starting as wives of physical workers, mostly miners, they have become educated employees who occupy, more frequently than their husbands, managerial positions.[38]

This attitude finds its expression in performing female roles assigned to them by the traditional division into the work-related male role, that of being the major breadwinner, and the female role, consisting of homemaking, tending to offspring, and organizing the family's home life and budget. This division, despite having been implemented in differing variants, may be regarded as recurrent in industrialized societies throughout the world:

Although opinions and attitudes towards women and mining were unequal in different societies around the globe, domestic ideology in Europe and North America, originating from eighteenth- and nineteenth-century debates on 'women's nature,' was adjusted to the particular circumstances of the Industrial Revolution, providing a moral rationale for keeping women out of the mines and at home. A domestic ideology and the male breadwinner ideology concealed the concrete meaning of the gender division of labour for women's work in mining households, as well as the value of women's unpaid labour to the mining industry.[39]

The fourth of the above series of quotes equates "emancipatory attitudes" with "the propensity to undertake a professional career." I put forward a thesis that this suggestion is buttressed by a fundamentally false division, and therefore, the contentions voiced by the quoted researchers and journalists

---

[37] Witold Mrozek, *Rodzina górnicza: Przekształcenia społeczne w górnośląskim środowisku górniczym* (Katowice: Wydawnictwo "Śląsk," 1995), 194.
[38] Urszula Swadźba and Monika Żak, *Od żony górnika do naukowca: Zmiana systemu wartości i ról społecznych kobiet na terenach poprzemysłowych Górnego Śląska* (Katowice: Wydawnictwo Uniwersytetu Śląskiego, 2016), 165.
[39] Romano and Papastefanaki, "Women and Gender in the Mines," 194.

are, in fact, axiological – they judge women as "less than" men and "less than" non-Silesian women, who have adopted more progressive attitudes.

In cases of discussing the portraits of working-class women in Silesia, works conducted by feminist Marxists that question the standard definitions of 'progress' and 'modernization' are much more fruitful. Silvia Federici sheds light on the fact that the transition from the pre-capitalist order to the capitalist one not only did not facilitate the "liberation" of women, supposedly exemplified by their undertaking of professional careers, but to the contrary, appropriated their work in a twofold way and excluded them from access to communal assets.[40] Even more so, the women themselves became "communal assets" of sorts, managed by both men within the institution of the family and by employers in the workspace. Frederici calls it a "historic defeat" for women.

> This was for women a historic defeat. With their expulsion from the crafts and the devaluation of reproductive labor poverty became feminized, and to enforce men's 'primary appropriation' of women's labor, a new patriarchal order was constructed, reducing women to a double dependence: on employers and on men. The fact that unequal power relations between women and men existed even prior to the advent of capitalism, as did a discriminating sexual division of labor, does not detract from this assessment. For in precapitalist Europe women's subordination to men had been tempered by the fact that they had access to the commons and other communal assets, while in the new capitalist regime women themselves became the commons, as their work was defined as a natural resource, laying outside the sphere of market relations.[41]

The transition from a precapitalist economy to a capitalist one is plainly visible against the backdrop of mining history and this its development. The role women played in this regard was strictly demarcated and remained outside the sphere of production only ostensibly. Their reproductive role was what truly ensured the proper level of production output in the capitalist system. Moreover, in the workers' families, female exclusion from access to income was the main condition of their subjugation to males.

---

[40] Silvia Federici, *Caliban and the Witch: Women, the Body and Primitive Accumulation* (New York: Autonomedia, 2004), 114.
[41] Ibid.

Although in mining communities, women and girls had limited options for paid work outside the home, they managed the family budget or contributed to the family income through many informal activities. Invisible women's labour in the mines and in mining areas tended to take the form of informal paid or unpaid activities (such as taking in lodgers, taking in laundry, baking bread, sewing, being engaged in small-scale subsistence agriculture). Women's contribution to family income was extremely important in times of crisis, illness, or unemployment. In the case of the Sardinian mines in the 1940s and 1950s, women could contribute to the family's income through their waged work in the mines and by helping to buy the land on which to build the family house. In South Africa's coal-mining areas, women were responsible for agricultural production and diverse forms of reproduction (from preparing food to selling sex). The prostitution that developed in mining regions and company towns in diverse national and colonial contexts from the mid-nineteenth century seems a permanent and complex phenomenon of capitalist development.[42]

This abovementioned shift of paradigm makes a huge difference in analyzing the narrations of Silesian working-class women. Instead of following liberal notions of feminist emancipation understood as a space of freedom assured by the possibility of a professional career, I propose to look at housewives as subjects who are the main nexus of a nascent and dynamic capitalist economy, and not deny their activity as a fundamental base of social reproduction. I believe that a thorough analysis (this paper is merely an introduction of narrations of women's everydayness) needs a solid reconstruction from a researcher's standpoint. It leads, in this case, to developing a critical approach to Western feminist liberal theories of emancipation that are being adjusted for implementation in non-Western conditions of work and life.

LITERATURE IN THE FACE OF TRANSFORMATION

I will now proceed to briefly analyze a number of twenty-first-century Polish literary texts, both prose and poetry.[43] All cited texts will concern unnoticed women's work, but they cannot be treated as "testimonies" to or commemorations of women's efforts and existence. I would see them rather as elements of "programming" social machines: family relationships, social

---

[42] Romano and Papastefanaki, "Women and Gender in the Mines," 218.

[43] This paper is intended to be exclusively devoted to Polish and Silesian literature. The comparative analysis of German (Horst Bienek et al.) and Czech literary texts will be done in the next phase of the research.

relations, and labor relations. As Federici puts it, the process of literary and cultural labelling played a huge role both in creating the new social function for women and in degrading their social identity and was meted out against them as a means of expropriation.[44]

If we look at the texts that deal with an uneasy Silesian past and are published in the Polish and Silesian languages, we can see a strong tendency to romanticize and mythologize familial histories drawn against the background of historical and social changes. It is to be found not only in socialist realism in the literature of the Polish Peoples' Republic during 1949–1956, but much later, present in various forms in the literary production of the twentieth and even twenty-first-centuries, although texts from those times build a different version of how the "great powers" went about managing the described worlds. The fact is that the romanticized narratives of the early twentieth century (narrated in twenty-first century poetry and novels) rarely contain any fragments devoted to domestic work:

> – Again with this messy morass… – Momsy's vexed voice can be heard from downstairs; she is peeking from behind a scullery window at the mud gathering in the backyard.
>
> – Momsy's in the scullery early – says Josef's younger brother, who has already woken up.
>
> Momsy had been there yesterday, she ground pepper and allspice and juniper berry, coriander, and ginger with auntie. They ground them and made them into handsome tiny mounds alongside fine raisins and pouches of marjoram, alongside stale bread rolls – the 'żymłas' – all diced up; and how splendidly they crack when being diced up, how bountiful the way the żymłas crumble. And my, how it all did smell – delicious and titillating all at once.[45]
> (Szczepan Twardoch, *Drach*)[46]

> the underground seams seemed to descend into chaos,
> some were ready to give in, others ready to fight,
> some craved sunlight, others averted their eyes,
> yet the coal itself, formerly a forest,

---

[44] See Federici, *Caliban and the Witch*.

[45] All translations from Polish-Silesian literary and non-literary sources by Krystian Wojcieszuk.

[46] Szczepan Twardoch, *Drach* (Wydawnictwo Literackie: Kraków, 2014), 7–8.

> wanted to go upwards, to the surface,
> completely surrendered
> whilst rushing upwards in tramcars likened to coffins,
> it expanded, and relaxed euphorically
> once again sunlit and permeating the skies above
>
> it was finally free and happy
> even combusted in a stove, atop which Luca brewed
> bread soup for Pietrek,
> straight from his mine shift, sitting ravenously at the table[47]
> (Dorota Szatters, *The Coal*)

The quoted fragments come from books that vary in terms of their genres; Twardoch's novel is a nostalgic family saga, while Dorota Szatters' book of poetry tries to reproduce the 'Great Myth' of the (lost) mining world in Silesia. What they share, however, is a strategy of depicting Silesian women as guardians who uphold the integrity of the working-class "modern family;" the model whose pillar is the unpaid reproductive work of the full-time homemakers. The image of this work is shuffled down to the corner of the entire frame and, as can be observed from the fragment of Twardoch's novel – more attention is devoted to crumbs of bread (or the *żymła* crumbs, to be more precise) than to the woman dicing it up, who, incidentally, was merely a background character for the plot of the entire book. The process of mythologization of the female figures leads to their alienation. They often become stripped of their own bodies and deprived of their place in the main historical narrative.

Along with new currents in Polish literature and new questions that are for literary critics and scholars, new languages and voices have appeared. There is a strong interest in narratives that deal with the challenge of rewriting postwar history from below. That is also why we can find more female voices in contemporary literature. One example of such different portraits of female labor is found in the novel by Anna Dziewit-Meller *Od jednego Lucypera* (2020). It is the story of Marijka (an aunt of the main storyteller, Kasia), a Silesian women born before the Second World War. The narrative concentrates on the case of her mysterious death. "A straightforward gal puffing away on *Sports* [cheap Polish cigarettes – MG]," whose female ancestors are also described in the novel as Silesians "with their faces always

---

[47] Dorota Szatters, "Węgiel," in *Szychta* (Katowice: Górnośląskie Towarzystwo Literackie, 2017), 10.

contorted,"[48] has just started her work at a chemical plant, which then goes on to constitute the bulk of the novel's storyline. However, prior to working at the plant, Marijka's working life is described in the following way:

> Marijka took up a job at the chemical plant soon after the war when the workforce needed all the hands it could get; the post-war reconstruction had just commenced, and every volunteer was priceless.

> It is not to say that she hadn't worked prior to this. Every day after school, whether still the German one or already the Polish People's one, or sometimes instead of frequenting them, her mother made her tend to the house, to her sister, and later on, to her brother, so she didn't know whether she was coming or going, day in, day out, from dawn till dusk. She dug up potatoes from the field near the Azoty plant, scrubbed the floor on her hands and knees using a rice root brush, meticulously, systematically, inch by inch, doing the laundry, hanging it out to dry, ironing the laundry, baking cake, baking bread, and hand-plucking a chicken when times were good – normal chores, staying busy, not to mooch off others.[49]

> So that she'll go out into the world, as did the village girls before her in droves, first as maid to the Master and Mistress, and then to steelworks and factories, to the world apart that was bound to be a better one – well, it was a different one, that's for sure.[50]

Both the manner of depicting Marijka in Dziewit-Meller's novel and the book's narration "program" raises questions. We see the characters of Silesian grandmothers, aunts, and mothers through the eyes of the female narrator, and she is the protagonist who "stirs up" the emotions of the readers. Those emotions are quite problematic mainly because of her complicated relationship with Silesia – she decisively cut herself away from her Silesian roots, only to remain conflicted by having abandoned both Silesia and her family. The novel's reconstruction of Marijka's life story is a strategy of remembrance of her life and death, yet the narrative is still not free of the symbolic violence employed by the teller – her grandniece Kasia – who presumes that only her actions may bestow any meaning upon her grandaunt's death. Her grandaunt's life by itself is not enough to be grieved. Those voices describe their life experiences as women;

---

[48] Anna Dziewit-Meller, *Od jednego Lucypera* (Kraków: Wydawnictwo Literackie, 2020), 199, 7.
[49] Ibid., 45.
[50] Ibid., 18.

daily lives and problems are discussed honestly and openly. But the frame of the main storytelling line identifies all the problems I have discussed. The emancipation project is much more complicated than the challenge of women's liberation as they all were the same, had the same needs, and lived in nearly homogenous worlds.

Yet another literary example is the poetized story of "Grandma Helena," written by Joanna Fligiel, where two additional threads are woven into the topic of women's work. One of them is related to the issue of rethinking one's lower strata origins, while another is an illness caused directly by physical work performed in a laundry. Fligiel reconstructs her family stories on the pages of her previously published books, but this one is particularly interesting because of the ineffable question of whose effort of rebuilding "all of Poland" it was. Helena, never seen as grandma with a "worn-out body," was functioning as a pure, beautiful, female body, which hers never was. Deprived of it, she becomes invisible, and all the contributions to the development of the new Poland she made will never be recognized.

No one called Grandma Helena 'Grandma',
when she wandered in her tailor-made pantsuit,
men, who know how to behold beauty, fell
off scaffolding, and back then, all of Poland
was being built anew.

The catcalling always piqued Grandpa,
yet he linked arms with Helena as if
taking credit for her appearance.

Helena was doing the wet-work
for all of Katowice: rubbing, wringing,
hanging, ironing, engulfed in
vapor, smelling like
soap flakes. So industrious was she
that her coming from
the wrong bank of the Przemsza River
escaped his attention.

The rheumatoid arthritis first afflicted her palms
and then the rest of the worn-out body.[51]
(Joanna Fligiel, *Nie mów do mnie "babciu"*/ *Don't call me 'Grandma'*)

---

[51] Joanna Fligiel, the poem has not yet been published; available courtesy of the author.

Literary stories reconstructing the role of women at the beginning of the twentieth century (till the post-war time in Twardoch's dating) present them as merely underdeveloped stand-ins whose works are considered transparent, immaterial, and inconsequential for the circular economy (whether highly centralized or laissez-faire). In contrast, Dziewit-Meller's novel and Fligiels' poem deal with the post-war implementation of party policies promoting the employment of women. Those are two radically different narrative strategies for shaping the memories of women's roles in society, and shaping the definitions of women's emancipation. The first two do not present women as active agents, while the latter ones call into question forced employment as a source of emancipation, showing us the backstage of the exploitation of women's bodies.

CONCLUSIONS

Therefore, when we think about how enormous the research work that lies ahead for both female researchers and writers, to symbolically reverse the multi-layered expropriation of women, we need to go back to those moments of social degradation and reconstruct the underlying circumstances preceding the implementation of various models of femininity. It is clearly visible that "the history of struggle to free or discharge women from working in mining testifies to the numerous women – the wives and daughter of miners – who worked. Although wages were increasing, economic considerations were waning. This, coupled with formal prohibitions, led women to leave the mining industry as a profession."[52] The process of leaving it, in my opinion, is not tantamount to a conservative turn. Virtually all sociological and historical studies on the subject feature a thesis of the progressive emancipation of Silesian women, which is equated with their taking on a professional career and, by the same token, more often than not, resultant social advancement. Indeed, one cannot deny that undertaking work in industry translated into the entrance of women into the public sphere. At the same time, however, we may observe from a brief historic outline of their presence in mining that industrialization did not lead to a higher employment rate for women overall. Quite the contrary, it led to the re-domestication of women, coupled with restricting them to reproductive work. But we have to be aware that it was not an individual decision, but an effect of long-term political strategy that was strictly connected to the history of economic crises.

However, I believe the greatest challenge is to elaborate an entirely different way of narrating and remembering the latter kind of work. What constitutes a

---

[52] Górnikowska-Zwolak, *Szkic do portretu Ślązaczki*, 99.

stake in this game is putting an end to the default interpretation of women's departure from the workforce as an example of the backlash against the emancipatory struggle, and instead reconstructing the circumstances leading to those transformations of everyday life and awarding reproductive work the status of material work aimed at reproducing the labor force. Only then will we be able to transform particular forms of collective memory, and not so much make Silesian mothers, wives, and female workers visible, but tell their stories in a form that shall not ascribe value to them *a priori* by cutting them down to size or weighing them against the visions of social progress that ignore reproductive labor and equate modernization with the advancement of capitalism.

REFERENCES

Barragán Romano, Rossana, and Leda Papastefanaki. "Women and Gender in the Mines: Challenging Masculinity Through History: An Introduction." *International Review of Social History.* 65, no. 2. (August 2020): 1–40.

Berger, Stefan, and Peter Alexander, eds. *Making Sense of Mining History: Themes and Agendas.* London, New York: Routledge, 2020.

Błaszczak-Wacławik, Mirosława, Wojciech Błasiak, and Tomasz Nawrocki. *Górny Śląsk: Szczególny przypadek kulturowy.* Kielce: Wydawnictwo Naukowe Jan Szumacher, 1990.

Bukowska-Floreńska, Irena. *Rodzina na Górnym Śląsku.* Katowice: Wydawnictwo Uniwersytetu Śląskiego, 2007.

Dziewit-Meller, Anna. *Od jednego Lucypera.* Wydawnictwo Literackie: Kraków, 2020.

Federici, Silvia. *Caliban and the Witch: Women, the Body and Primitive Accumulation.* Autonomedia: Brooklyn, NY, 2004.

Frąckiewicz, Lucyna. "Możliwości i konsekwencje aktywizacji kobiet w województwie katowickim." In *Górnośląskie Studia Socjologiczne*, vol. 11., edited by Wanda Mrozek, 57–77. Katowice: ŚIN, 1975.

Górnikowska-Zwolak, Elżbieta. *Szkic do portretu Ślązaczki. Refleksja feministyczna.* Katowice: Wydawnictwo Śląsk, 2000.

Haraway, Donna. "Situated Knowledges: The Science Question in Feminism and the Privilege of Partial Perspective." *Feminist Studies* 14, no. 3 (Autumn 1988): 575–99.

Hastrup, Kirsten. "Out of Anthropology: The Anthropologist as an Object of Dramatic Representation." *Cultural Anthropology* 7, no. 3 (August 1992): 327–45.

Jaros, Jerzy. "Z dziejów górnictwa węglowego." In *Górniczy stan: W wierzeniach, obrzędach, humorze i pieśniach*, edited by Dorota Simonides, 7–26. Katowice: Śląski Instytut Naukowy, 1988.

Komosa, Agata. "Żony górników nie powinny pracować? Szef Solidarności oderwał się od rzeczywistości." Accessed October 20, 2021. https://natemat.pl/130091,kopalni-nie-mozna-zamykac-bo-zony-gornikow-nie-powinny-pracowac-to-jeden-z-argumentow-piotra-dudy.

Lusek, Joanna, and David Skrabania, eds. *Kobiety o kobietach na Górnym Śląsku: Frauen über Frauen in Oberschlesien. Archiwum Historii Mówionej* 6. Gliwice, Opole: Dom Współpracy Polsko-Niemieckiej, 2018.

Markowska, Barbara. "Silesian Women's Situated Identity and the Question of Subjectivity: The Power of the Past and Promise of the Future." In *Gender and Energy Transition Case Studies from the Upper Silesia Coal-mining Region*, edited by Katarzyna Iwińska and Xymena Bukowska, 153–70. Cham: Springer, 2022.

Mountjoy, Eileen. *"A Woman's Day: Work and Anxiety."* Accessed October 12, 2021. https://www.iup.edu/library/departments/archives/coal/people-lives-stories/a-womans-day-work-and-worry.html.

Mrozek, Witold. *Rodzina górnicza: Przekształcenia społeczne w górnośląskim środowisku górniczym.* Katowice: Wydawnictwo "Śląsk," 1995.

Linek, Bernard, ed. *Narracje górnicze z terenu Zabrza: Kopalnia to je do mie wszystko.* Zabrze: Muzeum Górnictwa Węglowego w Zabrzu, 2016.

Gołębiowski, Bronisław, ed. *Pamiętniki górników.* Katowice: Wydawnictwo Śląsk, 1973.

Harpreet Kaur Paul, and Dalia Gebrial, eds. *Perspectives on a Global Green New Deal.* London: Rosa-Luxemburg-Stiftung, 2021.

Piłat-Borcuch, Magdalena. "Konflikt ról społecznych – przypadek kobiet na Górnym Śląsku." *Górnośląskie Studia Socjologiczne* 4, no. 8 (2013): 133–47.

Piotrowski, Jerzy. "Zawód a struktura rodziny." In *Rodzina a zawód* (Biuletyn ŚIN nr 39), edited by Wanda Mrozek, 18–32. Katowice: Śląski Instytut Naukowy, 1963.

Przybyłka, Arkadiusz. "Przywileje socjalne związane z pracą w górnictwie w okresie PRL-u." *Studia Ekonomiczne: Zeszyty Naukowe Uniwersytetu Ekonomicznego w Katowicach*, no. 353 (2018): 48–58.

Riccardo Cristiani, and Barbara Rosenwein. *What is The History of Emotions?* Oxford: Polity Press, 2017.

Rosenbaum, Sebastian, ed. *Rok 1918 na Górnym Śląsku: Przełom społeczno-polityczy i jego konsekwencje.* Gliwice: Instytut Pamięci Narodowej – Komisja Ścigania Zbrodni przeciwko Narodowi Polskiemu & Muzeum w Gliwicach, 2020.

Spence, Jean. "Women, Wives and the Campaign against Pit Closures in County Durham: Understanding the Vane Tempest Vigil." *Feminist Review* 60, Feminist Ethics and the Politics of Love (Autumn 1998): 33–60.

Swadźba, Urszula, and Monika Żak. *Od żony górnika do naukowca: Zmiana systemu wartości i ról społecznych kobiet na terenach poprzemysłowych Górnego Śląska.* Katowice: Wydawnictwo Uniwersytetu Śląskiego, 2016.

Szatters, Dorota. *Szychta.* Katowice: Wydawnictwo Śląsk, 2017.

Szczepański, Marek S. "Rodzina w procesie restrukturyzacji: instytucja zapoznana? Przypadek województwa katowickiego." In *Kobiety wobec przemian okresu transformacji*, edited by Krystyna Faliszek, Elisabeth McLean Petras, and Kazimiera Wódz, 187–197. Katowice: Wydawnictwo Śląsk, 1997.

Twardoch, Szczepan. *Drach.* Kraków: Wydawnictwo Literackie, 2014.

Vanja, Christina. "Mining Women in Early Modern European Society." In *The Workplace before the Factory: Artisans and Proletarians, 1500–1800*, edited by Thomas M. Safley, and Leonard N. Rosenband. Ithaca, NY, London: Cornell University Press, 1993.

INSTEAD OF AN AFTERWORD: FOUR UKRAINIAN ESSAYS ON LITERATURE AND MEMORY

Abstract: This section of the book addresses the complex relationship between memory and literature in Ukraine in the context of the ongoing full-scale Russian war of aggression. Through a variety of lenses and in the form of essays, the authors show how memories of the Holodomor, the Soviet past, war, and identity are represented and constructed through literature. They reflect on the role of literature in shaping and reflecting individual and collective memory, and how it can be used as a tool for remembering and forgetting. The essays also consider the ethical and political implications of memory, highlighting the tensions between personal and national memory and the potential for literature to both challenge and reinforce dominant narratives, both in Ukraine and abroad. The section covers works by Vasyl Barka, Oleksandr Irvanets, Sofia Andrukhovych (among others), and examines the broader cultural and political contexts that inform their writing.

Keywords: Memory, Literature, Ukraine, *Holodomor*, Soviet Past, War, Identity, Ethics, Politics, Russian war of aggression

***

Essay 1:
Are Pushkin and Bulgakov to Blame for Russia's War against Ukraine?

Olha Tkachenko

Polish Academy of Sciences, Poland

In today's Ukraine, it is crucial not to say that the war started on February 24, 2022, as that was the day Russia's full-scale invasion of the country began. The truth is that Russia's most recent war against Ukraine started in 2014—the real, not metaphorical, war with weapons, human victims, and annexation of territories. However, since the collapse of the Soviet Union, on cultural and historical levels, the war did not end. Although the Russian and Soviet empires seized to exist as structural political units, they did not give up their colonial practices. Therefore, there are still over one hundred monuments to the Russian poet Alexander Pushkin (1799–1837) in Ukraine. Interestingly, aside from the Ukrainian national poet Taras Shevchenko (1814–1861), no other cultural or political leader can compete with Pushkin on the number of monuments erected in Ukraine. There is a similar situation with streets and squares named for Russian writers and poets. Even though many monuments of communist leaders were dismantled in Ukraine as a part of the decommunization process, Russian culture and history are still ubiquitous in the Ukrainian urban space. One may say that there is nothing harmful about the presence of Pushkin, Mikhail Lermontov (1814–1841) or Mikhail Bulgakov (1891–1940) as monuments or names of streets in Ukraine, and that they are just people of culture. However, if we consider the reasons for such evident visibility of Russian but no other culture in the Ukrainian urban space, we can understand that this is hardly the case.

Literary scholar Ewa Thompson very clearly explained the imperial nature of Russian literature in her famous book, *Imperial Knowledge: Russian Literature and Colonialism* (2000) and alarmed the need for revision of Russian literature in the global context of literary studies. However, in today's arguments about the need to diminish the presence of Russian culture in Ukraine, Thompson's book is forgotten, both in Ukraine and abroad, and some people still refer to the humanism of Russian literature. As a response, Ukrainian literary scholar Vira Aheyeva, in her book *Za lashtunkamy imperii* (*Behind the Scenes of the Empire,*

2021), clearly describes how the "humanism of Russian literature stopped on the Ukrainian question."[1] She argues that the loss of the colonies, firstly Ukraine, meaning the end of Russian imperial ambitions, has always been perceived as a catastrophe for Russia. The literature was an instrument for imperial ideology, regardless of the form of the state, whether it be the Russian empire, the Soviet Union or the Russian Federation.

The sites of Russian cultural heritage in Ukraine are nothing other than the attempts of an imperial policy to create an alleged common history and artificially form a common cultural space of the metropolis and its colony. According to Antony Smith's classic work, national identity is defined, among other things, by a common historic territory or homeland, common myths and historical memories, and common culture. The Russian Empire, the Soviet Union and then the Russian Federation consistently and obstinately implemented the policy of unification in Ukraine. Visual signs of Russian cultural and historical persons are meant to establish and support the feeling of belongingness to some common imagined community of Russia and Ukraine, with the supervision of the first, of course, which undeniably leads to unification in terms of identity. This process is well-known as the narrations about the "brotherhood" of Russia and Ukraine or "one nation" (*odin narod*), which has been cultivated and voiced to artificially create a common cultural and historical space between the two separate countries.

After Ukraine gained independence in 1991, it took two decades to enter the active phase of de-communization. In 2014, after Euromaidan, the fall of the monuments to Vladimir Lenin and then the renaming of toponymical features slowly led to the elimination of Soviet colonial heritage in the Ukrainian urban space. However, the changes were mainly introduced by dismantling the monuments to communist leaders and removing the communist names from public spaces. After February 24, 2022, when Russian missiles and bombs started to destroy Ukrainian land, monuments and streets named after Russian writers, composers, and other people of culture began to be removed, along with Russian literature in the school programs.

For centuries, Russian culture has been an instrument for establishing imperial superiority and controlling the colony. To explain the reasons for removing Russian writers', poets' and composers' names from Ukrainian urban spaces, school programs, cultural institutions and other aspects of people's lives, Ukrainian philosopher Volodymyr Yarmolenko recently wrote:

---

[1] Vira Aheyeva, *Za lashtunkamy imperii* (Kyiv: Vikhola, 2021), 131.

When Russia destroyed Chechnya in the 1990s, sparked artificial separatist struggles in Moldova and Georgia in the 1990s, invaded Georgia in 2008, and invaded Ukraine in 2014, these acts of brutality had their intellectual underpinnings in the great Russian literary classics and their authors' attitudes toward the empire's colonies and conquests. To this day, these authors and their works are telling Russians that there is nothing to respect in the lands occupied by Russian soldiers. When Pushkin depicted Ukrainian Cossacks as bloody and cruel, this was just the 19th-century version of today's propaganda narrative about Ukrainians as alleged Nazis whose historical fate is death and submission. When Tyutchev presents 19th-century Russia as Europe's glorious savior from democracy, he is echoed in Putin's fight to overturn color revolutions in Ukraine and elsewhere.[2]

Ukrainian scholar and literary critic Rostyslav Semkiv, in his article "How Russian literature serves the Empire" (2022), also emphasized the imperial and chauvinistic anti-Ukrainian motif in the renowned works of Russian writers. He stressed, among other things, the imperialist and anti-Ukrainian discourses of Bulgakov's novel *The White Guard* (*Belaya gvardiya*, 1925). "His novel *The White Guard* is imbued with convictions about the supremacy of Russian culture and lamentations about the demise of the empire",[3] Semkiv writes.

The question of Bulgakov and his legacy in Ukraine remains open, especially concerning the Bulgakov museum in Kyiv. Russia's full-scale invasion of Ukraine activated the de-russification and decommunization processes. Today there is a campaign to remove the Bulgakov Museum and replacing it with one dedicated to Ukrainian composer Oleksandr Koshyts (1875–1944).[4] The main reasons lie in the facts of imperial and openly anti-Ukrainian motifs in Bulgakov's writings. However, many influential and well-known people in Ukraine are against the abolition of the Bulgakov Museum, calling it a brand of the city of Kyiv. Additionally, Bulgakov has been retained in the Ukrainian school program. People who support the idea of closing or dedicating the Bulgakov Museum to someone else emphasize his Ukrainophobia and imperial position. Famous Ukrainian writer Oksana Zabuzhko has explained

---

[2] Volodymyr Yermolenko, "From Pushkin to Putin: Russian Literature's Imperial Ideology," *Foreign Policy*, June 25, 2022.

[3] Rostyslav Semkiv, "Yak rosiyska literatura sluzhyt imperii." *Ukrainskyi Tyzhden*, March 7, 2022.

[4] Oleksandr Koshyts (1875–1944) was a Ukrainian choral conductor, arranger, composer, ethnographer, writer, musicologist and lecturer. He helped popularize Ukrainian music around the world. His performance also popularized Mykola Leontovych's "Shchedryk" in his concert, which Peter Wilhousky later translated into the popular "Carol of the Bells."

many times, in her interviews and articles, the need for Ukraine to bid farewell to "Russian *Kiev* and Bulgakov."[5]

In 2015, Zabuzhko wrote an article about the Mikhail Bulgakov Museum, often called "Bulgakov's House." Zabuzhko presented the history of the building in Kyiv at Adriivskii Uzviz 13 and its real progenitor owner—the Ukrainian architect Vasyl Lystovnychyi (1876–1919). The fact that people still call this building "Bulgakov's House" is due to the Soviet authorities, which deprived the building of its historical owner and corresponding name, kidnapping a large part of the historical memory of Kyiv.[6]

At the same time, Russian missiles deliberately physically destroyed Ukrainian culture. The first museum that was bombed by Russia in Ukraine was the Local History Museum in Ivankiv near Kyiv. The museum's most valuable exhibits were artworks by the Ukrainian painter Maria Prymachenko (1909–1997).[7] After the fire, only the walls remained at the museum; many artworks and showpieces were lost. Yet another example: on the night before May 7, 2022, the Russians destroyed the museum of the Ukrainian philosopher Hryhorii Skovoroda[8] in Kharkiv Oblast. As of 24 October, UNESCO has verified damage to two hundred and seven sites since 24 February – eighty-eight religious sites, fifteen museums, seventy-six buildings of historical and artistic interest, eighteen monuments, and ten libraries. Therefore, against the background of the physical destruction of Ukrainian culture, the removal of the sites of Russian imperial and chauvinist anti-Ukrainian culture from the city spaces in Ukraine is very reasonable and helpful in dismantling the myth about a common Russian-Ukrainian cultural space and "brotherhood."

REFERENCES

Aheeva, Vira. *Za lashtunkamy imperii.* Kyiv: Vikhola, 2021.

Drozdova, Yevhenia. "'Ya pomniu chudnoe mgnovene'… raketa vluchyla u dim. Chomu Ukraina mae pozbutysya pamyatnykiv i vulyts' Pushkinu." *Teksty.org.ua*, March 30, 2022. https://texty.org.ua/articles/106161/ya-pomnyu-chudnoe-mhnovene-raketa-vluchyla-u-dim-chomu-ukrayina-may e-pozbutysya-pamyatnykiv-i-vulyc-pushkinu/?fbclid=IwAR1c8Zi7bVtju9SIR Rl7LsUAP-g4OR95XXzz-_HqHlskKF4DR5PINrikOYY.

---

[5] Oksana Zabuzhko, "Zachukhanyi provintsializm – tse koly v Kyevi tilky 'pereshyvayut te, shcho v Moskvi nosyat." *Insider*, October 5, 2015.

[6] Oksana Zabuzhko, "Tsei proklyatyi 'kvartyrnyi vopros'." *Radio Svoboda*. June 18, 2015.

[7] Maria Prymachenko (1909–1997) was a Ukrainian artist and representative of a naïve art.

[8] Hryhorii Skovoroda (1722–1794) was a Ukrainian philosopher, poet, writer and theologist. His philosophy was mainly focused on different aspects of ethics and had enormous influence on future generations of people of culture in Ukraine.

Semkiv, Rostyslav. "Yak rosiyska literatura sluzhyt imperii." *Ukrainskyi Tyzhden,* March 7, 2022. https://tyzhden.ua/Culture/254500.

Smith, Anthony. *National Identity.* Harmondsworth: Penguin Books, 1991.

Thompson, Ewa. *Imperial Knowledge: Russian Literature and Colonialism.* Westport, CT and London: Greenwood, 2000.

UNESCO. "Damaged cultural sites in Ukraine verified by UNESCO." Accessed October 28, 2022. https://www.unesco.org/en/articles/damaged-cultural-sites-ukraine-verified-unesco.

Yermolenko, Volodymyr. "From Pushkin to Putin: Russian Literature's Imperial Ideology." *Foreign Policy,* June 25, 2022. https://foreignpolicy.com/2022/06/25/russia-ukraine-war-literature-classics-imperialism-ideology-nationalism-putin-pushkin-tolstoy-dostoevsky-caucasus/?fs=e&s=cl&fbclid=IwAR2zm_WR9zWe1njjr_HxWeU6306RCbyfg7zIi5SrvjG14pavtLMdHXM3qOo.

Zabuzhko, Oksana. "Zachukhanyi provintsializm – tse koly v Kyevi tilky 'pereshyvayut' te, shcho v Moskvi nosyat." Interview by Yevhenii Stasinevych. *Insider,* October 5, 2015. http://www.theinsider.ua/art/oksana-zabuzhko-lyutii-zachukhanii-provintsializm-tse-koli-v-kiyevi-tilki-pereshivayut-te-shcho-v-moskvi-nosyat/.

Zabuzhko, Oksana. "Tsei proklyatyi 'kvartyrnyi vopros'." *Radio Svoboda,* June 18, 2015. https://www.radiosvoboda.org/a/27079412.html.

Essay 2:
Memories of Famine in Ukraine. Vasyl Barka's Novel *The Yellow Prince* (1962)

Maria Ivanytska

Taras Shevchenko National University of Kyiv, Ukraine

HISTORICAL DIGRESSION

One of the greatest tragedies in the history of mankind—the *Holodomor*, the purposefully created famine in Ukraine, which destroyed between six and nine million lives in 1932 and 1933—was concealed for a long time. The Communist Party of the Soviet Union did everything to hide information about the famine: the Soviet press was instructed to write about the happy life of the people, sometimes mentioning only the difficult years of bad harvests. Journalists coming from abroad were shown only the successes of the Soviet Union and were forbidden from visiting towns and villages without permission. Only Gareth Jones (1905–1935), a journalist from Wales, managed to secretly visit and report the truth about the starving Ukraine, but he was killed shortly thereafter. Ukrainian writers living in the Soviet Union at that time were also subject to mass reprisals, branded enemies of the people, arrested, shot, and exiled to Siberia. As a result, only those authors who lived in exile wrote about the famine. The first longer narrative about the Holodomor was written by Ulas Samchuk (1905–1987), the Ukrainian writer who lived in Prague in the 1930s. His work *Maria* was published in 1934 in Lviv (which was then part of Poland, not the Soviet Union), becoming the first novel about the violent Soviet collectivization and famine in Ukraine.

MEMORIES AND AUTOBIOGRAPHY

In 1943, another exiled Ukrainian writer, Vasyl Barka (1908–2003), began to write a longer piece about the famine. Born in Central Ukraine (Poltava region) as Vasyl Ocheret, he graduated from a pedagogical college and started working in the Donbass region. During the years of the famine, he lived in the city of Krasnodar, in the center of the historic Kuban region. Barka visited his brother's family in Ukraine, and the starvation and suffering of the people he saw touched him deeply. Barka was on the verge of starvation himself. Thanks to these first-hand encounters, he was later able to speak to the true psychological depth of the Holodomor experience in his literary work and to properly depict its horrors to the readers.

At the outbreak of the Second World War, Barka was called up to the front, got injured, and finally landed in a DP camp in Germany. There he began documenting his experiences and eyewitness accounts of the Ukrainian famine. In 1950, Barka emigrated to the USA, where he began to edit materials he had collected to integrate them into a novel on Holodomor. As Marko Stekh writes, Barka "got up every day before sunrise with unwavering discipline and worked until nightfall, by the river or in the woods, and in an empty barn during bad weather. Convinced that a well-fed writer would not be able to properly describe the sufferings of starvation, he refused to eat for several days while writing the saddest chapters of the novel."[1] According to Stekh, "Barka believed that without this second [experience] of fasting, he would not have been able to re-create, as he said, 'those fibers, shades of feeling: the abyssal, the worst in a human being.'"[2] This is how *The Yellow Prince* was born, the book considered to be the foremost work of Ukrainian literature.

Almost all of Barka's works, Stekh notices, concern the most excruciating periods of Ukrainian history, such as Stalin's terror in the 1930s and the catastrophe of the Second World War, and yet, surprisingly, they are all imbued with "the warmth of human kindness and the secret light of divine providence."[3]

MEMORIES AND WORK FOR SOCIETY

The Yellow Prince belongs to Ukrainian politically engaged exile literature written in the 1940s and 1950s that describes the totalitarian reality of life in the Soviet Union and whose ultimate goal was to tell the world the truth about the tragic fate of the Ukrainian people.

It should be noted that Ukrainian literature, in many periods of its development, was politically and socially driven. The reason for this was the fact that for several centuries, Ukraine was not an independent, sovereign state. Vast parts of Ukrainian territories belonged to the Russian Empire for roughly 250 years. During this time, the Ukrainian language was often banned, Ukrainian literature could not be developed without restriction, and

---

[1] Marko R. Stekh, "Pyshuchy roman pro Holodomor, Vasyl Barka po kilka dniv vidmovliavsia vid yizhi." *ZIK:* 23.11.2017. Accessed October 14, 2022. https://web.archive.org/web/201 80312145047/https://zik.ua/news/2017/11/23/marko_r_steh_pyshuchy_roman_pro_golod omor_vasyl_barka_po_kilka_dniv_1211579

[2] Ibid.

[3] Ibid.

Ukrainians were discriminated against and oppressed for social, religious, and national reasons. Hence Ukrainian authors fought for freedom through their words, such as national poet Taras Shevchenko (1814–1861) or the poets of the so-called Executed Renaissance before the Second World War. By the same token, the post-war Ukrainian authors in exile saw literature as an instrument to fight for truth and enlightenment and thus to oppose the propaganda of the Soviet Union.

When the prominent Ukrainian literary scholar Mychailo Rudnyc'kyi (1889–1975) discussed the question as to why Ukrainian literature became *literature engagée*, he compared Ukrainian and European literary Romanticism. He noticed the flight of imagination in European Romanticism and the closeness to reality in Ukrainian Romanticism, the strong personality of a free writer in European literature and a sense of duty to society in Ukrainian literature, the predominance of feelings over reason in European literary works and the prevalence of pragmatic considerations on labor in Ukrainian literary works. "European Romantics were inspired by folk poetry, drank from it, and forgot what they owed it. Ukrainian Romantics drew only from folk song sources, immediately returning what they had borrowed. They did not demand inspiration for themselves [...]," Rudnyc'kyi wrote, adding that "all Ukrainian Romantic literature is the most Romantic in sacrificing itself on the altar of the homeland—both works and talents. Those with no talent sacrificed what they could do for the common good [...] Without Ukrainian Romanticism, the Ukrainian national movement would be unthinkable."[4] Much of the same can be said about the later generations of Ukrainian authors and their emphasis on the role of literature as a socially important phenomenon. This also concerns Ukrainian post-war exile literature, including Barka's oeuvre. Through his literary works, Barka sought to keep the world alert, to give testimony to the greatest tragedies of the Ukrainian people, and to ensure that humankind would not look away.

MEMORIES AND POETRY

Barka also wrote poetry. His modernist poems and their deep religious symbolism are connected to social issues on a philosophical level; the issue of the Soviet famine was present in his poetry much earlier than in his prose. For example:

---

[4] Mychailo Rudnyc'kyj, "Die Eigenart der ukrainischen Romantik." *Slavische Rundschau*, no. XI (1939): 181–192.

Sunflowers pray.
Thunder on a cloud reads the Bible ...
The poplar whispering: how terrible
is your weeping, Isaiah!
Sunflowers pray.
Famine. The mother kills the baby...
The poplar cried: so is
my paradise, Isaiah![5]

This poem, "Paradise," is considered a key text for understanding Barka's works, as it synthesizes the most important characteristics of his oeuvre: the genuine religiosity that penetrates every line of Barka's poem; the concern for the fate of those who are suffering, which is the core of Christianity; the interest in the literary tradition while searching for new forms of expression; and finally, a metaphorical language combining the spheres of the earthly and the mystical.[6] "Paradise" belongs to the post-war collection of Barka's poems entitled *The White World*. The "white world" refers to the simple humanity, the Christian faith, and the traditional morality of the Ukrainian people rooted in their pantheistic love of nature. This gentle, seemingly defenseless white world, is contrasted with the demonic challenges of the twentieth century, which the poet saw with his own eyes and experienced directly.

The interplay between nature, poetic-philosophical imagery, and harrowing metaphors is typical of Barka's prose. His poetry, however, is considered neo-baroque, following the traditions of Hryhorii Skovoroda (1722–1794), a Ukrainian poet and philosopher of the Baroque period who combined the poetic world of the Bible, prophet motifs, and pantheism, appealing to universal values.

A MEMOIR OF THE APOCALYPSE

Based on documents and his own memories and reflections, in *The Yellow Prince* Barka develops a comprehensive portrait of an apocalyptic world where lawlessness, degradations, abuses, humiliation, gross violence, and heartlessness prevail. The novel has a unique resonance because it connects two paradigms, bringing the reader "into the world of the Bible and the *Divine Comedy* of Dante. This world is dominated by peculiarly mystical, at times prophetic intonations which help depict the terrible images of the Holodomor

---

[5] Vasyl Barka, *Bilyi svit.* (Munich: Ukrainska trybuna, 1947), 9.
[6] Bohdan Boichuk, "Rannia poeziia Vasylia Barky." *Svitovyd.* no. 4 (1998): 42–50.

in a uniquely symbolic way."[7] The twentieth century is seen, then, as an apocalyptic time in which the most important struggles take place not in world politics, but in the souls of ordinary people. Of the books of the Bible, Barka was particularly drawn to the Book of Revelation. Like in the Bible, every human emotion in Barka's work has a religious significance. *The Yellow Prince* contains countless images that imply apocalypse on many levels—through individual human fates, peoples' actions, and the degradation of the character's souls. The novel is full of heartbreaking and appalling facts and events: the author depicts how a whole family dies of starvation or how in a village dying of hunger, its inhabitants go insane, which ultimately leads to acts of cannibalism. Despite everything, the novel's main protagonists, the Katrannyk family, remain faithful to human values and Christian morality. *The Yellow Prince* also describes in detail the Soviet policy towards the Ukrainian people: how the Soviet officers took away the last crumbs of bread and thus deliberately condemned whole families to death, how they beat and tortured peasants, and how starving villagers were not allowed into the cities or to cross the border into the neighboring Russian SFSR. Barka interprets the tragedy of 1933 as a biblical prophecy and at the same time as the result of a programmed genocide carried out by the Communist Party and its leaders.

By vocalizing what he had experienced in the 1930s, Barka managed to slightly alleviate his trauma. In this sense, his case was typical: many Ukrainian authors aimed both to give testimony to what they had suffered, and also to commemorate and reflect on the tragedy for themselves and their compatriots. Their texts are philosophically and aesthetically processed narratives about real events, evaluations of traumatic experiences, and attempts to warn the world about inhumanity, totalitarianism, and autocracy. *The Yellow Prince* can be defined as a social-psychological novel, but also as a document of the epoch that develops deeply symbolic images on the micro and macro levels. For this reason, some researchers consider Barka's novel to be "material for research and possibly a source for scientific works in sociology and psychology, (and) a document of the epoch of totalitarianism which could be used in the international court on Bolshevism."[8] Barka also wrote in the preface to the first edition of his novel in Ukraine: "The author is not a judge in his work, but ... a witness for the court: he tells what happened in life."[9]

---

[7] Natalia M. Tymoshchuk, "Antytotalitarnyi pafos ukrainskoi prozy XX stolittia: problema holodomoru." *Aktualni problemy slovianskoi filolohii: Mizhvuzivskyi zbirnyk naukovykh statei,* no. IX (Kyiv: Znannia Ukrainy, 2004): 417–424.

[8] Oleg S. Hryniv, *Ukraina i Rosiia: partnerstvo chy protystoiannia? (Etnopsykholohichnyi analiz).* (Lviv: Instytut narodoznavstva NAN Ukrainy, 1997), 204.

[9] Vasyl Barka, *Zhovtyi kniaz: Roman.* (Kyiv, Dnipro, 1991), 26.

UKRAINIAN PEASANTS: BETWEEN DEATH AND MORALITY

The fate of the Katrannyk family is closely connected to Christian and ecclesiastical imagery, illustrating the episode of a golden chalice that the Ukrainian peasants managed to hide from the Soviet officials. It is Myron Katrannyk, the locally respected and venerated father of the Katrynnyk family, chosen to keep this treasure safe. Despite being captured by the Soviets and tormented to death, Myron refuses to reveal where the chalice is hidden. In Barka's novel, the golden chalice becomes a symbol of the true Ukrainian soul that values faith, honor, cohesion, loyalty, and honesty over material things.

Of the entire Katrynnyk family, only the youngest son, Andriyko, survives. At the end of the novel, Andriyko has a piece of bread and is ready to share it with an unknown starving woman. With this, *The Yellow Prince* ends on an optimistic note: a new day begins, and it brings hope for the rebirth of life.

THE STRUGGLE BETWEEN GOOD AND EVIL

The novel's plot is narrated from three different perspectives.

The first is a look at the daily life of the Katrannyk family—their attempts to survive while moving and wandering in search of food.

The second is a psychological one that offers an analysis of the remarkable changes in the human soul while it is faced with the experience of mass hunger. As Barka notices, even though the starving people strived for food, they still kept compassion for others at the bottom of their hearts. Particularly in comparison with the Soviet authorities who created the famine, the starving Ukrainian peasants retained their humanity.

The third perspective is metaphysical and spiritual: it is a vision of an uncanny supernatural world on the one hand and a heaven that is open to pure, faithful, and simple people on the other, which immediately brings the topos of the eternal struggle between good and evil to the forefront of the novel. *The Yellow Prince* portrays the confrontation between good and evil as the struggle between God and the devil, between the truth and the lie, and between the pure souls of the Ukrainian peasants and the soullessness of the Bolsheviks.

THE SYMBOLISM OF THE COLOR YELLOW

The title of Barka's novel, *The Yellow Prince*, carries deep symbolism. The "yellow prince" is an allusion to a rider from the Book of Revelation who is believed to bring death, sorrow, suffering, total destruction, and devastation not only to the earth, but also to human souls. "I looked, and there before me was a pale horse! Its rider was named Death, and Hades was following close behind him. They were given power over a fourth of the earth to kill by sword, famine and plague, and by the wild beasts of the earth."[10]

But the title *Yellow Prince* can be interpreted in different ways; it can be seen as the embodiment of the soulless new government led by Stalin, the "Antichrist", whose mission is to kill, and a symbol of the hunger that reigned on the streets of suffering Ukraine. In the novel, the color yellow is a symbol of death and the destruction of the world and the human. Yellow is the color of dried weed and grass on the quiet streets of half-dead villages; it is the color of the corpses of people who died of hunger. Everything touched by the inhuman Soviet power turns yellow, as if breathed on by the fire of hell. The image of the yellow prince permeates throughout the novel, as it is both symbolic and multifaceted. He "rules in the air," and "he and his demons rule over souls like hawks over chickens."[11] The apotheosis of the unity between the devil and the Soviet state is depicted in the yellow walls of the official buildings.

Yellow is thus a symbol of sadness, separation, and horror. The bare figure of the "yellow prince" is embodied in Hryhoryi Otrokhodin, the representative of the Soviet regime in the village where the Katrannyks live. Ostrokhodin's appearance is quite striking: he has teeth made of gold; he wears jackets similar to the one Stalin wore; his glasses are frameless, just like Beria's: and he has a yellowish complexion. He hates and does not understand Ukrainian peasants, especially those like the Katrannyks.

On the other hand, the evil in Barka's novel is juxtaposed with good, which is also related to the yellow color, as it is embodied in the image of the sun. *This* yellow has a different hue: bright, warm, and pleasant. Its rays rise, illuminate the wheat fields, and save human lives. The sun is an eternal image of goodness, hope, warmth, and harvest; it cannot be overcome by dark forces. As the color of the life-giving sun, ears of corn, and bread, yellow becomes a symbol of life and renewal. Similarly to the golden chalice, it becomes a symbol of light that overcomes darkness and gloom, despite all oppression.

BARKA'S NOVEL AND THE PRESENT

The first volume of *The Yellow Prince* appeared in 1962 in *Suchasnist* magazine (New York—Munich). In 1981, the novel was published in France by the prestigious publishing house Gallimard as *Le Prince jaune*, translated by Olga Yavorska, with a preface by Pierre Ravich. In Ukraine, *The Yellow Prince* was not published until 1991. Barka's novel also formed the basis for Oles Yanchuk's film *Hunger-33*. In December 1991, the day before the referendum

---

[10] Revelation 6:8.
[11] Barka, Vasyl. "Zhovtyi kniaz. Tom 1: Povist." *Suchasnist*. no.7 (Munich, New-York, 1962): 12.

on Ukraine's independence, the film ran on all channels of Ukrainian television and most likely influenced people's decision to vote for Ukraine's politictal sovereignty.

Nowadays, Russia still refuses to acknowledge the Holodomor as a genocide. The communist crimes that were investigated shortly after the collapse of the Soviet Union have again been closed to examinations. Joseph Stalin is seen as a model statesman who made the Soviet Union a world power other countries throughout the world were afraid of and whose citizens were genuinely proud of it.

Precisely such narratives made Russia's present war against Ukraine possible. Reading Barka's novel in 2022, I see a repetition of the events that took place almost a hundred years ago: the way Russians/Soviets aim to destroy the heart of Ukraine, the peasantry; the way Russian/Soviet troops bury the corpses of the murdered Ukrainians in mass graves; the wish to eradicate the existence of the free people and to subjugate the entire country to the Kremlin. However, we believe that Ukrainians will stand firm and that the peaceful sun will rise again over Ukraine, as it once did for Barka. We, like Myron and Andriyko, do not give up.

REFERENCES

Barka, Vasyl. *Bilyi svit.* Munich: Ukrainska trybuna, 1947.

Barka, Vasyl. *Zhovtyi kniaz: Roman.* Kyiv: Dnipro, 1991.

Barka, Vasyl. "Zhovtyi kniaz. Tom 1: Povist." *Suchasnist.* Munich, New-York, 1962, no.7 (19): 5–38; no.11 (23):5–55.

Boichuk, Bohdan. "Rannia poeziia Vasylia Barky." *Svitovyd.* 1998, no. 4: 42–50.

Hryniv, Oleg S. *Ukraina i Rosiia: partnerstvo chy protystoiannia? (Etnopsykholohichnyi analiz).* Lviv: Instytut narodoznavstva NAN Ukrainy,1997.

Rudnyc'kyj, Mychailo. "Die Eigenart der ukrainischen Romantik." *Slavische Rundschau.*1939, no. XI: 181–192.

Rudnytskyi, Leonid. "Literatura z misiieiu." *Slovo i chas.* 1999, no. 9: 41–45.

Samchuk, Ulas. *Mariia.* Lviv: Ukrainska biblioteka, 1934.

Stekh, Marko R. "Pyshuchy roman pro Holodomor, Vasyl Barka po kilka dniv vidmovliavsia vid yizhi." *ZIK:* 23.11.2017. Accessed October 14, 2022. https://web.archive.org/web/20180312145047/https://zik.ua/news/2017/1 1/23/marko_r_steh_pyshuchy_roman_pro_golodomor_vasyl_barka_po_kilk a_dniv_1211579.

Tymoshchuk, Natalia M. "Antytotalitarnyi pafos ukrainskoi prozy XX stolittia: problema holodomoru." *Aktualni problemy slovianskoi filolohii: Mizhvuzivskyi zbirnyk naukovykh statei.* Kyiv: Znannia Ukrainy, 2004, no. IX: Linhvistyka i literaturoznavstvo: 417–424.

Essay 3:
Remembering a Bright Soviet Past. Scatology and Necrophilia as Metaphors of a Diseased Memory in Oleksandr Irvanets's *Rivne/Rovno* (2001)

Valentin Peschanskyi

University of Münster, Germany

Oleksandr Irvanets's *Rivne/Rovno (Stina). Nibyto roman* (*Rivne/Rovno* (*The Wall*). *A Quasi-Novel*) of 2001 portrays a gloomy dystopia: with Russia's help, Ukrainians yearning for a bright Soviet past occupy almost all of Ukraine. The counterfactual (quasi-)novel employs two metaphors for this Soviet nostalgia that are as bold as they are amusing: scatology and necrophilia.

1. A DAY TRIP DOWN MEMORY LANE

Ten years after the collapse of the Soviet empire, Irvanets' has his literary revenant Shloima Etsirvan spend a day roaming the streets of the city that lends its name to the novel. That city is, as the title *Rivne/Rovno* implies, divided into two parts by a wall—a division that is also reflected in different time zones, languages, and political systems. The eastern part, Rovno, belongs to the Neo-Soviet Republic of Ukraine, abbreviated to the telling acronym S.R.U. ("I shit"), a vassal state of Moscow that, with Russia's help, has almost swallowed up all of Ukraine. The western part, Rivne, which, like West Berlin, forms an enclave within the S.R.U., is administered by the European-oriented West Ukrainian Republic.

The renowned, roughly forty-year-old writer Shloima Etsirvan lives in the western sector, Rivne. After a four-year wait, he receives permission to visit his family in the eastern part, Rovno, the very day his play *The Day After Tomorrow's Schedule* premieres. The date of his visit, a September 17 sometime in the 2000s, could not be of greater historical symbolism: it was on this day in 1939 that the Soviet Union began its occupation of Eastern Poland under the pretext of protecting the Ukrainians and Belarusians living there. The invasion was followed by the excesses of Bolshevik terror and the incorporation of the territories into the Ukrainian and Byelorussian Soviet Socialist Republics. The novel thus at once evokes two Soviet occupations bookending the Second World War—the divisions of Poland and Germany—and projects them into the Ukrainian present.

Etsirvan's foray through Rovno is structured by contemplative cigarette smoking that shapes his perception of time and space. As he is numbed by the smoke, his gaze repeatedly slips back to the past. Rovno is, as Yurii Andrukhovych writes in the foreword to the German translation,

> an almost timeless concentration of everything Soviet, anachronistic, and dead. And yet it is also about a territory of nostalgia, memory, sentimentality, a zone of the lost time one unexpectedly finds once again, a space of the reconstruction of dreams.[1]

The encounters with different people, the bleak streets, buildings, and parks evoke different episodes from Etsirvan's Soviet childhood and youth. The number of cigarettes he has left in his packet of red Gauloises serves as a chronometer, and the butts he leaves behind at various places mark the space he traverses like fairytale breadcrumbs. Etsirvan's crossing the border from Rivne to Rovno is not only a spatial movement but also a temporal one: the day in Rovno conjures up his entire life, the history of the city, the region and ultimately the entire Soviet empire.

2. SEWERAGE AND SCATOLOGY

As Etsirvan moves through the city space, he also moves into a different time: on the surface, Rovno seems like a harmless museum of the Soviet past, but via the power of memory, this past soon awakens, penetrates the present, and finally takes possession of it. In the text's last fifth, Etsirvan pays a heavy price for his nostalgic trip: it turns out that the S.R.U. is using a technology with the equally telling name D.U.P.A. ("ass") to control the thoughts of Rovno's inhabitants, including all the characters who have crossed Etsirvan's path. It transpires that the Rovno authorities staged the playwright's entire day in order to collect compromising material and blackmail him. The Rovno neo-Soviets' plan is simple: using a mechanism found in the basement of the theatre in Rivne, of all places, they force Etsirvan to open the bars separating parts of the shared sewage system so that the S.R.U.'s "special units", dressed "in special anti-fecal suits" (*R/R*, 147), can enter the western part and reunify

---

[1] Juri Andruchowytsch. "Ein Blick hinter die Mauer. Vorwort," Oleksandr Irwanez, *Pralinen vom roten Stern*. Trans. Alexander Kratochvil. Vienna: Haymon, 2017, 11–12.

the city under their flag.[2] Things get even worse when Etsirvan finds out that all the inhabitants of the democratic western part are in on the plan and urge him to realize it. The theatre's German guest director Maul'vurf ("mole") has gone so far as to integrate the real attack into the premiere of Etsirvan's play *The Day After Tomorrow's Schedule*. Even Etsirvan's tomcat Bonifatsii is in on the conspiracy and brings him the key he needs to operate the fatal mechanism that opens the bars. The only one who doesn't know what's going on is the writer himself, who, blinded by his illusions, refuses to recognize that the depths of hell are opening up before his eyes.

In a second metaleptic leap, in the novel's last paragraph, we learn that Rivne probably never existed and was merely a nice daydream on the part of Etsirvan that materialized on the pages we are reading. In order to merge Rovno with Rivne, he simply has to wake up and allow the typical Soviet indifference and apathy to take possession of himself:

> I unite two streams of filth, two fecal worlds, two seas of shit surging from both East and West whose separation is really only unnatural and artificial. They would unite in the future without me anyway, perhaps a little later, they would eat up, corrode these very symbolic bars and come together. [...] The city merges with the city, the imaginary with the real city and the latter will be the former, just as it should be. You, my dreamed-up, my unreal city, you never existed, you exist only on the previous few dozen pages of this book. Never before and never again, just here and now, when the reader reads these lines that are nearly the last. [...] And that is the end. The end of the novel and the end of the independent city, the enclosed city. The end of West Rivne. The wall doesn't fall, it simply disappears, dissipates into evening mist. The city unifies, unites, becomes one. (*R/R*, 185, 187)

The dichotomy between Russian totalitarianism and fragile European democracy that allegedly divides Ukraine is resolved in an instant. The stream of feces in the sewer functions as an allegory of the Soviet past fermenting in the subconscious of the inhabitants of *both* parts of the city and threatening to surface at any time. As Alexander Kratochvil notes, the novel's scatological imagery evokes, through the juxtaposition of Rivne and Rovno, the juxtaposition

---

[2] The abbreviation *R/R* refers to Oleksandr Irvanets. *Rivne/Rovno (Stina). Nibyto roman.* Lviv: Kalvariia, 2002. All quotations from the novel are translations from the Ukrainian by Valentin Peschanskyi.

of *hivno* und *govno*—that is, "Ukrainian" or "Russian" shit.[3] As long as people hold on to a Soviet nostalgia for a bleak but supposedly simple past that promised a glorious future, the names for the city or the feces of its inhabitants are irrelevant—it doesn't change the quality, consistency or smell of the shit they have in their minds.

3. THE DEAD BODY AND NECROPHILIA

In addition to scatology, *Rivne/Rovno* employs a second metaphor of poisoned memory: necrophilia. The S.R.U. blackmails Etsirvan with a video showing him having sex under the influence of morphine with the love of his youth Olena Bliashana, or Oblia ("Oh fuck!") for short. They threaten to put the video online if he doesn't comply with their demands. That would sound rather banal or harmless if Olena were not the embodiment of the memory of a corpse symbolizing the Soviet Union. Etsirvan's necrophiliac lust for the past, I claim, is the root cause of the "tragic" turning point—his transformation from a Western democrat to a stooge of the Rovno regime.

Before Etsirvan meets the adult Olena in the present, she is frequently the object of his reminiscences, one of which is of particular importance for our context: shortly after their first kiss, the fifteen-year-old Etsirvan accompanies Olena to her father's workplace, the local morgue. When the father and daughter briefly leave him on his own, Etsirvan walks up to a metal table on which lies the corpse of a beautiful twenty-year-old suicide. Equally fascinated by "death and the naked maiden", the boy slowly uncovers the body and enjoys the erotic sight of the corpse that has not yet become stiff and cold.

> It was the first naked girl's body he had seen in his life. At the same time, it was the first dead human body he had seen in his life. And overall, it was the strongest impression in his life thus far as a fifteen-year-old boy. [Arkady] Gaidar commanded a squadron at his age, Alexander the Great gathered an army for his Asia Minor campaign. [Jean-François] Champollion sank his teeth into the hieroglyphics. Shloima Etsirvan, on the other hand, saw for the first time a naked and dead girl's body. (*R/R*, 66)

The erotically charged visual exploration of the dead female body proves to be the direct continuation of the innocent attempts at French kissing with Olena. It is, as it were, a perverted transitional rite in tension between Eros and

---

[3] Alexander Kratochvil. "Postmodern History/Postmodern Stories," *Harvard Ukrainian Studies* 32 (2011), 504.

Thanatos that ends with Etsirvan recognizing his sexuality and, at the same time, his mortality, and with them birth and death as his life's limits.

The beautiful corpse turns out to be the critical nexus of Etsirvan's identity, of the spatiotemporal structure of the fictional world and hence of the entire novel. Etsirvan's interactions with Olena, both in his memory and in the present, are directly associated with the dead body—Olena carries the memory of the corpse lying on the metal table. The fateful carnal act, which just so happens to take place in a hospital near the Rovno morgue, is not only the culmination and climax of Etsirvan's day trip but also the realization of a phantasma he had put off for a quarter of a century. Afterwards, as he drifts off into the world of dreams, drunk on love and morphine, he imagines the corpse rising from the metal table and giving him a "cold biting kiss on the lips" (*R/R*, 95).

Let us take a step back at this juncture and examine this necrophiliac attraction to the beautiful corpse from the higher plane of literary and cultural theory. One of the core theses of Elisabeth Bronfen's seminal study *Over Her Dead Body: Death, Femininity and the Aesthetic* (1992), based on Edgar Allan Poe's "Philosophy of Composition" (1846), states:

> By dying, a beautiful Woman serves as the motive for the creation of an art work and as its object of representation. As a deanimated body, she can also become an art object or be compared with one. [...] Because her dying figures as an analogy to the creation of an art work [...], 'the death of a beautiful woman' marks the *mise en abyme* of a text, the moment of self-reflexivity, where the text seems to comment on itself and its own process of composition, and so decomposes itself.[4]

The beautiful corpse functions, then, as the text's motive, material, topic, motif, telos and final tableau, as a picture within the picture in which the entire work is concentrated. It not only reflects the essential *semantic levels* and *structure* of the text, but, moreover, it also functions as a kind of *autoreflexive* metaphor for its creation.

The corpse in *Rivne/Rovno* illustrates Elisabeth Bronfen's theory in quite exemplary fashion. The dead body lying on the metal table is the fulcrum of the plot, and thus the novel's *structure*, since it—or, more precisely, the memory of it—is the aim of Etsirvan's (scripted) journey through Rovno. Its appearance also marks, then, the beginning of the text's decomposition:

---

[4] Elisabeth Bronfen. *Over Her Dead Body: Death, Femininity and the Aesthetic*. Manchester: Manchester University Press, 1992, 71.

whereas up until this point, the text was, despite its dystopian scenario, "realistic", thereafter it drifts into the realm of the fantastical, before finally disintegrating into postmodern linguistic play. This development, the blurring of the imagination and reality, is taken up by the novel's conclusion when it has the corpse appear in the form of an indexical sign: the opening scene of Etsirvan's play, which reflects the novel's plot as fiction within the fiction—that is, as a concluding *mise en abyme*—shows the protagonist Olesia, a fictional revenant of Olena or Oblia, "on a shiny metal chair on a gleaming metal table, very similar to the one back then in the morgue" (*R/R*, 173).

The *autoreflexive* moment in *Rivne/Rovno* is also striking. The very surname of the protagonist Etsirvan, a figure in the fictional realm and at the same time an anagrammatic double of the real writer (French *écrivain*) Irvanets', draws attention to the novel's manufacturedness and fictionality before addressing them explicitly in the book's final pages. Against this background, the corpse appears as a kind of dead muse that stimulates Etsirvan's (or: Irvanets's) creativity in order for him to produce the work that imagines a Ukraine oriented towards Europe but which remains a fiction within the work too.

For our context, however, the motif is even more significant on the level of *semantics*. Immediately before the sex scene, Olena and Etsirvan have a conversation about the beautiful corpse: "I knew her", says Olena when Etsirvan asks about her identity, "She killed herself. [...] She drank a whole bottle of vinegar essence. Apparently due to unrequited love. Her insides were, as Papa said, completely black, all burnt...", to which Etsirvan replies: "Funny. She was beautiful. I mean, on the outside she looked so beautiful..." (*R/R*, 93–94). The suicide with the deceptively attractive exterior concealing a corroded, repulsive interior symbolizes the main topic of the novel as a whole: the question of how to deal with the Soviet past. The nostalgic flirtation with its idealized surface leads directly to a situation in which its long suppressed, forgotten and invisible traumas, thought patterns and ideologemes, festering somewhere in the depths or indeed the sewerage of cultural memory, violently burst into the present. The great allegorical arc spanning *Rivne/Rovno* tells us that every flirtation with the Soviet Union or, more precisely, its cadaver, however brief and ostensibly harmless it might be, results in annihilation. The Soviet Union is a beautiful wrapper that is able to draw in the naïve, the nostalgic, and the cynical but, in fact, was always close to decomposition, not merely rotten and dead but also deadly.

4. THE PITFALLS OF MEMORY

The depths of the sewer and the burnt insides of the beautiful corpse in *Rivne/Rovno* symbolize the contaminated post-Soviet cultural memory. Scatology and necrophilia stand for a diseased and clouded memory that lusts after the decayed Soviet Union while overlooking the fact that behind the attractive surface of the Soviet kitsch cultivated since the 1990s lurk its vile, dead insides.

The differentiation between the surface and the innards that forms the central thematic axis of the novel also shapes its reception: upon an initial, *superficial* reading, one might gain the impression that the juxtaposition of Rivne and Rovno at the turn of the millennium merely represents an exaggerated portrayal of the (supposed) division between eastern and western Ukraine. Yet the obvious scatological metaphors show that the alleged political and linguistic differences between East and West do not hold. It is immaterial whether shit is called *hivno* or *govno*; the issue is rather the relationship with the Soviet tradition, its idealizations and suppressed traumas, which are equally relevant to both parts of the country.

The novel's slightly more subtle, more elusive, second metaphoric level borrows its images from the sphere of necrophilia: the long-since decomposed woman's body, an equivalent to Lenin's corpse, which has been on display for almost 100 years in the center of Moscow, is the embodiment of the "real" Rovno in the novel, which itself figures as an open-air museum for the dead and deadly Soviet past. The Rivne merely "imagined" by Etsirvan is a counterpoint to this Soviet nostalgia, a projection that can become the future reality that promises a new life. The divide between Rovno and Rivne is thus not so much geopolitical and spatial as mental and temporal. Because Etsirvan cannot let go of Rovno, he repeats the girl's infatuated suicide insofar as he sacrifices the vision of a European and democratic Rivne and thus the future to his unrequited desire for the Soviet past.

The dichotomies between beautiful appearance and vile essence, between the surface and the subconscious, between the manifest and the latent, between reality and imagination, between the past and the future are thematized once again in the novel's finale. Etsirvan takes the lift down to the basement of the theatre building to open the bars dividing the sewer's two parts, thereby enabling the rebirth of Soviet monologism:

> How long will the lift's motor keep growling up there under the ceiling … How long can it take to travel these one-and-a-half stories from the stage to the basement …? Or maybe you're already in some other dimension and are travelling through the years, through years gone by, forgotten and remembered, through their petrified deposits, through their dark mass, and they converge over your head like the rings in a tree stump, … the nineties, eighties, seventies, sixties … (*R/R*, 181)

Etsirvan's supposedly harmless time travel along the horizontal surface of Rovno to the beautiful corpse suddenly turns into a vertical, deadly plummet evoking the topos of the descent into hell. As simple as it is stark, this conclusion tells us there is no such thing as harmless wallowing in memory: memory is always political and even ostensibly innocent reminiscences can have deadly consequences.

The comforting thing about visions and projections of the future is that they are seldom fully realized. However, Irvanets's vision of the future is horrifyingly precise in its prediction of Russia's relapse into imperialism and its attack on Ukraine. Yet, in one respect, the prognosis falls short of reality. In 2001, he could hardly have imagined that only a few years later Ukraine would begin to rise forever from the Soviet imperialist slurry—while the Russian Federation continues to sink in further.

Translated from the German by John Heath

REFERENCES

Andruchowytsch, Juri. "Ein Blick hinter die Mauer. Vorwort." In: Oleksandr Irwanez, *Pralinen vom roten Stern*. Translated by Alexander Kratochvil. Vienna: Haymon, 2017, 5–12.

Bronfen, Elisabeth. *Over Her Dead Body: Death, Femininity and the Aesthetic*. Manchester: Manchester University Press, 1992.

Irvanets, Oleksandr. *Rivne/Rovno (Stina). Nibyto roman*. Lviv: Kalvariia, 2002.

Kratochvil, Alexander. "Postmodern History/Postmodern Stories." *Harvard Ukrainian Studies* 32 (2011): 495–508.

Essay 4:
Amadoka (2020) by Sofia Andrukhovych as an Archeological Novel about Memory

Olena Saikovska

Odesa I. I. Mechnikov National University, Ukraine

Post-colonial countries face the consequences of the manipulation of their national history by the colonizer (rewriting history, silencing the truth, imposing one's own interpretation of events etc.). For a long time, Ukraine was *deprived* of its own historical memory; its history was changed or destroyed by the colonial state. After Ukraine gained independence, the process of distancing and departing from the colonizer began, which led to the necessity and possibility of recalling and rethinking one's own history. This first applies to the period of the 20th century. In 2002, in response to public demand, the Centre for Research on the Liberation Movement (*Tsentr Doslidzhen Vyzvolnoho Rukhu*) was founded. The Centre is an independent scientific public organization that investigates the politics of national memory and the processes of overcoming the consequences of the totalitarian past in countries of the former USSR, and Central and Eastern Europe. Another organization, the Ukrainian Institute of National Memory (*Ukraiinskyi Instytut Natsionalnoii Pamiati*), was established in 2006 as a special organ for the restoration and preservation of the national memory of the Ukrainian people. It is the central executive body operating under the Cabinet of Ministers of Ukraine.

How does Ukrainian literature reflect the societal challenges? What are the topics and literary works devoted to memory and national history?

Ukrainian professor Olena Vitaliivna Romanenko (born in 1973), in her article *Identychnist natsii ta tekstu: Jak suchasna ukrainska literatura formuie intensyvni obrazy natsionalnoii identyfikatsii* (*The Nation and the Text's Identity: Creating Intensive Images of National Identification Using Modern Ukrainian Literature*, 2016) analyzed the Ukrainian literary process of 1985–2015 and determined that Ukrainian literature of that time went through two stages of a new perception of the past and formed two stages of Ukrainian national identity depicted in literary texts. She defined the first stage (1985–2000) as a "time gap" which uses destruction as a way of perceiving the past and the present. The second stage (2000–2015) is characterized by the underlining distance and mentality that "separates Ukrainian identity from the background of the post-Soviet." (p. 116)[1] Ukrainian society went through two revolutions and the beginning of the war. At this stage, a "transit identity" is formed, which provides the opportunities for rethinking historical memory. "This concerns the reformatting of attitudes towards the Holodomor, the OUN–UPA resistance movement, the events of the Soviet–German war of 1939–1945, the events of 1918, etc." (p. 113) Literature after 2015 continues to work with the historical past and its memory. Neo-mythologism and the revival of common historical memoirs are becoming the leading forms of artistic thinking. The texts by Ukrainian modern writers Sofia Andrukhovych, Maria Matios, Vasyl Shkliar, Oleg Shynkarenko, Yurii Vynnychuk, Oksana Zabuzhko, and Serhii Zhadan recode the mythologems of the Holodomor, the OUN–UPA movement, military events, the Soviet era, etc.

As literature with a "transit identity," Ukrainian literature is searching for suitable forms of expression and shows certain characteristics: the war as the main topic and the starting point for plot development; writing about the present; rewriting the past; rethinking the concepts of disappearance and memory; existing on social media platforms; the intermedial character of texts. All these features can be applied to the novel *Amadoka* (*Amadoka*, 2020) by Sofia Andrukhovych (born in 1982).

Amadoka is a novel about memory and its absence. Just as archaeologists find shards during excavations and put them together to form a whole vessel, Sofia Andrukhovych forms an idea of the past from the remnants of memory. The key word here is *idea* (hint) of the past. One cannot make a whole vessel from the shards, but one can understand its form, purpose, etc. The same applies to the past: it is impossible to form a true objective past from the remnants of memory. It is no coincidence that the characters' professions are related to excavation and storage (the literary archive worker Romana and the archaeologists – Bohdan Kryvodiak and Viktor Petrov).

The cover of the novel is very eloquent, which can also be interpreted as an excavation of collective and individual memory. It depicts pieces, shards, that try to form something whole – the whole world that is being blown to pieces; a lake that has gone underground; a broken mirror; an injured face of a person with lips (the only detail by which Romana recognized the Man); the reconstruction of the face from pieces by "sewing" them together in such a way that it will never regain its original appearance. In an interview with the author, the literary critic Vasyl Vovk notes:

---

[1] All quotations are translated from Ukrainian into English by the author of the essay.

The cover of the book is interesting in the aspect of providing several interpretations: someone sees the disfigured face of the main character Bohdan on it, someone sees fragments of the history of Ukraine, which form a complete picture only together, and someone sees a certain person who is involved in the creation of the national identity of Ukrainians in each fragment. (Vovk)

Sofia Andrukhovych explains her interpretation of the cover:

…these fragments are different parts of human identity, such a human split that is characteristic of almost everyone. The theme of this inner split, the contradictions of various human qualities, is one of the main themes of *Amadoka*. (Vovk)

Why is the excavation important in this novel? It can help to find remnants of memory. "Excavation" begins in the literary archive. The archaeologist Bohdan Kryvodiak brought several suitcases with the photos of his family to the archive where Romana worked. She took those photos to her home. In the archive, she met Victor, the grandson of a party censor (the author doesn't name him directly, but gives several options – Pryvdyk?, Pravdyk?, Pryndyk?) who had to read the letters of the Ukrainian writer Viktor Petrov–Domontovych to Sofia Zerova[2] and stole some of them.

The principle of excavation was realized in Pinchas's diary with ancient geographical maps (with the lake Amadoka) and scratches of the city Buchach. Pinzel's sculptures, the Professor's apartment, the museum of atheism in Zoe's apartment, social networks, the cemetery, photographs, video recordings, and social networks are chosen as other modes of archiving memories.

There are two groups of photos in *Amadoka*. The first group is "excavated" family photos, which Romana shows to her "husband," imposing unfamiliar memory on him. The text does not contain the photographs themselves, but Sofia Andrukhovych provides descriptions of them in order to enable the readers to "see" the photos in their own way. The second group is the photos that Romana shares on her Facebook page, creating her own diary restoring the Man's memory and reviving herself on the social network. She (a woman who almost does not exist in the real life of the text) created a whole life for display on Facebook.

---

[2] Sofia Zerova (1890–1985) – a wife of Mykola Zerov (1890–1937), a Ukrainian poet, translator, classical and literary scholar and critic, one of the leading figures of the Executed Renaissance, and Viktor Petrov.

In *Amadoka*, nothing and no one exists only in one dimension. In the beginning, it seems that Romana is a woman who intends to restore her husband's memory. The reader empathizes with this character, realizing that she is making an effort to return his husband to himself. At the end of the novel, it becomes clear that Romana imposed the memories of another person on the Man. An interesting observation emerges here: if someone else's memories and life are imposed on a person who is tabula rasa, the moment of recollection will still come. Extrapolating it to Ukrainian society means that the memory of the nation will be awakened, the recollection will still come, with the awareness of the treachery and meanness of those who have been imposing someone else's history.

One of the possible explanations for why Romana tries to impose on the Man from the East the memory of another man from the West during the war (that is taking place in the East of Ukraine) fits into the concept of multidirectional memory elaborated by Michael Rothberg, who understands it as a series of interventions through which social actors bring multiple traumatic pasts into a heterogeneous and changing post-Second World War present. Arguing with American literary theorist Walter Benn Michaels (born 1948), Michael Rothberg states in his book that Michaels takes up one of the most agonizing problems of contemporary multicultural societies: how to think about the relationship between social groups' histories of victimization. He adds that memory culture is often considered within the categories of "victim" and "perpetrators." "Victims" and "perpetrators" have become collective attributes that shape identity. Sofia Andrukhovych notes that *Amadoka* is a novel about "victims and executioners, about the love of victims for executioners and the love of executioners for victims. About the hatred of the rescued towards the saviors. About the fine line between the savior and the executioner and how easily these roles are swapped, how easily they are confused."[3]

One of the explanations of the Man's "quietness" after recalling is the assumption that Romana does not exist. As Sofia Andrukhovych emphasizes in an interview, Romana is not quite a person. Ukrainian scientist Ihor Kotyk noted the meaning of the name Romana as a name-narrative and the absence of direct speech in the article *Chest, viddanist, rozbitii labirint Minotavra* (*Honor, loyalty, the broken labyrinth of the Minotaur*, 2020). If we take this idea into consideration, the end of the novel becomes clearer. Romana – is the novel itself. [4] There is a lack of information about this woman, about her past and present in the text, but it is underlined that she only listens to other characters, collects testimonies, archives, and memories, and then tells her story – the novel

---

[3] https://blog.yakaboo.ua/ru/sofia-andruhovych/.
[4] The Ukrainian word for "novel" sounds like "roman".

Amadoka. And her novel is about the biggest lake in Europe – Amadoka, which also exists in several dimensions: depicted on maps until the seventeenth century, but it is not known whether it existed by mistake by Herodotus and other cartographers. Sofia Andrukhovych says that Amadoka is:

> Something very sensible, but at the same time invisible. Something that defines our lives today, but at the same time is very undefined. I think trying to capture the images of this lake with all the delicacy is something that is useful for everyone.[5]

None of the characters in Sofia Andrukhovych's novel can be interpreted unambiguously. This is constant in the history of Ukraine. Three stages (forgetting – inventing and imposing memories – recalling) embody the traumatic experience of Ukraine, which was first deprived of its memory before the Soviet authorities imposed their vision of history on it and, finally, the painful stage of recollection came.

Another question that Michael Rothberg discusses in his book is the connection between identity and memory. Sofia Andrukhovych *sews together* (Kotyk) individual memory, social memory, traumatic memory, selective memory, imposed memory, lost memory, other types of memory, and shows that they do not quite fit together but all embody Ukrainian society. To understand identity means to overcome the amnesia of the nation. *Amadoka* proves to be the text to excavate, define, analyze, and show the Ukrainian identity.

REFERENCES

Andrukhovych, Sofiia. *Amadoka*. Lviv: Vydavnysttvo Staroho Leva, 2020. 12

Freud, Sigmund. "Über Kindheits- und Deckerinnerungen." *Monatsschrift für Psychiatrie und Neurologie* 18 (1899): 285–310.

Kotyk, Ihor. "Chest, viddanist, rozbitii labirint Minotavra." *Zbruch.eu.* Accessed December 12, 2022. https://zbruc.eu/node/97917.

Romanenko, Olena. "Identychnist natsii ta tekstu: Jak suchasna ukrainska literatura formuie intensyvni obrazy natsionalnoii identyfikacii." *Literaturnyi proces: metodolohiia, imena, tendencii. Filolohichni nauky* 7 (2016): 112–120.

Rothberg, Michael. *Multidirectional Memory: Remembering the Holocaust in the Age of Decolonization.* Stanford: Stanford University Press, 2009.

Vovk, Vasyl. "Pro novyi roman, tuhu za Avstro-Uhorshchynoyu ta kino." *Weche.info.* Accessed December 12, 2022. https://www.weche.info/blog/liudi-8/post/pro-novii-roman-tugu-za-avstro-ugorshchinoiu-ta-kino-5685.

---

[5] https://youtu.be/EXR_OIMm23o.

Author Information

Philine Bickhardt is currently researching at University of Zurich (Switzerland). She holds a Master's Degree in Russian and Serbian Literature at the Humboldt University of Berlin (Germany). As a scholarship holder of the Friedrich-Ebert Foundation since 2017, she has studied abroad in Saint Petersburg (Russia) and Belgrade (Serbia). Since 2018, she worked as the web editor of *novinki.de*, an online newspaper for Modern Slavic Literatures published in German. Her main focus of interest is on the literary strategies of memory and the relationship between literature and historiography (including Varlam Shalamov, Svetlana Alexievich, Ales Adamovich, and David Albahari).

Jennifer Döring is a Ph.D. candidate and research assistant at the University of Tübingen (Germany) in the Department of Slavic Literatures and Cultures. Her research interests include East Slavic contemporary literature, memory studies, and disability studies. In her doctoral studies, she focuses on the disappearance of people in totalitarian systems in Russian, Belarussian, and Ukrainian contemporary literature.

Monika Glosowitz is an Assistant Professor in the Faculty of Humanities at the University of Silesia (Poland). She is a literary scholar and feminist literary critic. Her latest book publications include the monograph *The Affective Machineries. The Literary Strategies of Emancipation in the Recent Polish Women's Poetry* (2019, in Polish) and the collected volume *Imagines Geographies. Central European Spatial Narratives between 1984 and 2014* (2018, together with Aleksandra Konarzewska and Magdalena Baran-Szołtys). She was awarded the Poznań Literary Award *Stanisław Barańczak Scholarship* in 2020.

Melinda Harlov-Csortán is an Assistant Professor at Apor Vilmos Catholic College in Vác (Hungary). She is a heritage scholar and historian, researching memory and representation in the twentieth-century Central European context. Her recent English publications include "Betrayal of Memory in Hungarian Public Memorials of the 20th century" (in: *Traitors, Collaborators and Deserters in Contemporary European Politics of Memory. Formulas of Betrayal*, 2018) and "Remembering the Iron Curtain: Diverse Memory Events after 1989" (*Nationalities Papers*, 2022).

Alena Heinritz is a postdoc researcher at the Department of Comparative Literature, University of Innsbruck (Austria). Currently, she is working on a project on the interrelationship between literature and work/labor. Her latest book publications include the monograph *Postcommunist Modes of Writing, Narratives on Communism in Early 21st Century Novels* (2021, in German), the journal article "Grotesque Artifacts: State Socialist Lieux de Mémoire in Novels by Pavel Pepperstein and Jáchym Topol" (2021), and the journal article "Burying the Undead: Coming to Terms with the Soviet Past in Novels by Slavnikova and Lebedev" (2017).

Elisa-Maria Hiemer is a postdoctoral researcher at Herder Institute for Historical Research on Eastern Europe in Marburg (Germany), where she is about to finish a project on abortion trials and debates about illegitimacy in interwar Poland. Her publications on Polish literature include, among others, *Autobiographical Writing as an Issue of Aesthetics* and *Jewish Pluralism in Contemporary Polish and German literature* (2019, in German). She edited the *Handbook of Polish, Czech, and Slovak Holocaust Literature* (2021, together with Jiří Holý, Agata Firlej, and Hana Nichtburgerová). She is currently preparing a special issue for "Poznańskie Studia Slawistyczne" dedicated to pop-cultural representations of the Holocaust (together with Urszula Kowalska-Nadolna).

Maria Ivanytska is Professor at Taras Shevchenko National University of Kyiv (Ukraine); currently a fellow at the University of Tübingen (Germany). Her research interests lie in translation studies, cultural studies, German literature of the Bukovina, and German-Ukrainian literary contacts. She authored *The Personality of the Translator in Ukrainian-German Literary Relations, A Monograph* (2015) in Ukrainian, and over 90 scientific articles, and "Ukrainian Identity, Communicated to the Outside World: On the Ukrainian Image in German Literary Translations and in Literary Studies" (2017, in German).

Karolina Kołpak is a Ph.D. candidate at Yale University specializing in the Modern History of Eastern Europe and Russia, focusing on late nineteenth and early twentieth-century Poland and Polish-Jewish relations. Her work engages histories of nationalism and empire; antisemitism and fascism; civil society and democracy; childhood and minority histories. Her dissertation reconstructs the history of the Warsaw Summer Camps Society (1882—1939). At Yale, Karolina taught her seminar, "The Jewish Metropolis: Warsaw Before the Holocaust." She authored the introduction to Magdalena Kicińska's *Pani Stefa and the Orphans: Out of the Shadow of Korcz*ak, translated by Sean Gasper Bye (2021).

Aleksandra Konarzewska is an Assistant Professor in the Faculty of Humanities at the University of Tübingen (Germany). She is a literary scholar and a historian of ideas of East and Central Europe. Her latest book publications include the monograph *The Exit from the Immaturity: Sexuality, Cultivation, and the Disenchantment of the World in the Work of W. Gombrowicz and S. Brzozowski* (2019, in German), and the collected volume *Unsettled 1968 in the Troubled Present: Revisiting the 50 Years of Discussions from East and Central Europe* (2020, together with Anna Nakai and Michał Przeperski).

Anna Nakai is a part-time lecturer and research fellow for the Institute for Global Area Studies at the Tokyo University of Foreign Studies and a Ph.D. candidate at the Department of History, Central European University (Austria/Hungary). Her research covers the cultural and intellectual history of contemporary Central Europe, particularly focusing on the late socialist and post-communist era. She edited the collected volume *Unsettled 1968 in the Troubled Present: Revisiting the 50 Years of Discussions from East and Central Europe* (2020, together with Aleksandra Konarzewska and Michał Przeperski). Recently, she also deals with literary translations of contemporary Polish literature (Joanna Bator).

Valentin Peschanskyi, born in Odesa, studied Slavic Studies, Comparative Literature, German Literature and Philosophy at the University of Tübingen. He received his doctorate in Slavic Literature and Culture with a dissertation on *The Dead Woman as an Icon, The Relationship Between Death, (Sacred) Images and Femininity in the Works of Fyodor Dostoevsky, Vasily Perov,* and *Ivan Turgenev and Yevgeni Bauer.* He is an Assistant Professor (*Akademischer Rat*) at the Institute of Slavic Studies at the University of Münster. He is working on *A Narrated Day in Literature, Film and Computer Games* with a focus on Polish, Russian and Ukrainian culture.

Antonina Puchkovskaia is a Lecturer in Digital Humanities at the Department of Digital Humanities at King's College London (United Kingdom). Her research and pedagogy take place at the intersection of cultural history, spatial humanities, cultural heritage, and digital humanities. She focuses on how technical processes have shaped the field of Humanities at the forefront of conceptualising and analysing its sources as data. More recently, she has primarily engaged with the GLAM sector, exploring the (in)visibilities of cultural data and approaches to its representation. Her latest publications include a study on race in *Slavic Review* and others.

Olena Saikovska is an Associate Professor in the Philological faculty at the Odesa I. I. Mechnikov National University (Ukraine) and DAAD Fellow in Eberhard Karls University of Tübingen (Germany). She is a literary scholar of Slavic literature (Bulgarian and Ukrainian). Her scientific interests concern modern Bulgarian and Ukrainian literature, intermedial studies, the questions of war and literature, and memory studies. Her latest publications include essays to the Cassandra-Project (2022, in German and English), articles "Intermediality of Pavel Vezhinov's prose" (2019, in Ukrainian), "Fundamentals of National Identity in Bulgarian and Rusinian Literature (Based on the Works by Hristo Botev and Alexander Dukhnovych)" (2021, in Ukrainian), "Intermediality codes in *A Ballad for Georg Henig* by Victor Paskov" (2022, in Ukrainian).

Justyna Tabaszewska is an assistant professor at the Institute of Literary Research of the Polish Academy of Sciences. She specializes in literary and cultural studies, especially memory studies. Her latest publications include the monograph *Servile Humanities* (2022, in Polish) and the paper "Affective Future and Non-existent History" (*Memory Studies*, 2022). She holds a scholarship (Bekker NAWA Programme) at the Goethe University Frankfurt and works on a project concerning the issue of affectiveness of Polish literature and on a book *Affective Memory. Dynamics of Polish Collective Memory after 1989* is to be published in December 2022.

Kseniia Tereshchenko is an independent researcher and translator with degrees in Finno-Ugric Philology and Digital Humanities.

Olha Tkachenko is a researcher at the Institute of Slavic Studies, Polish Academy of Sciences. Her academic interests encompass media and identity studies, Polish-Ukrainian relations, Central and Eastern Europe as a concept, language of the media, and critical discourse analysis. Her publications on Ukrainian identity include, among others, *Discourse of Ukrainian Identity in the Polish Opinion-Forming Press during the Orange Revolution and the Euromaidan. Media Linguistic Analysis* (2022) in English. She edited the collective monograph *Searching for Identity: Personal Experiences and Methodological Reflections* (2021, together with Ayur Zhanayev). Currently, she works on the representation of the war in Ukraine in foreign media.

Index of Names

Index of Terms

Printed in the USA
CPSIA information can be obtained
at www.ICGtesting.com
LVHW010619191023
761502LV00007B/271/J